THE WAY OF KNOWLEDGE

THE WAY
OF
KNOWLEDGE

IN THE REIGN OF
ANTICHRIST

OLIVER ST. JOHN

The Way of Knowledge in the Reign of Antichrist
© Oliver St. John 2022, 2024

All rights reserved. No part of this publication may be reproduced, distributed, or transmitted in any form or by any means, including photocopying, recording, or other electronic or mechanical methods, without the prior written permission of the publisher, except in the case of brief quotations embodied in critical reviews and certain other noncommercial uses permitted by copyright law.

Cover design and graphics © Oliver St. John 2022
The front cover symbolises the end of Kali Yuga
The back cover symbolises AVM

ISBN 978-1-7391549-9-8
Paperback Edition (June 2025)
ORDO ASTRI IMPRIMATUR
www.ordoastri.org

TO THE FELLOWSHIP OF THE HEART

CONTENTS

Concerning Metaphysics	i
Preface	iii
The Dark Age	1
The Reign of Antichrist	3
Vincit Omnia Veritas	7
Knights of the Cross	9
The Chivalric Order	16
The Ass and the Ark	21
Sat-Chit-Ananda	26
The True Self	29
Anaximander and the Infinite	35
Andromeda	40
Sacred Magic of Abramelin	45
Satanic Inversion of the Angel	51
Knowledge and Conversation	55
Name and Form: Nama-Rupa	61
The Two Adams	64
The Recording Angel	68
Oracle of Isis	79
The Throne of Ra	80
Postmodern Shamanism	97
The Key of Magick	101
I Am That	105
Mysteria Magica Sexualis	110
The Sacred Heart	117
Don Juan	125
Oracle of Nuit	129
Dual and Non-Dual	130
The Eagle	133
Dreaming Attention	136
The Grail Castle Revisited	139

Gradations of Samadhi	146
Considerations on Yoga Practice	152
Kundalini Yoga	155
Egyptian Yoga	159
Dual Symbolism and Symbolic Inversion	163
Brahmacharya	170
The Star of Man	176

Illustrations and Figures

Vincit Omnia Veritas	6
Jacques de Molay	8
Dante: Symbolism of *The Divine Comedy*	10, 13
The Descent into Hell and Ascension	12
The Great Year (cyclical manifestation)	14
The Sphinx: Cycle of Ascent and Descent	15
Mudra of Shiva: Sign of Protection	16
Brahma: Stone Sculpture	32
St. Matthew and the Angel (Guercino)	54
Hieroglyphs for 'heaven' and 'sky'	81
Hieroglyph: Fourfold division of the heavens	84
Hieroglyph: Sekhem sceptre	86
Akh or Crested Ibis (celestial being)	88
Lugh (or Loki) of Three Faces	102
Yantra	113
Hieroglyph: Ab vessel or 'heart'	117
Hieroglyph: Ab vessel with more detail	118
Yantra with *bindu*	120
Sri Yantra	123
Dove and Grail Tree of Life symbolism	142
Gradations of Samadhi	150
Hieroglyph of *heh*, 'Eternity'	169
Hieroglyph of Khabs	176
Metaphysical point in the circle	177
Hieroglyph: Hand of Orion	178

Concerning Metaphysics

Before metaphysics can be explained by discursive means, the terms used must be redefined. Metaphysics is meant here in the etymological sense of the word, which is to say, 'beyond the physical', and so nothing to do with the chemical state of the body or brain, or the psychological domain. Metaphysics refers to the infinite, unlimited universal doctrine that can only be known metaphysically. As it depends from a supra-human source, it can never be a branch of philosophy or some other science. Indeed, philosophy and the other modern theoretical sciences were originally derived from metaphysics and not vice versa.

Symbolism is the only way to convey metaphysical reality without direct knowledge; language itself comprises a set of symbols. Ancient languages, with all their subtlety of etymology, roots of words and phonetics, are nonetheless well equipped to symbolise metaphysics, which is solely concerned with principles that amount to pure knowledge. Such principial knowledge is most adequately set down in the Hindu Vedas and Vedanta. Such knowledge is not in any way derived from an individual author, as is the case with all Western philosophical theories. With the Vedanta, the goal is always that of pure knowledge: untransmissible, infinite and absolute reality. That is what we mean by 'metaphysics'.

This knowledge is not then in any way apprehended by reason or argument as it is derived from a supra-human source. All dialectics of the ancient sciences, including Hermeticism for example—something that in itself has been confused with profane science—form only an outward veil of that which is truly esoteric, which is inevitable. The ordinary meaning of the term 'dialectic', derived from Greek (διαλεκτικη), means 'a discussion', and that word derives from analysis, which is necessarily confined to the domain of reason. The limitation imposed by this is such that the conventional modern dictionary definition, 'enquiry into metaphysical contradictions and their solutions', is confused in its very nature and rests on total misunderstanding of the word's meaning. Such an enquiry removes the enquirer from anything metaphysical, even in the etymological sense. There can be no contradiction in metaphysical or principial reality, which is infinite and contains all possibilities within Itself without any disharmony entering therein. The dictionary will even inform us that metaphysics is concerned with 'abstraction' that has 'no basis in reality'! This owes to the fact that modern science imagines 'concrete existence' to be the only reality.

Some scholars have even attempted to reduce the meaning of metaphysics to the level of the utterly inane, until it becomes no more than 'in addition to' or 'after', as with the appendices of a book![1]

Inevitably, some Sanskrit terms must be used when expressing a metaphysical idea, for there are no words in modern languages to describe Atma or Brahma, for example, let alone the vast array of other technical terms and their different contextual uses. Sanskrit has the vocabulary of a complete science of consciousness itself; this is better understood if the universe is considered as ontological and not material; unfortunately even that completely escapes the grasp of ordinary rational comprehension and is only truly conveyed by direct knowledge. The means of acquiring such knowledge is the subject of the *Yoga-Sutras*, for example, but few are prepared to make the intense and prolonged effort that is needed.

We must then rely on symbolism and language, whatever its shortcomings, if we are to communicate anything at all. That limits our scope to a few that are prepared to work diligently towards an understanding, putting aside any preconceived notions they might hold. It is these few persons that we are addressing, for the rest are as in a deep sleep, lacking the strength or will to awaken. In fact, these sleepers are even the enemies of the knowledge that is our subject and our ultimate goal, which means they will never acquire it. As it is put very succinctly in the alchemical text *Aurora Consurgens*,

> Fools despise this glorious Science of God, and the Doctrine of the Secrets, and the Secret of the Philosophers, and the Medicine of the Physicians, because they do not know what she really is. ... And nor is this kind of wisdom suited to the ignorant because everyone who is ignorant of her is her enemy, and not without cause, as the Observer of All Things says. ... Nor will the spirit of this Wisdom enter into a coarse body, and nor can a fool ever grasp it, due to the poverty of his reasoning, because the wise have not spoken to the foolish, for he who speaks to a fool speaks to someone who is asleep.[2]

---

[1] We refer to S.M. Cohen, 'Aristotle's Metaphysics' [Stanford Encyclopaedia of Philosophy, California].
[2] Book I: 111.

Preface

Sophia is our Guiding Light.

With this book we pass beyond the syncretism of occultism to the synthesis of the metaphysical gnosis, which is necessarily the view from the 'centre'. All true initiatic paths lead to the same goal and only differ from the point of view of the outsider who only sees the appearance. The outward differences of paths owe to cultural or other modifications, as is necessary, and none of that is of any consequence to initiation at all.

We must deal with the conditions of the world that we now find ourselves in. While we will not avoid the subject, it is necessary to point out that this book is not a comment on social conditions or the more or less extraordinary phenomena that is all part of the 'signs of the times'. We will not research to produce evidence of truth, or of the deviation that has afflicted an entire civilisation, for that would only add to the layers of confusion through 'information' that already exist everywhere. Our purpose is to set forth in the clearest possible terms the ways now open to us given the circumstances of our times. We will also deal with some of the ways that lead nowhere. The false or counterfeit ways are multitudinous yet increasingly homogenous. It is easily possible to dispose of them, therefore, without giving them more attention than they deserve.

Owing to the great acceleration towards the ending of an entire Cosmic Cycle, or Manvantara, we have found the need to adapt and readapt our methods.[3] At the beginning we developed rituals and yoga that owed largely to the modernist influence of the nineteenth and twentieth century occultism, as typified by syncretism. This was natural as our mentors were in the third generation from the nineteenth century Order of the Golden Dawn, as it has come to be known. Whether these offshoots of the Golden Dawn were 'dissident' or not, as declared by some, is a moot point.[4] The 1888 Order was composed from the remnants of earlier traditions, including ancient Operative Masonry, in so far as that existed at the time, mixed with Neo-Rosicrucianism and the very influential but counter-initiatic Theosophical movement.

---

[3] See 'Cosmic Cycles', *Nu Hermetica—Initiation and Metaphysical Reality*.
[4] The occultist and surrealist painter Ithell Colquhoun composed a directory of 'regular' and 'dissident' factions in *The Sword of Wisdom*, which was in many ways a defence of Golden Dawn founder MacGregor Mathers.

Although no evidence has yet been found other than hearsay, it seems likely that Egyptologist E.A. Wallis Budge provided resources and even room space at the British Museum for the performance of some of the rites and ceremonies. The latter included the use, in the subtle realm, of artificial Egyptian Godforms. It is a fact that Budge's hieroglyphic copies were used on some of the temple furnishings—notably the two pillars of the temple in the Hall of Neophytes.

Amidst the syncretism of the Golden Dawn and other influences mentioned, apart from those that are now known to be anti-initiatic, there is nonetheless one frequently overlooked factor that supplies continuity. The Rosicrucian and alchemical source text *Chymical Wedding of Christian Rosenkreutz* begins with a vision of Isis. This strangely echoes the conclusion of *The Golden Asse* by Apuleius, written fifteen centuries earlier.[5] The latter was written sometime around the 2nd century AD, when the initiatic rites of Isis were still performed, quite often in countries other than Egypt such as Greece and Rome. Archaeologists dug up a temple of Isis in London not so many years ago. In Elizabethan England, the Christian Hermeticist, astrologer, scientist and cartographer John Dee entered into a ten-year long communication with various angelic intelligences, resulting in what is now known as the 'Enochian System'. The operation was launched following the persistent manifestation of the Shakti in the form of an audacious young woman named Madimi. Taking all into consideration, Madimi is comparable in some ways to Lolita or the Kumari of the Tantras. According to MacGregor Mathers, the Golden Dawn founder, it was a vision of Isis that prompted the founding of their first Lodge, named Isis-Urania.

The way of the devotee of Isis, the Soul of Egypt, is implicit in the (Egyptian) Book of the Law, in spite of the unsuitability of Aleister Crowley, who wrote the book down. Thelema, when understood as a spiritual path, has nothing whatsoever in common with the anti-initiatic developments of Crowley and has even less in common with the fantasies of the postmodernists that followed in his wake, making the way darker through deliberate ambiguity and the inversion of symbolism. We have for many years regarded the Book of the Law as a source text, in part at least, while retaining strong reservations regarding the material that was added to it by Crowley or that simply mirrors his line of thought. Crowley was a clever and subversive agent of the counter-initiation, and who ruthlessly pursued a profane agenda; inevitably the Book of the Law is rendered all the more obscure owing to this.

---

[5] *Chymical Wedding* was published 1616.

We have always rejected all 'official' commentaries on the book sourced from Crowley and his epigones. The 'voice' of Nuit-Isis in that book should nonetheless be recognisable to anyone who has studied Gnostic texts and those of the Upanishads and Tantras, even more particularly the Egyptian 'Thunder Perfect Mind', which dates to about the 1st century AD. The latter is a far purer source text than the Book of the Law, as it contains no admixture of thoughts from occultists and was certainly not received by the means of spiritism, which was an invention of the nineteenth century. This will very likely be the subject of our next book, as the text has not yet been dealt with sufficiently.[6]

The voice of the Goddess or Shakti grows in strength and power even though her rites were forbidden and forgotten two thousand years ago. Our universal Gnostic path is inclusive of the way of the devotee of the Shakti, whether she is known as Nuit, Isis, Hathoor or by any other name. Our work includes ritual and yoga, and the goal of the work is no different—and cannot possibly be any different—from Advaita Vedanta as defined by Shankara and more recently by René Guénon.[7] That does not mean that we are asking anyone to become a Hindu or to imagine they are an ancient Egyptian.

Over time the Way of Knowledge has become increasingly divided to the modern mind, so that we now have forms of Westernised 'yoga' that are exclusively concerned with physical fitness and so completely divorced from the principle of yoga, which is knowledge through union with first God (or Shakti) and then the Infinite.[8]

Owing to this division of the Western mentality, devotional practices, the discipline of pure knowledge and the path of yoga are frequently seen as separate disciplines, each one representing a specialisation—a word that has no real meaning in ancient doctrines. All ways or paths must serve the one purpose of ultimate deliverance (Sanskrit *moksha*), or at least 'salvation' as according to the strict limitations of religious paths, which are necessarily exoteric. Over a century ago, Sri Ramakrishna said that in the Age of Kali Yuga it is difficult to do the ancient rituals and that it is efficacious now to follow the way of the Tantras.[9]

---

[6] See *Thunder Perfect Gnosis* (first published September 2023).
[7] *Introduction to the Study of the Hindu Doctrines* [Sophia Perennis].
[8] The latter is better described as 'dissolution' than union as such.
[9] See p. 62, *Nu Hermetica*.

Many centuries ago the great sage Shankara (Shankaracharya), who is best known for his commentaries from the point of view of Advaita or Non-dualism, composed very fine hymns to the Goddess, Mahadevi Shakti.[10] The sages were well aware of the Kali Yuga or Dark Age, and the impact this would have on the path of knowledge. Advaita, the way of the non-dual, is the crown, the conclusion of the path that must have one goal only, which is deliverance. Beneath that crown, however, is the body of essential yoga, meditation, devotion and ritual. Indeed, Shankara's name means 'incarnation of devotion'.

The core practice on the Way of Knowledge is here defined as Egyptian yoga. In this, we apply the principles of Vedic yoga to the metaphysical doctrine that is veiled by the ancient Egyptian neteru, hieroglyphs and sacred texts, as well as other source texts. We are not 'mixing traditions' here. Our viewpoint is universal and Gnostic.

Sophia be-with-us forever.

Oliver St. John

Revised for the Second Edition Sol in ♋ Luna in ♏ 2024

---

[10] Shankaracharya is thought to have lived and taught his disciples at some time during the 8th century AD.

The Dark Age

René Guénon has spelled out some facts regarding the Cosmic Cycles that are of vital significance to the Way of Knowledge at the present time.[11] He speaks of the Age of Kali Yuga that commenced approximately 6,000 years ago, and in fact only lasts about 6,000 years until the end of a Great Year and of an entire Manvantara. That brings us to the present time, in which this book is being written. We have already explained the technical side of such matters.[12]

> Since that time, the truths which were formerly within reach of all have become more and more hidden and inaccessible; those who possess them grow fewer and fewer, and although the treasure of 'non-human' (that is, supra-human) wisdom that was prior to all the ages can never be lost, it nevertheless becomes enveloped in more and more impenetrable veils, which hide it from men's sight and make it extremely difficult to discover. This is why we find everywhere, under various symbols, the same theme of something that has been lost—at least to all appearances and as far as the outer world is concerned—and that those who aspire to true knowledge must rediscover; but it is also said that what is thus hidden will become visible again at the end of the cycle, which, because of the continuity binding all things together, will coincide with the beginning of a new cycle.

The 'new cycle' is our work now; it coincides with the ending of the old, which we now see breaking down around us. Intellect and reason are two different things. Intellect is already largely a thing of the past; those who still have it will not be heard or understood. Reason alone prevails, and it has reached its end limit now. Hearts, minds and souls are destroyed on a daily basis; confusion, complexity, doubt and unknowing are promoted to serve the financial interests of governments and corporations. The worst-case scenario imagined by the visionaries has now come about. A great deal of sugar is needed to swallow a very bitter pill, and that sweetness is the urge to self-preservation. The peoples of all the nations have blindly welcomed in totalitarianism in masked form. In putting this across—and there are by now many instances where it is unwise to do so—we will get confusing responses that are frequently self-contradictory. Guénon has described the epistemology of the modern world. Technically, this corresponds to the Qliphoth of Aquarius, of which we wrote,

---

[11] Cf. 'The Dark Age', *The Crisis of the Modern World* [Sophia Perennis].
[12] Cf. 'Cosmic Cycles', *Nu Hermetica*.

> When the dissolution of ego implicit on this path is resisted but the force remains irresistible—the forward momentum too great to overcome—then there is a reversion to type; the return to Nuit manifests in its degraded form as loss of consciousness in bestiality or sexual perversion ... the failing ego may also seek a refuge in collective consciousness, finding a temporary strength in the pose or attitude of the crowd, the approval of a peer group.[13]

There are petrified ones, who practice silent obedience. There are even those, persuaded by New Age counter-initiatic ideas borrowed from tradition but taken out of any doctrinal context, that imagine they must *surrender* to 'what's going on out there', which is no less than the System of Antichrist—a term that we shall shortly explain. It does not occur to them that this notion of 'surrender' was originally used in relation to *surrender to God*, or the will of God. They have completely inverted the meaning so as to conclude that a spiritual attitude means helping others like them to surrender to a force of evil and darkness! Then there are the others that take up the totalitarian cause with great zeal, wishing to invest in their share of the power. When tyrants rule the world, there are always legions of small or petty tyrants that want to be like the big ones.

The perversion of the sex-force may take multitudinous forms. Sadomasochists have long favoured masking or covering the face. The perversion is so complete that there is no joy in any sexual relations, and certainly not in any relations of love, for the damned are those who have shut out all possibilities of love and truth. Power is sought in every kind of restriction of the sex-force, in destruction of the possibility of love and the perversion of all natural feelings, which are necessarily complex, into fear and loathing, which are very simple, brutal emotions. When totalitarianism is worked through extreme 'health and safety' measures, the biological urge to self-preservation is channelled into the enforcement of self-isolation. It is the ultimate tyranny of the ego that denies truth and embraces self-destruction and the destruction of all real meaning in anything as the final solution to the dilemma invoked by belief in a lying spirit.

---

[13] 'Qliphoth of Aquarius' *The Flaming Sword Sepher Sephiroth*, entry for the number 323.

The Reign of Antichrist

Saturn, the planetary principle of Aquarius, concerns order and structure. The seven-headed beast described in the biblical book of Revelation as arising at the end of time symbolises the inverse or Qliphoth of the Saturnian force—the demonic aspect. It is incoherent, 'without a word'. Embracing the ascendancy of collective power and scientism, on the other hand—which is that seven-headed monster of the Apocalypse—can make a person sick forever so they lose their chance for the order and structure of an immortal soul. We have already explained how causal determinism has played a vital part in bringing about this degraded state of affairs.[14] Causal determinism is the basis of modern civilisation. It goes back at least 25 centuries, but the seeds were sown 6,000 years ago, at the very beginning of political history—which also happens to be the onset of the Age of Kali Yuga. We are in the time of the utterly dark. Yet this focuses the mind, for those who will not succumb to the force of evil. There is no room for doubt or confusion. Confusion is the primary means of the forces of anti-initiation. Truth prevails, even if it is invisible to nearly all.

We are undergoing a very rapid acceleration towards the great dissolution (Sanskrit *mahapralaya*). The Antichrist is the totality of the anti-spiritual force in man. This is sometimes seen as a kind of cosmic evil or force but really the kingdom of Antichrist only extends to the limit of the psychic realm and that of reason—and these two are not as far removed from each other as some like to imagine. Both realms have no real existence beyond the body or corporeal state. In that way the Antichrist only has a relative existence, though it is real enough within its own strictly limited sphere.

For these reasons we will refer to the 'System of Antichrist', as that is descriptive of the completely inhuman and mechanical entity we are up against. The System of Antichrist requires that an entire civilisation must be in a continual state of fear and anxiety. If it isn't a 'plague' it could be anything, staged terrorism or even carefully managed and orchestrated industrial wars, for example, as we have seen very recently. 'Health and safety' has now become the primary means of imprisoning entire populations and subjecting them to technological brainwashing, so they believe and obey the commands given them, whether directly or through hypnotic means.

---

[14] Cf. 'Lapis Philosophorum', *Babalon Unveiled! Thelemic Monographs*.

The aforementioned campaign has been remarkably successful. Agents of subterfuge also work through the 'alternative' groups and information. The agents can be sincere in the belief they are helping and 'healing'. According to René Guénon,

> It can happen that those who think they have escaped from modern materialism fall a prey to things that, while seemingly opposed to it, are really of the same order; and, in view of the turn of mind of modern Westerners, a special warning needs to be uttered against the attraction that more or less extraordinary phenomena may hold for them; it is this attraction that is to a large extent responsible for all the errors of 'neo-spiritualism', and it is to be foreseen that the dangers it represents will grow even worse, for the forces of darkness, which keep alive the present confusion, find in it one of their most potent instruments.[15]

While we are not likely to see a return to Victorian 'table turning' and other experiments in mediumism, for a century or more we have seen elements taken from esotericism and made subject to confusion or even complete inversion. These are presented as products with a pretended scientific basis, and a wide range of supposedly beneficial properties. Sometimes machines are made to produce phenomena. The world of 'information' is another matter entirely. The Internet is a free-for-all where 'facts' can be created and modified in seconds, and this is true not only of reported events but of the ever-shifting sands of pseudo-esotericism. However, while restraining this would clearly amount to censorship, new laws were passed in 2020 that make it easily possible now for governments and service providers to censor any information that contradicts 'real' facts about any 'event of public interest'. Thus governments and corporations can now determine for us what is real and what is not real. Whether news is fake or not depends on who is paying for it and who owns it.

We may see the present world situation symbolised as a Great Wall. Most humans are now on the side of the Wall governed by Antichrist. Knowingly or unknowingly, that is what they serve and no other, be they psychologists, sociologists, medics, teachers, trade unionists or even those in the so-called arts. The 'alternatives', the healers, dieticians and fake gurus of the New Age, were always at the vanguard of the anti-spiritual movement. Postmodernism across all its 'disciplines' rejects all possibilities of anything existing outside the self, the human mind (including psyche) and body.

---

[15] 'Conclusions', *The Crisis of the Modern World* [Sophia Perennis].

When chaos and disorder reign fully and all unifying principles are rejected or attacked, power is the only thing left—the power to govern and enslave by the same chaotic anti-rule of confusion and terror. The state of affairs will continue until the Wall comes down at the end of the cycle. Before that happens it starts to break apart.

The degradation of the intellect, even the ordinary reason, has occurred side by side with the degradation of our language, and this is to such an extent that there are generations now accustomed more to icons and pictures than textual information, for whom thought has been replaced by mere reaction. The following quotation from René Guénon from an article about Saint Bernard might serve to illustrate this point.[16]

> For those who consider it impartially, this life [of Bernard] confounds and upsets all those preconceived ideas of 'scientific' historians, who consider ... that 'the negation of the supernatural constitutes the very essence of critical thinking', something we readily admit, though for the reasons that we see in this incompatibility the exact opposite of what they do: the condemnation, not of the supernatural, but of 'critical thinking' itself. Truly, what lessons could be more profitable for our time than these?

Guénon wrote that some 70 or more years ago, and since then the degradation that he saw everywhere has vastly accelerated. So much so that there will be some who read that and will not understand it at all, even if they read it several times. And it is even quite likely they will see in it the very opposite meaning to that intended, such is the extent of the educational, cultural and environmental brainwashing they have undergone.

The ways of initiation are not open to those who serve Antichrist and his ministers, which are truly legion in the world. It is impossible for them to know of anything outside themselves or anything that even reflects (as a symbol) a true image. None of this is a ground for despair, however, as, apart from the fact that despair only places us in the hands of the System, even the sad state of our world can be an *apa-guru* for those who stay awake. An *apa-guru* can be anything, a person, a thing or even a situation that will teach us and lead us to truth—a journey that begins on the other side of that Great Wall, the Veil of Illusion. Such truth includes the realisation that 'our world' is but a minute, impermanent fraction of the totality of being let alone that which lies beyond it. Initiation is a path to unlimited freedom.

---

[16] 'Saint Bernard', *Insights into Christian Esoterism* [Sophia Perennis].

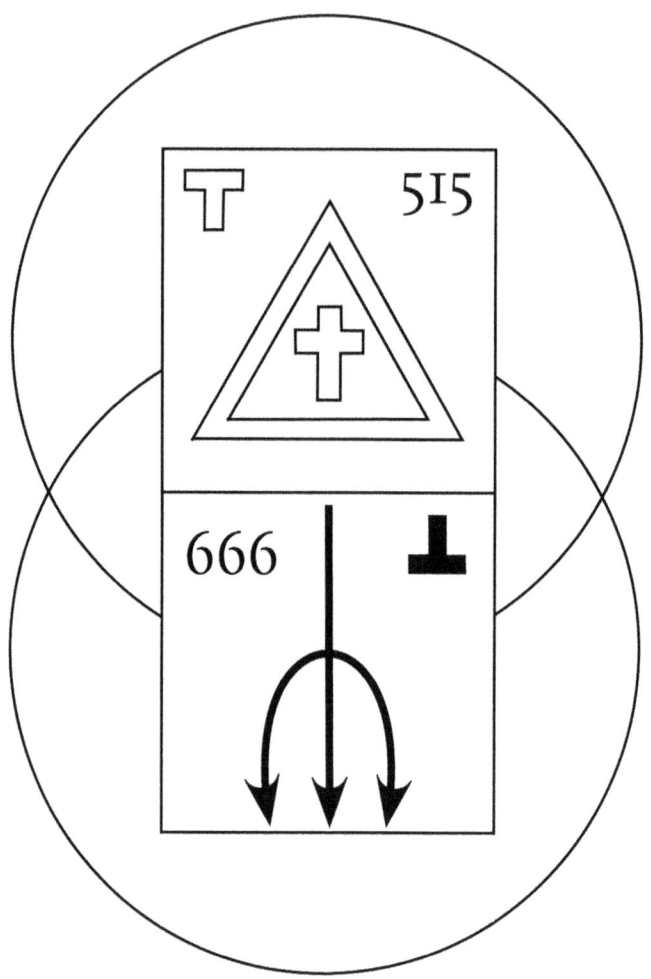

Vincit Omnia Veritas

Vincit Omnia Veritas

The illustration on the facing page depicts the formula of knowledge as expressed from the particular point of view of the restriction placed upon the Reign of Antichrist at the End of Time. The *vesica piscis* in the background depicts the world, as well as the new Manvantara emerging from the old. Geometrically, the *vesica piscis* is a means of forming an equilateral triangle, which is the perfect expression of 'unity'.

The System of Antichrist is depicted on the lower half of the Double-Cube, or Altar of the Universe. The inverted trident and inverted Tau show the repression of spiritual knowledge and the way of darkness and ignorance. The symbolism of the trinity itself is thus inverted. For example, the Way, the Truth and the Life become Obscurity, Lies and Death; Love, Life and Liberty become Hatred, Death and Oppression or Restriction. The number 666 is a dual symbol, not necessarily evil, but in this case it is the number of the 'beast' that arises from the pit in the book of St. John's Revelation to commence the Reign of Antichrist.

The Way of Knowledge is figured in the top half of the Double-Cube. The Cross and Triangle is to show Love and Sacrifice, and the descent of the Light into the darkness of the world to rescue the soul. This symbol is also a protection against evil. The Tau symbolises the Way of Truth and Life. The number 515 was used by Dante in his *Divine Comedy* to depict initiation and the means of freedom from the restriction of Antichrist. It reduces to the number 11 and thus symbolises the union of the macrocosm with the microcosm, the 6 and the 5. As a 'five' (divisible by 5), 515 is also a number of the pentagram, as is 15, and the Energy of the Great Work.

It should be noted that the midpoint of the two cubes or squares crosses the exact centre of the *vesica piscis*, which is the 'eye' or 'centre of the world', also the Sacred Heart. Initiation necessarily involves a descent into Hell and then an ascent, or re-ascent, and this mirrors the Cosmic Cycles.

The whole figure is to signify *Vincit Omnia Veritas*, 'Truth is Triumphant over All'. The Reign of Antichrist is necessarily short-lived and 'seeming', for the triumph of evil is only an apparent one. At the conclusion of the Manvantara the Angel of Judgement comes to exact Justice upon the earth: *Igne Natura Renovatur Integra*.

Jacques de Molay, Last Grand Master of the Knights Templar

Knights of the Cross

There are cycles within cycles, the lesser and the greater. When Dante penned *The Divine Comedy*, his first draft coincided with one such cyclical change, a change that had catastrophic consequences for all of time to come. The Knights Templar was outwardly a Catholic organisation that had the primary purpose of guarding the way to the Holy Land for true pilgrims. It was thus essentially a chivalric Order, though it grew in power and wealth, and had business as well as military interests—most of its members were not actually knights. It was an initiatic Order and the guarding of the way to the Holy Land was the outward aspect of a function that was essentially esoteric, for the Knights Templar preserved links between exoteric Christianity and its esoteric core. As the custodians of the Primordial Tradition, their 'secret' as such was the universality of this knowledge. They maintained links with other civilisations than that of Christendom, including Hinduism, Islam and the Hebrew and Persian traditions.

The Order of Knights Templar, founded in 1118, was destroyed to all intents and purposes when King Phillip IV of France, who owed it a very large debt, had the Templars charged with heresy, which in those days was a foregone conclusion. No matter how fantastic the accusations, confessions were exacted by torture. Many of the French Knights Templars, including the last of the Grand Masters, Jacques de Molay, were arrested on Friday 13th October 1307, tortured into giving false confessions and burned at the stake. Pope Clement V was persuaded by Phillip to officially disband the Order in 1312. It is well documented that many of the Templars nonetheless escaped, and the Scottish Rite in Masonry, for example, still carries certain elements of their symbolism, though some masonic organisations later erased it, having forgotten its meaning.

Dante, as has been unequivocally demonstrated by Guénon, was an initiate of organisations linked to the Templars.[17] King Phillip IV and others like him were agents of the Antichrist as far as Dante was concerned. He thus had to make changes to the poem to conceal his affiliation and the true purpose of the mission of the Templars. The devastating and irreversible consequences of the dissolution of the Templars cannot be overestimated. The Western world and that of Christendom had brutally severed all links with the esotericism that alone gave it life and real meaning.

---

[17] See Guénon, *The Esoterism of Dante* [Sophia Perennis].

To understand the real esoteric purpose of Dante and of the Knights Templar we have to at least summarise the symbolism of the Cosmic Cycles that is cleverly woven into the structure of *The Divine Comedy*. Our purpose for so doing is not for historical interest, but to clarify the Great Work in the present time. Dante had first to place himself symbolically at the midpoint of a Great Year, which as we have explained, is approximately 13,000 years, half of a precessional cycle.[18] This represents an entire 'world', a lesser cycle in the greater scheme of things. Dante therefore said that there were 65 centuries behind him, and 65 more until the end of that 'world'. As we shall see, this was necessary so that he was able to descend into Hell in the *Inferno*, rise to *Purgatory* and enter *Heaven*.

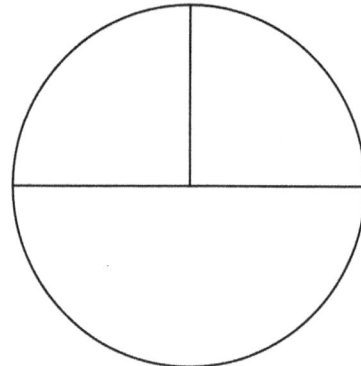

The horizontal line divides the precessional circumference into two hemispheres, each of 13,000 years, chronologically speaking, making one complete precessional cycle in all. Each hemisphere symbolises one Great Year as it was termed by the Greeks and the Persians. One may make a starting point anywhere on the outer circumference of a circle and it must always reach its completion at that same point, which is at the same time the commencement of a new cycle. The error of Nietzsche and some others has been to assume that time and events must replicate exactly. Nietzsche used this to concoct his 'eternal recurrence' theory, while others have used the idea of things eternally repeating themselves as evidence that the Hindu doctrine of Cosmic Cycles is absurd. The absurdity rests on the incomprehension of those that have made a superficial study of it, simplifying and reducing its meaning to almost nothing. Things do not replicate, even when 'returning' to a point where they have correspondence. There is change in the state of Being.[19]

---

[18] See 'Cosmic Cycles', *Nu Hermetica*.
[19] Cf. 'The Key of Magick'.

Although cycles can appear to replicate themselves, time is not quantitative but qualitative in reality, and no measurements of time are ever exact, only an approximation—in the same way, the means of the 'squaring of the circle' is only an approximation, as with the use of the *pi* (π) ratio, called an 'irrational number'. Furthermore, owing to the change in the state of Being that takes place, which is only seen as a progression in time from the corporeal point of view, the succession of cycles is better understood as spiralic—the point of the return is in fact a point of departure that nonetheless retains a link or relation with the previous; in fact, the whole progression is unified, not in any way separate or interrupted. There must be an indefinitude of possible cycles; any number, such as 360 degrees, is analogous not actual.[20]

Dante, as has been said, placed himself at the midpoint of the temporal cycle, which symbolises the polar axis or terrestrial centre, Jerusalem in the Christian symbolism—and the way to that place was literally guarded by the Knights Templar. The way to the centre was therefore cut off when the Templar was dissolved. The terrestrial centre is also a geographical centre, Jerusalem being the centre for Christianity in the same way that Heliopolis was at one time the centre for Egypt, at other times Thebes. The centre of any sphere, however, is halfway down the vertical axis, and it is the point of maximum gravity. On the diagram (above) this is shown where the radius meets the horizontal or diameter. To ascend to the Heavenly Jerusalem, which is described at the end of the Apocalypse of St. John, one must first descend along the vertical axis. The centre is then also the bottom or lowest point, since when that is passed, an ascent begins towards the circumference on the opposite side of the place where one started. The first part of *The Divine Comedy* is the *Inferno*, with its nine circles, of which the ninth and lowest is the place of Lucifer at the peak of the inverse mountain of hubris. He is seated on a rock surrounded by a frozen lake—for materialisation is complete here, a total solidification. Individualisation has nowhere further to go; the ego is alone, separate and cut off, in a state of more or less complete isolation from spiritual reality. Lucifer can only be passed by *turning around* him. The ascent then takes place, which in Dante's poem is symbolised by the mountain of *Purgatory*. At the top of Purgatory is the terrestrial Eden or paradise. Beyond this is the Heavenly Jerusalem. This commences a new cycle of manifestation, a Great Year or greater Manvantara, in terms of the Hindu doctrine.

---

[20] The cycles are indefinite, not eternal; they are within manifestation—but not necessarily in *time*. They exist both inside and outside of time.

The descent and reascent of Dante forms a funnel or double cone, similar to that included with the diagrams of the Orbicular Tree of Life, or Tree of Life in a Sphere.[21] In the case of the Orbicular Tree, the double cone or funnel is to show the thread of the Ain Soph, by which all worlds are connected as a 'string of pearls'. It is the thread that passes through a string of pearls by which each world is related. The vertical axis is non-temporal, and it was only by placing himself at the centre, on the axis, that it was possible for Dante to observe everything without being affected by it, even while undergoing full descent into Hell.

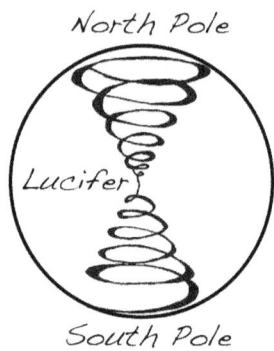

Notably, the only way to pass Lucifer, enthroned upon his frozen lake, is to turn around him, as previously mentioned. Although the direction of movement continues from the North Pole to its antipode, by *rectificando* there is nonetheless a change of direction that is a qualitative one, not a geometrical one. It is only by following the golden thread that rectification is accomplished. It is the complete meaning of the well-known alchemical acronym VITRIOL, *visitae interiora terrae, rectificando invenies occultum lapidum*. 'Go ye forth to the centre of earth, by rectification ye shall find the hidden stone of the wise.' The Company of Heaven, or Celestial Jerusalem, is not reached by a continued descent, even if it appears that way geometrically. Once the centre has been passed the direction is no longer downwards but *upwards*. The change of direction implicit in rectification is a real and permanent change in the state of the being, if this is regarded in terms of initiation. Such a symbol is effective both cosmologically and in terms of the individual Great Work, and this is equally true of the doctrine of the Cosmic Cycles.[22]

---

[21] See *The Enterer of the Threshold*.
[22] Cf. René Guénon, 'The Chain of the Worlds', *Symbols of Sacred Science* [Sophia Perennis].

A further analogy can be made with the 'two doors' or two paths, the Gate of Man and the Gate of Gods.²³ Dante enters through the Door of Man (summer solstice) at the midpoint, so as to arrive at the centre. The centre is the lowest point of the sphere and also, by inverse analogy, the highest—for it is at the centre that the thread of spirit penetrates, where one contacts the Solar Ray or suprahuman influence. At the very centre, Dante loops around Lucifer, changing direction, yet still continues on his course to emerge at the South Pole, the winter solstice, Gate of the Gods. The rectification at the centre is a reversal of point of view so that one realises the world, or the soul, as a reflection of the Real—the two unite when the journey is complete. It is literally true, of course, that the magnetic pull reverses on either side of the earth's equator.

It is the thread of spirit that effects the reversal since each state is threaded upon it as a bead upon a necklace; the curve of the thread pulls the direction around, so that the being or world is properly placed, rectified. By travelling the thread, passing through each state is to follow the cycle of the necklace. At the clasping, or stopping point, the end and the beginning, one exits manifestation altogether.

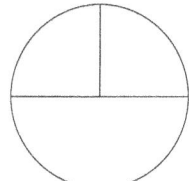

It remains to understand the concealed purpose of Dante and of the Knights Templar, and how this relates to our purpose now, as we near the end of a Great Year and entire Manvantara. Dante's symbol happens to be identical with the Hermetic symbol for the 'mineral kingdom', which is no accident. This symbol can be found on some of the older Tarot decks, especially the one designed by Oswald Wirth.²⁴ As symbol of Imperial Power, it is often surmounted by a cross. The mineral kingdom, or kingdom of stone, naturally includes gold and silver. Dante's vision included the establishment of a Holy Empire, not the Holy Roman Empire but a restoration of the earth to her true spiritual governance. This was viewed quite literally, but it goes without saying, from the present perspective at least, that it was not possible to accomplish such a restoration within our own time cycle, when the Age of Darkness had already been in existence for more than 5,000 years. Nonetheless, the cosmic vision of the Knights Templar was no different from that of the Great Work in all ages.

---

²³ See 'The Gates of the Sun', p. 93, *Nu Hermetica*.
²⁴ It is unfortunate that hardly any of Oswald Wirth's books have been translated into English. Most of them, apart from the Tarot, are available in French editions only.

The completion of a cycle is represented by another Hermetic symbol, which is the circle-cross with both vertical and horizontal axes in full extension. This is called the 'vegetable kingdom', but since trees are the most apt form descriptive of its function, we could also call it the Kingdom of Trees. The plant and tree symbolism not only indicates the terrestrial Eden but also, and most importantly, includes the assimilation of the seeds of a previous cycle so they can be carried forward to the next.[25]

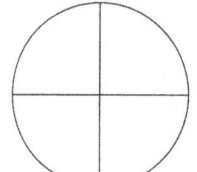 Some time ago we produced a symbol called *The Sphinx—Life-cycle of Consciousness*.[26] The symbol is a cosmological form of the Great Year, where at the top or north pole of the circle is placed the precessional Age of Leo the Lion, or Egyptian 'First Time'. The antipode is that of the Age of Aquarius and the present time.[27] The right-hand half of the circle depicts the precessional ages starting from a time that approximates with the ending of the last Ice Age and the beginning of the present Great Year. This was also the time of the great deluge that brought about the disappearance of Atlantis, seat of the Primordial Tradition in the previous Great Year. The left-hand side of the circle does not take place in time, but depicts the full descent into Hell followed by the reascent. This does not take another 13,000 years to effect but occurs simultaneously, as soon as the end of the present Manvantara is reached and the final dissolution.

Regarded as a type of 'clock', our present position on the cusp of Aquarius is seconds away from the end of time. While a very few have already witnessed the full descent, it remains for others, that have the possibilities latent, to follow—a path that they are hesitant or even reluctant to accept, which is of course quite understandable. When the last attains initiation, the new cycle commences.

---

[25] It has become necessary to mention that the tree and plant kingdom, as understood Hermetically, and in the present context, can have nothing whatsoever to do with so-called entheogenic plants or 'plant medicines' that are by now widely used in certain countries where they are native. Even the word 'entheogenic' implies a complete inversion of spiritual truth—'divinity' cannot be produced out of any plant substance, or from the human psychic realm. Cf. 'Postmodern Shamanism'.
[26] *The Ending of the Words*.
[27] See *Law of Thelema—Hidden Alchemy* (2024), 'The Sphinx, Time and Alchemy'. The diagram has been retitled 'The Sphinx: Cycle of Ascent and Descent' (see facing page).

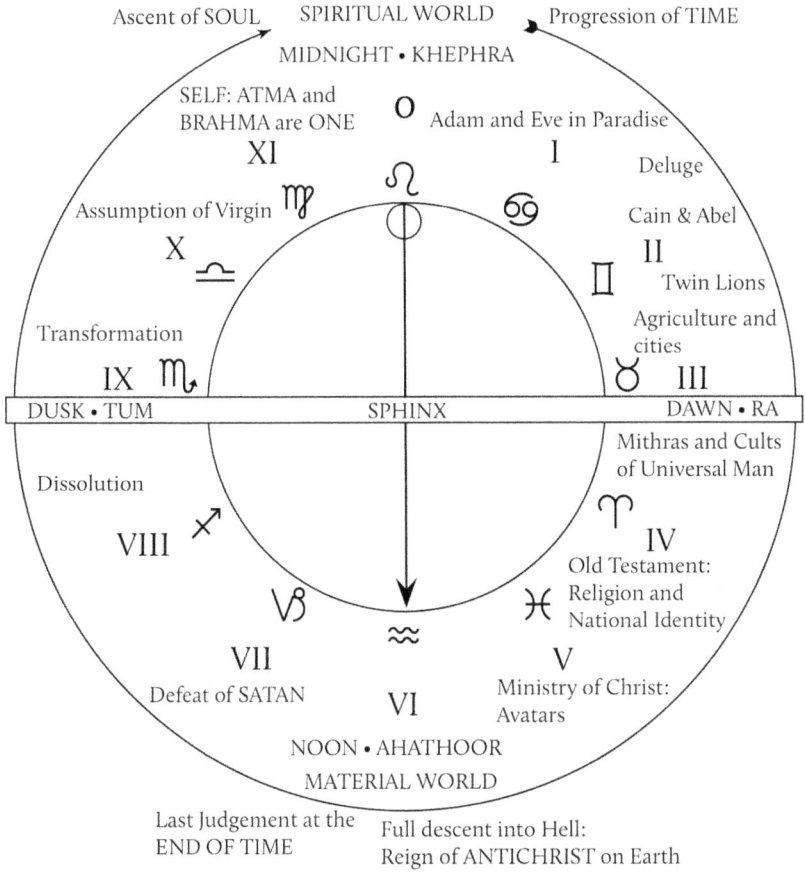

The Sphinx: Cycle of Ascent and Descent
(reproduced from *Law of Thelema—Hidden Alchemy*)

The Chivalric Order

The preceding 'Knights of the Cross' article received comments and questions from a number of readers, most of whom probably had no idea previously of the affiliation of the poet Dante with the Knights Templar.[28] The subject is a very interesting one and is scarcely written about from an esoteric point of view, so it is worth taking up a few of the points that were raised in more detail.

The right hand of Shiva Nataraja ('Lord of the Dance') forms the 'sign of do not fear'. In his left hand he holds the trident of fire. His left foot is raised in deliverance, and his right foot treads down the foe. Hear the tale of Shiva Nataraja, in his overcoming of the forces of darkness!

The evil ones conjured forth a great tiger, which rushed at him, but smiling he skinned it with his little fingernail and wore it for a garment. They then conjured forth a gigantic cobra serpent and sent it against him. Shiva then took it and wore it around his neck for a garland. They finally, in desperation, sent a malignant dwarf, which he trod upon with his foot, breaking its back. He then continued the dance. Om Nama Shiva-ya!

A chivalric Order within the outward veil of the grades and degrees of a collegium can and certainly does exist: When we alluded to a link between the work of the Knights Templar and that of our own, that was not a mere vague or romantic whim, as is so often the case when persons make such a claim. In our times, the world is in a perpetual state of war, but it is not the temporal war of the forces of lies, chaos and oppression that are alike to both sides in any such conflict that we are concerned with. It is the spiritual war that is the greater one, and which nonetheless has ramifications now in the 'ordinary lives' of all of us. The Adversary is that which we have referred to as the System of Antichrist, the anti-spiritual force in man. Such is the nature of this 'beast' however, that the slaves of that power never realise the fact, and will even think they are on the side of 'freedom'.

---

[28] This article was first published in *93 Current Journal* No. 82, Aquarius.

Curiously, the three holy vows of the Knights Templar are agreed to at the very outset, if not signed as an oath, by every person that even begins a Probationership. But how many of those truly uphold it, even when they have passed through grades? The ones that do uphold it are veritably Knights of the Holy Grail, and these will also never be fooled by Antichrist, his prescriptions or fake ideals, even though he is a veritable master of disguises. These will never accept or surrender to his rule, and will fight to the end—they will not demonstrate publicly, as is the way of the slaves of the System of Antichrist, but will wage war spiritually and so invisibly.

The group of poets known as Fideli d'Amore ('faithful of love') were in reality esotericists that used poetry to convey ideas that can only be symbolised, and this became even more the case once the Templar was destroyed on the orders of King Phillip. Apart from the writings of Guénon (*Esoterism of Dante*), much confusion abounds on this subject; confusion that is mainly due to the usual scholastic incomprehension of initiatic matters. One may find some doubting that the group even existed, owing to a lack of 'documentation', even though such documentation, if it had existed, might very easily have placed Fideli d'Amore in the hands of the Inquisition! Apart from that, there is confusion between 'sects', a term that can only justly be applied to religious organisations, and 'fraternities' of an esoteric nature. These are also confused with 'societies' that can only be exoteric by definition. One may commonly find the work of the poets described as Erotic Poetry; one might suppose that those who have that mentality in common might think the same about the biblical Song of Solomon.

The Templar, which was to a large extent founded by St. Bernard, who wrote the rules, was a chivalric order. The Templars were monks as well as knights, and therefore combined sacerdotal authority with temporal power, for example the way of the Brahmin with the way of the Kshatriya. Chivalry, in its outer or exoteric form at least, is both romantic and mystical, since love is its whole foundation. Guénon has defined mysticism as only existing within a religious context, as the emotional basis precludes real knowledge.

There are, however, degrees of knowledge or initiation, and this is reflected in what are typically represented as numbered grades or degrees, following an orderly hierarchy from the basis to the height or principle itself. Naturally, there are always those who mistake this kind of hierarchy with a system of temporal governance that can only represent very ordinary powers, but that is of no consequence as they are merely exhibiting their profanity.

There are also those who are inclined to think of the grades as a quantifiable standard applicable to all indiscriminately—a kind of profane thinking that, while seriously wrong, is understandable given the educational and cultural conditioning we have all been subjected to. No two beings are identical in all of creation or manifestation; initiation is likewise experienced differently and uniquely, even if the principles involved are invariable. The grade system is a way that we can mark progress or development, as are the 'magical powers' along the path of the chakras, but it is not a way, in itself, of ascertaining the real level of initiation or knowledge of other persons. That can certainly be done, but it is not done 'by numbers', it is a qualitative, not a quantitative evaluation.

In the (Egyptian) Book of the Law, I: 51, Aiwass tells the first recipient that while he might know a little concerning the lesser mysteries, he will never know anything at all of the greater mysteries; in fact, from the wording of the verse, it seems that he will not truly enter the 'palace' of the central mystery:

> *There are four gates to one palace; the floor of that palace is of silver and gold; lapis lazuli and jasper are there; and all rare scents; jasmine and rose, and the emblems of death. Let him enter in turn or at once the four gates; let him stand on the floor of the palace. Will he not sink? Amn. Ho! warrior, if thy servant sink? But there are means and means.*

The above verse, which is descriptive of the sephiroth grouped about Tiphereth at the centre of the Tree of Life, describes the pilgrim's 'way to the centre', that was guarded by the Knights Templar, the warrior monks. The 'sinking servant' mentioned in the penultimate line of the verse has baffled commentators but in Hermetic source works it refers to the corporeal form. In particular, the Sethian Gnosis is very exact. We have commented on this previously:[29]

> The practice itself, or one of its primary aims, is called 'stripping off the Servant-form', which is to discard the enslavement to the Beast or Leviathan, the Dragon of Time and Death. This is the task of the 'perfected' or Universal Man, of which the pharaohs and Christ, or other avatars, are the type. To liberate oneself, the body of flesh must be transformed into a Celestial Garment. The Celestial Garment equates to the incorruptible soul, which the ancient Egyptians called the Sahu. The body of the King—the human ego or *ahankara* in Tiphereth—dissolves as aromatic essences that return to the heart of Nuit in her infinite or principial aspect.

---

[29] 'The Sethian Gnosis', pp. 176–177, *Nu Hermetica*.

For he that is not qualified, the very centre of the 'palace', the Holy City or terrestrial Eden, has a floor that is like quicksand—there is a fall back to the world of the profane. The verse continues to list other means, as being the way of the ordinary person whose concerns are limited to the corporeal state—a way that has the possibility of religious salvation, so long as the law is obeyed.[30]

Now when we said in the previous chapter that 'very few have witnessed the full descent', that applies on more than one level. Firstly, there are few real initiates in the world today, in the full sense of what that means. This owes to the postmodern mentality, which makes it almost impossible. For more than a century there has been a total inversion of spiritual symbolism so that it comes to mean the opposite of what it once did. Even consulting a dictionary will prove this. According to the dictionary, 'metaphysics' is only 'abstraction', and cannot be anything real in itself, because there is nothing about metaphysical reality that can be weighed or measured by the means of material science.

The same applies to many words in modern languages. According to the dictionaries, *eidolon* only means 'an idealised person or thing', or even, 'a spectre or phantom'. The writers of dictionaries cannot conceive of *eidolon* as being anything other than an abstraction or a phantasmal illusion. And yet in some of the rituals we speak of the 'eidolon of the Holy Guardian Angel'. Is this a phantasmal thing that does not exist, or a mere conceptual ideal? To those afflicted with the anti-spiritual force, it does not exist and for them it never will. The etymological meaning of *eidolon* really concerns 'essence' (Sanskrit *purusha*) but owing to the limitations of Greek scholastics, this was confused with 'form', which was then further degraded to an 'ideal' form. Finally, in modern times it comes to mean practically nothing at all, a mere phantasm of the mind.

The governance of Antichrist will not last long, but neither will our world. However, only very few persons can see that as a reality. Most do not see it at all, and so, if they should happen to read this they will think that we live in some imaginative realm and do not know reality. But the reverse is true.

---

[30] In the case of the (Egyptian) Book of the Law, Nuit has a more or less identical rôle and function to that of the Virgin Mary in Catholicism, the Grail itself—and which was indeed the real subject of the 'erotic' poetry of Fideli d'Amore. Unfortunately, Thelema is not a religion, no matter what some may like to claim of it for tax purposes—a religion must have three things: ritual, doctrine (or dogma) and moral teaching, or it is not a religion.

Most persons in the world today are completely unable to discern the true from the fictitious. Initiates have gone through a 'turning around', just as described by Dante, and while their gaze is most often fixed on eternity, not on ephemeral or contingent things, they can see very clearly what is going on in our world today. In fact, such a gap between real knowledge and that of the 'wordly wise' is not by any means unique to the present time. According to John, 3: 12:

> If I have told you earthly things, and ye believe not, how shall ye believe, if I tell you of heavenly things?

Yet even those who aspire to initiation still cling to delusion and false hope. They are very resistant to confront reality, to know the true state of affairs, so that a 'Great Wall' now exists. Most are on the side of the wall governed by Antichrist. A very few are on the other side of it and what they see and know cannot be comprehended in any way by those on the side governed by Material Illusion. While to a certain extent that has been true for 6,000 years or so, we have recently seen a great acceleration towards the dissolution (*mahapralaya*), and a corresponding real degradation in human intellect and even ordinary reason. Reason is in any case not at all the same thing as intellect, in the true sense of the word. Reason can believe anything it wants and reject truth entirely if that truth is uncomfortable. Reason has by now rejected truth for so long that most of the human race has accomplished the turning around as described by Dante, but in the wrong direction. They have turned their faces against all spiritual possibilities and, instead, have self-identified with Luciferic pride. If they should even suspect the existence of the Knights of the Holy Grail, they would think them mad and possibly even fear them as a danger to humanity. 'To know, to dare and to keep silence' is indeed a practice that may be interpreted on more than one level.

The Ass and the Ark

It is frequently said that the Ass must carry the Ark into the Holy City. When Jesus entered the gates of Jerusalem on Palm Sunday, before the Passover (Christian Easter), he rode upon an ass.[31] Palms were strewn in the way, for these symbolised both peace and victory in various Mediterranean cultures. The exoteric meaning of this is that Christ Jesus is no worldly kind of king but is the saviour of the world, to whom all will flock. Through him all nations will be assimilated into the Holy City, or Jerusalem. The riding upon an ass, or donkey, was prophesied in the book of Zachariah 9: 9–10, with regard to King Solomon—for both Solomon and Christ Jesus were supposed to be descended from the House of David.

> Rejoice greatly, Daughter Zion!
> Shout, o Daughter Jerusalem!
> See, your king comes to you,
> righteous and victorious,
> lowly and riding on a donkey,
> on a colt, the foal of a donkey.

> I will take away the chariots from Ephraim
> and the warhorses from Jerusalem,
> and the battle bow will be broken.
> He will proclaim peace to the nations.
> His rule will extend from sea to sea
> and from the River to the ends of the earth.

While the symbolism owes directly to the Judaeo Christian tradition, it has universal meaning and import. The final assimilation of all nations into the Holy City takes place at the end of time, or the end of a Manvantara or Cosmic Cycle, according to the Hindu metaphysical doctrines. This 'event', and the preceding Reign of the Antichrist, is recounted in St. John's book of Revelation, or Apocalypse. From the corporeal point of view it is essential that the Ass must carry the Ark into the Holy City. The Ark will not carry the Ass, however much we might like to have it that way. To act as though the Ark will carry the Ass is a recipe for endless delusion and if it is thought of as 'magick' then the delusion is only reinforced, sometimes permanently.

---

[31] Palm Sunday is the first day of Holy Week, and is celebrated on the Sunday before Easter in the Christian tradition.

The Ass must carry the Ark from the corporeal point of view because of course it does not matter to the Ark whether it is carried into Jerusalem or not. It *is* both Jerusalem and the principle. Atma, the principle also called the True Self, is not changed, modified or conditioned by anything. The Ass may symbolise the corporeal state or the human ego (Sanskrit *ahankara*). This is usually understood in terms of a necessary 'sacrifice' for the accomplishment of the Great Work, although from the initiated point of view the ego does not truly exist so nothing can actually be 'lost' and in fact, everything, the whole world as it were, is gained. The 'world' here means the sum totality of all states of Being, of which the human state represents only one degree. Nonetheless, initiation must start from the human and physical state, or else it would have no meaning.

There were two Adams mentioned in the book of Genesis.[32] Adam Kadmon or primordial Adam is the first created, in which Adam and Eve are the one androgynous being. The same primordial state of existence is called Universal Man in the Arabic tradition, and there is comparison to be made with the *purusha* and *prakriti*, 'essence' and 'substance' in Hinduism. It is to this Adam, not the fallen Adam that is born into separation and death, that the Kingdom or restored Eden belongs. Fallen man, that is to say the human state of man, must realise fully the existence of Adam, the true King of the World, otherwise his fall is fatal or irrevocable, for he is easily seduced into believing the lies of the System of Antichrist, the anti-spiritual force.

Both the Ass and the Ark are needed, therefore, but to think that the Grail can carry the human, or that it is there to serve contingent human needs and concerns, amounts to a satanic inversion of all spiritual knowledge. It is symptomatic of our times, as we draw towards the end of the Manvantara, that those who would promote a counterfeit spirituality will insist on this very subversion of the true principles, and will work to convince others of the delusion that the Ark can carry the Ass by magick, or otherwise by some extraordinary means. It is more often the case, in fact, that this goal is sought through some perfectly ordinary psychic means, including all the applications of knowledge of neo-spiritualism, usually for 'healing' or some perceived improvement to the health of body and mind.

---

[32] Cf. 'The Two Adams'.

It can hardly be a coincidence that the practitioners of such black arts are among the most ardent supporters of the System of Antichrist. When world governments, institutions and corporations implemented the 'lock-step' strategy in the spring of 2020, holistic centres took up the call and enthusiastically relayed the 'keep safe' propaganda, all the while keeping a close eye on ways to maintain their profits and sell new products.[33] The term 'black arts' is used here because such practices, which for some are fatally seductive, take the degraded remnants of traditional knowledge and remove them entirely from any principle beyond the human domain. Hence there is a need that we convey in unequivocal terms the inversion of spiritual and natural law that is veiled by the humanistic hypnosis that pervades all such practices.

The word 'yoga' has an etymological link across several languages with 'yoke', and this provides a clue to the union between the Ass and the Ark that is implicit in the practice of yoga. The Holy City is the world 'centre', sometimes symbolised as the World Egg encompassed by a serpent. The heart is also used to depict the same, and it has been said, 'there are four gates to the one palace'.[34] The 'four' is a square, and always symbolises the completion or 'squaring of the circle' in manifested states of being. The completion of a cycle is simultaneous with the new commencement, as at the end of a Manvantara. The symbolism of Cosmic Cycles, in common with all traditions that retain something of the primordial, has a counterpart in the Great Work of initiation itself, and so the 'circle squared' is used to denote grades or degrees in an Order. In the Kali Yuga or Age of Darkness the practice of yoga, taken in its true context, of 'union with God' or knowing the Real, is absolutely essential.

While the celebration of Easter takes place at springtime in the northern hemisphere, it has a reciprocal relation with the autumn. Easter follows the spring equinox, when the Sun enters the zodiacal sign of Aries and then passes to Taurus. At the autumn equinox the Sun enters Libra, the Scales, then passes to Scorpio. The ancient Egyptian festival of Sokar, the Hawk-headed Lord of Death and Resurrection, took place at a time approximating our Easter. Sokar was carried around the temple on a wooden barque following a circular route.

---

[33] Notably Glastonbury in England is one such holistic centre, built around the psychic residues of the ancient stone and other buildings that proliferate there, so as to syphon what remains and redirect it towards improper ends.
[34] The (Egyptian) Book of the Law, I: 51. Cf. 'The Chivalric Order'.

Upon the barque of the white-shrouded Sokar was placed an ark, which contained a mystery no less than the mystery of Sokar himself, as the solar principle. It was the official duty of the high priest of Memphis to place the ark upon the vessel before it was carried around. Such a priest very often was a son of the pharaoh, and so possessed all the attributes of a priest-king or divine intermediary between heaven and earth.[35] The symbolism of the Cosmic Cycles is implicit in this rite.

Taurus and Scorpio are opposite signs in the Zodiac, or rather, they are complementary as no zodiacal sign can be understood without reference to its opposite on the wheel of time. Life and death are the two most vital functions within manifested existence. While life is the principle of existence itself, and the 'breath of spirit', death marks any change of state in the being, especially the permanent change of state that is indicated by initiation in the real sense. Thus the death and resurrection of Christ Jesus is, or was once at least, celebrated at Easter, and we celebrate the entry of the Sun into Scorpio at autumn with the ritual of the black hawk Sokar. Sokar is also the Lord of the Labyrinth that lies hidden beneath the sands of Sokaris, called by the Greeks and others a 'Necropolis', a land of the dead, but known to the Egyptians as the City of God and the land of life everlasting.

The labyrinth serves two purposes. Firstly, it is the initiatic way to the centre or palace that was previously mentioned. The person must overcome various obstructions to reach it, or otherwise follow the 'golden thread' so as not to get lost or detained in the underworld. The thread (Sanskrit *sutratma*) is that which strings together the worlds of existence as beads on a necklace. The worlds of existence are the appearance, the manifest states, but the thread itself is Atma, the Real, without which they could not exist at all. In the second case, the labyrinth protects and guards the initiatic way from the profane, so that only true pilgrims may reach the centre.

---

[35] Aiwass, communicant of the (Egyptian) Book of the Law, was at one time the high priest of Memphis.

Sat-Chit-Ananda

While the Egyptian initiatic symbolism most certainly has a complete metaphysics, the knowledge vanished away with the language at least two thousand years ago. While we can retranslate and comment on some of the texts, recovering the full knowledge of what was largely an initiated oral tradition from the hieroglyphs that remain presents us with a difficulty. As with the Hindu doctrines, while there is a unified body of knowledge, there is great diversity in the *darshanas* or 'points of view'.

Fortunately, the Hindu doctrines have a complete metaphysics that is written down, and as all such doctrines must originate from a primordial tradition, they are always in agreement. Thus, we can apply the Hindu doctrines as revealed by René Guénon, especially as he always kept in view the universality of all traditional knowledge. In all other writings there are problems with the translations from Sanskrit into modern languages and subsequent interpretation. It seems that few people are aware of the distortions that have taken place through abridgements and uninitiated commentaries.[36] Greatly confused explanations of Sanskrit terms relating to aspects of mind and consciousness are commonplace, especially in relation to yoga. These errors are so extensive that it would not be worthwhile trying to list them. Instead, we will look at a few of the key metaphysical Sanskrit terms and clarify their meaning, for it is impossible to use merely one word as is frequently done. It soon becomes clear that with accuracy and care in translation the Hindu doctrines can act as a key to deciphering the Egyptian as well as other sacred texts with a reasonable degree of certainty.

Atma and *Brahma*. According to the Vedanta, 'Atma and Brahma are one', for in the principial domain of the Real there is difference but not separation. Atma is the principle of the Real when considered outside and beyond all particular conditions that determine the states of manifestation. While Atma can be symbolised geometrically by the solar point in a circle, 'unity' is a determined state and so secondary to the Real. Even 'zero' is an imperfect analogy.

---

[36] The Vedas, often falsely described as 'religious texts', are a substantial body of works. The Vedanta consists of the luminous commentaries made on these. Most of what we have in the English language is fragmentary, inaccurate, overly simplified and substantially reduced and degraded in meaning.

Brahma is the equivalent of Absolute Nuit in Egyptian terms (not the appearance of Nuit). While Brahma does not 'cause' anything to manifest or be produced, the reflected light or radiation of Atma in extension (as radii to a circumference) is the basis of first formless manifestation and then manifestation in the worlds of form. Hadit is thus the Egyptian equivalent of Atma, though we must be careful to distinguish Hadit 'not extended' from Hadit in extension, where he becomes the Serpent of Knowledge, which is the near equivalent of *jivatma* (see below), perceiving only Ishvara, the 'Lord' or 'Divine Personality' (Demiurge), as a distorted reflection in the most inferior realms of the psychic or subtle states. At the highest level, however, Ishvara is the state of Pure Being and not subject to determination.

Maya is the Sanskrit equivalent of the Egyptian Nuit when Hadit 'causes' her appearance through his reflected light.[37] Maya is often personified as a goddess of the same name in Hindu art (*kala*). She is very frequently misconstrued in modern language interpretations, which usually involve gross over-simplifications of the Vedanta, for example the translations and abridgements of the commentaries of Shankara. It is quite incorrect to think of Maya as being 'illusion' and therefore even non-existent. While that which appears to the senses is of an entirely illusionary nature from the point of view of the Real, it is real enough on its own plane, even if that reality is conditioned. It is better to think of Maya as that which works upon the substance of the universe, its 'fabric' or 'weave', to produce all things that appear to the senses, whether subtle or physical.

Sat-Chit-Ananda. Firstly, *chit* is not to be understood in the sense of individual thought. It is the total consciousness of the Self in relation with *ananda*, 'beatitude', which is in itself not different from *sat* or pure being. Thus *sat-chit-ananda*—which essentially belong together as one entity—is wrongly described by orientalists and occultists as 'being, consciousness, bliss', and so is degraded in its meaning. The 'one entity' of the three principles is in fact the unconditioned Atma.

Jivatma is the 'living soul' and so the near equivalent of the Hebrew *nephesch*. While its essence is nonetheless Atma, as the sole reality, Atma is here only perceived in a conditioned state and is subject to determinations and contingencies.

---

[37] Nothing is really 'caused', but rather manifestation is produced or comes about through various interactions and subsequent determinations.

Ahankara is the root of self-awareness. It is the near equivalent of what we term as ego or ego-consciousness—though the Sanskrit term has far greater accuracy when it is taken in its doctrinal context, which is necessarily far more complex than modern 'psychological' terms. The *ahankara* is that which divides the world into 'mine' and 'not mine'—it is thus separative, not unitive. By identifying all things and qualities in the world, the *ahankara* enables the soul to relate to perceived objects. If the soul is in a state of ignorance (*avidya*), then *ahankara* may lead itself to be separate from the divine source, the Real. The ego is the soul when that is considered as attached to a body, the corporeal state. There are (at least) three other aspects of mind:

Boddhi is the pure or transcendent intellect, the attributes of which are formless. It is able to know universal principles. One must understand that this is not discursive thought or reason but is direct intellectual intuition. 'Intuition' here must not be confused with that which is of a merely sensorial and vital order. It has nothing to do with the psychic realm.

Manas is the mental faculty or inward sense, which includes reason, memory and imagination. It is individual thought and corresponds to form.

Chitta, not to be confused with *chit*, from which it is derived, is the faculty that gives form to ideas and so associates them one with another. Through *chitta*, the individual ego self (*ahankara*) may lead the soul into delusion through identification with a perceived object, which then binds the self to that object. The last two terms are not modes of consciousness as such, but without them nothing can be perceived:

Purusha is 'essence' (sometimes 'spirit'). It is said in the Upanishads that it resides in the pure heart of Brahma and that heart is concave or hollow. Through self-polarisation *purusha* divides, or at least appears to do so, and becomes *prakriti*, 'substance'. Purusha and *prakriti* are not really separate and can be analogously understood as the northern and southern extremities of a vertical axis.[38] Neither *purusha* nor *prakriti* are within manifestation in any degree but *prakriti*, through the action of *purusha* upon her, is able to produce living forms and creatures. Prakriti is thus personified as a goddess, who, like Maya, weaves the tapestry of life and of all living forms.

---

[38] Cf. 'Metaphysical Basis of Love and Will', *Nu Hermetica*.

The True Self

It is common among those who think they choose a path that 'suits them' to speak of wanting to know their True Will or to discover their True Self, as though that were a possession. The ordinary will of the individuality (*jivatma*) is subject to all of the countless contingencies of the corporeal state and has no meaning in relation to the spiritual Will or True Self, which is immutable. The tendencies of the individual are so confused in the present times that it takes more than an ordinary effort even to fulfil *dharma*—a word for the true nature that has no exact equivalent in modern languages.

The True Self is only one of countless terms to have suffered abuse through being removed from any doctrinal context and made to fit the modern mentality. The psychological influence on the occult movement, and the various schools of postmodern art and literature, means that everything but rational, atheist humanism is excluded. It rests on theory instead of real knowledge, as do all modern sciences, and is therefore anti-metaphysical and anti-spiritual.

The Soul, for example, as referred to in modern translations of the Vedanta, is Atma, the supreme principle.[39] It has nothing at all to do with the soul as conventionally understood, which limits it to the body and mind (these two are quite intimately associated). Such distortions are so widespread that it is easily possible to develop a completely false notion of the Self, for Will can be interpreted in many ways. The True Will, to use this very particular expression, has its nearest equivalent with the Sanskrit *dharma*, which, when applied to an individual, is the true nature of that being in its current mode. That can have nothing to do at all with the libido of Freudian analytical psychology. Yet this Will has been reduced until it means no more than an 'unconscious' force within the human domain, which renders it lower in the scheme of things than reason.

While the True Self is frequently used as descriptive of the goal of the work, the term is used without qualification, as though everyone would know what it means. Inevitably it becomes confused with the individuality, which is really no different from the ego, the nearest equivalent to the Sanskrit *ahankara*, which is separative.[40] We must then make a clear difference between Self and ego.

---

[39] Cf. 'Sat-Chit-Ananda'.
[40] Ibid.

To further our understanding of the human being in relation to the Vedanta, René Guénon has made clear this distinction. He has explained in detail the possibilities of the Self, as relative to the manifestation of the human form, and in strict accordance with the metaphysics of the Hindu doctrines:

> The 'Self' is the transcendent and permanent principle of which the manifested being, the human being for example, is only a transient and contingent modification, a modification that, moreover, can in no way affect the principle ... The Self, as such, is never individualised and cannot become so, for since it must always be considered under the aspect of the eternity and immutability that are the necessary attributes of pure Being, it is obviously not susceptible of any particularisation, which would cause it to be 'other than itself'. Immutable in its own nature, it merely develops the indefinite possibilities that it contains within itself, by a relative passing from potency to act through an indefinite series of degrees.[41]

Furthermore, the Self achieves this, as Guénon goes on to say,

> through a multiplicity of modalities of realisation, amounting, for the integral being, to so many states, of which states one alone, limited by the special conditions of existence that define it, constitutes the portion or rather the particular determination of that being, which is called the human individuality.

From this we can see how far from any metaphysical truth it is to confuse the Self with the human individuality, or to go even further and treat the Self as though it were merely an aspect of the human individuality. To make this clearer, we need to understand that:

> The Self, in relation to any being whatsoever, is in reality identified with Atma, since it is essentially beyond all distinction ... The Self is not therefore really distinct from the Atma, except when one considers it particularly and distinctively in relation to a being, or more accurately, in relation to a certain definite state of that being, such as the human state, and insofar as one considers it from this special and limited point of view alone.

The modern mentality will often mistake ego (or 'self') for Self, which as we have seen is no different in its essence than the Sanskrit Atma. Rationalistic thought reduces the universal nature and possibilities of being to the human individual level. This has the effect of sealing off all ways to the higher intellectual intuition (Sanskrit *boddhi*), which alone has the possibility of knowing formless and universal reality.

---

[41] *Man and His Becoming According to the Vedānta*, Chapter Two [Sophia Perennis].

Our ideas of ego and individuality have come about through modern education and psychological theories, in which there is no discernment possible between the ego and the Self as is understood from the traditional or metaphysical perspective. The idea of the Self as it is conveyed in the Hindu doctrines is reduced, since reason does not attain to knowledge beyond the corporeal state of being, to which it is attached. This point of view is vacuous, spiritually empty, for it totally excludes the realisation of any higher principle or source. The individual ego self is then mistaken as the object to which all else is subject, as if it was a complete, self-contained unit. The individual is thus considered to be the direct cause for everything. By such anti-metaphysical assumptions, the understanding of our true nature and whole range of possibilities is limited. All possibilities are restricted to those pertaining to the individual nature alone.

Through the popular 'alternative' spiritual deviations, traditional teachings are misunderstood or otherwise changed so as to conform and fit with the modern mindset. This mentality is not exclusive to any particular school of thought; everything of a spiritual nature is seen as a valid target by the reductionist mentality. Neo-spiritualists, for example, sometimes adopt the Greek aphorism *Know Thyself*, which is supposed to have been written at the entrance to the temple of Apollo at Delphi. The neo-spiritualist or New Age interpretation solely concerns psychological knowledge, which is always directed towards the goal of 'improvement'. In so doing, even the idea of a temple is reduced to a facility for psychological self-improvement, whereas in fact the word 'temple' really means 'consecrated place' (as derived from the Latin *templum*).

New Age 'spiritual' enterprises and 'self-help' books have further contributed to this confusion. Alternative therapeutic culture seeks only to reinforce the ego through the self-hypnotism of 'positive affirmations'. Occultists, on the other hand, misunderstanding the Advaitans, assume that 'annihilation of ego' means doing without the ego altogether, as if we could exist in the human state without the individual faculty, which is impossible. The ego is better considered as the human individual state, one in which limitation is necessarily imposed by definition. The notion of sacrificing the ego is then even sometimes confused with Deliverance, the final liberation (*moksha*) from the cosmological sphere and departure from all determinations permanently and forever. The postmodern mentality asserts, on the other hand, as though it were higher wisdom, 'going with the flow', in relation to completely ordinary life and circumstances.

It would be as though a kind of renunciation of ordinary will-determination could, in the absence of will, somehow allow spiritual forces to intervene, which is nothing more than fantasy. The ego is still exclusively concerned in this case with its own preoccupations in the corporeal state, thus perpetuating an isolated sense of self-existence. As nothing existing beyond the human individuality is understood or is even deemed as possible or in any way acceptable, various ways of gratifying the ego are all that remains. This has the effect of closing the self off from all possibility of spiritual realisation; anything that transcends the merely mundane is ignored, as it does not exist at all from the point of view of the corporeal state. The true nature of the Self, which is only known through direct knowledge (*atma-boddhi*) is restricted; the spiritual source is lost.

Ishvara Prānidhana is the fifth *Niyama* ('Observance'), from Patanjali's *Yoga-Sutras*. This is usually interpreted as 'surrender to the Lord', or to Ishvara. Ishvara is the Divine Personality, which can further be considered as the True Self of Brahma. The nature of the Arabic *Al-fana* ('extinction') in Islamic esotericism is a return to the primordial state in which the ego is annihilated; it is through the dissolution of the ego by which the soul is able to arise transcendent. This involves a real, actual change in the state of the being, which is in the nature of a 'death' to all previous states, for these cannot be returned to. From the transcendent point of view, it is life, for it involves the realisation of all possibilities of the being instead of confinement to one degree of existence—a limitation that excludes even human possibilities. From the point of view of the True Self, there is nothing to be annihilated as the ego has no existence from its own side—something frequently misunderstood when destruction of the ego is referred to in traditional teachings or translations of them. Any 'destruction' is therefore only as seen from the corporeal point of view, which is strictly limited, having a relative existence.

The Self has been defined as the principle of essential 'unity', which is transcendent and permanent. The manifested human being is a particular modification of this. It cannot affect the principle itself. The person exists by virtue of the principle of manifestation, the 'essence', which is the spirit of Self. The True Self is not in any way individualised or particularised, since it is Atma Itself. If the being only knows Self as ego—or identifies the sum total of the being as human individuality—the knowledge of reality is sealed off from beneath so it becomes completely obscured. The knowledge of higher states of the being requires that described in the Hindu doctrines as the *boddhi* intellect, and not the human reason.

Brahma, stone sculpture from Elephanta, 8th century

It is the higher intellectual intuition—which is not to be confused with the instinct or emotion—that is capable of the transcendent spiritual realisation, also called 'knowledge of the heart'. Everything within manifestation has its source in the infinite, the supreme principle. All that is outside of the spiritual or principial state is a reflection of the source—provoked by the presence of the principle, but not as a consequence of anything that the principle does.

The modern mentality can understand nothing existing beyond the world of physical form and sense. Anything outside of time is therefore seen as illusion. The 'Universal Man' is a term derived from Arabic that denotes the knowledge of total existence, in which both worlds—manifest and unmanifest—coincide as a continuous cycle from beginning to end. This is not in any way comprehensible to the modern mentality and so all symbolic references to it in different traditions are either thought of as imaginary or non-existent, or are otherwise reduced to the level of a psychological function within the human individuality.

In various schools of Hinduism, the Sanskrit words Brahma and Ishvara can have multiple interpretations. Brahma has different and highly technical meanings, depending on the spelling and context. An accent or mark for example, can highlight either the masculine or feminine quality. The Hindu Trinity or *Trimurti* unifies the divine Shakti triad of triple manifestation: Brahma, Vishnu and Shiva. In the Trimurti, Brahma is the highest reality, the impersonal and supreme principle in which Ishvara (the Supreme Being) is a lesser degree of its universality. Ishvara as the Divine Personality is the principle of universal manifestation. So being, in the sense of Self, is not in any way separate from Brahma and in the same way spiritual knowledge is not in any way separate from the principle, as when a yogin attains supreme realisation of Atma and Brahma as being one, 'not two' or separate.

The intellectual *boddhi* is considered to be formless and not of the world of form—and for this reason it is able to apprehend what is in its very essence formless. The 'personality', in context of the Hindu doctrines, is universal and has nothing to do with the personality as conventionally understood. It cannot exist independently of Atma, the universal spirit or principle that permeates all things in the light (*jyotis*) of being. By analogy, the individual ego is as a cloud hiding the sun; the true nature of Self, symbolised as the sun as the light of existence, is the heart of being—the Tiphereth of the Tree of Life.

Our conventional notion of the ego is therefore simplistic. There are differences to discern between individuality and personality, and even greater differences between ego and Self (Atma). The Self is not separate from Atma, as Atma is not separate from Brahma. The term 'ego' is prone to misunderstanding when not qualified, as is so often the case. It is not something entirely good, nor is it an evil to be done away with, for that is not possible until the dissolution of the Final Deliverance (*moksha*).

Yoga, or 'union with God', is the means of uniting with the universal principle, bringing about the restoration of the spiritual or primordial state. The dormant possibilities of the individual are thus raised to the higher states of knowledge and being. The ego then has its natural place or function within the individuality, while the True Self extends beyond this into the state of Pure Being, the sum total of all possibilities of being. To conclude with some further words from Guénon touching upon the True Self:

> From all that has been said, we see that real knowledge is not based on the path of reason, but on the spirit and the whole being, for it is none other than the realisation of this being in all its states, which is the culmination of knowledge and the attainment of supreme wisdom. In reality, what belongs to the soul, and even to the spirit, represent only degrees on the path toward the intimate essence that is the true self; this self can be found only when the being has reached its own centre, all its powers being united and concentrated as in the single point in which all things appear to it, since they are contained in this point as in their first and unique principle; thus the being is able to know everything as in itself and of itself, as the totality of existence in the oneness of its own essence.

Anaximander and the Infinite

The Greeks lacked a word for the infinite, or, if they had one, it became confused by commentators that were unable to distinguish between 'eternity' and that which is manifested and therefore not infinite but *indefinite*. Anything in the world of manifestation, however great or small that is perceived—which itself is a quantitative measurement—is necessarily limited. The world of the infinite, or of eternity, is not within space and time, it does not occupy space and is truly without limits since it has no beginning or end. Manifestation is understood as cyclical, not linear. Although there can be an indefinite number of points drawn along a circle's circumference, any movement around the circumference eventually returns to the place it started. This metaphysical doctrine has been confused, so that some have thought, notably the philosopher Nietzsche, that 'history' or time repeats itself infinitely.[42] In fact, the circle itself is only a simple analogy. To be more exact, cyclical manifestation consists of open circles and not closed ones, so that manifestation takes on a spiral form, if we view that as taking place within a geometric sphere. There is a change in the state of the being, upwards or downwards, using the spherical analogy. Nothing within manifestation ever replicates itself exactly; otherwise the two things would be the same thing.

The Greek word that appears to have given rise to the confusion is *apeiron* (απειρον), conventionally translated as 'that which is unlimited', 'boundless', 'infinite' *or* 'indefinite'—which betrays total confusion or an otherwise total ignorance of metaphysics. The word literally means 'without end', 'without a limit'.[43] Apeiron is central to the cosmological theory said to have been created by Anaximander, a 6th century BC pre-Socratic Greek philosopher whose work is mostly lost. Firstly, metaphysics in any true or authentic sense cannot be the invention of any individual, but scholars insist this must be so as they cannot conceive of anything depending from a non-human origin. So they will always look for evidence of 'authenticity' to support the case for invention or creation of one person.

---

[42] Nietzsche, misunderstanding the Hindu doctrine, concocted his own false notion, which he called 'eternal recurrence'.
[43] The prefix 'a' is the negation, 'without'; *peirar* (πειραρ), 'end', 'limit', 'boundary', which is the Ionic Greek form of *peras* (περας).

The works of Anaximander, what he wrote down, are lost. What remains of his cosmology is very much like pure metaphysics. This has been so misconstrued by others that he is rather admired as a type of the 'first scientist', dedicated to experimentation and theory—which can have nothing to do with pure metaphysics. However, it is impossible to know what Anaximander knew, or even what he said or wrote, as nothing survived other than the references others made to him. It is possible that he learned something of the Hindu doctrine, or otherwise such remnants of the primordial tradition that had survived within Greek culture, and then misunderstood or otherwise misapplied it, as scholastics have been doing for millennia, making out of it a rationalist philosophy. But we cannot know that with any degree of certainty.

From existing fragments we learn that Anaximander posited that the beginning or ultimate reality (*arche*) is eternal and infinite, or boundless (*apeiron*), subject to neither old age nor decay. Apeiron perpetually yields fresh materials from which everything that we can perceive is derived. The *apeiron* generates the pairs of opposites, or complementaries, such as hot and cold, wet and dry, which in turn act upon the creation of the world.[44] Everything is generated from *apeiron* and then it is destroyed by returning to *apeiron*. Infinite worlds are generated from *apeiron* and then they are destroyed as according to the natural order.

So much more or less accords with traditional knowledge, even though it is attributed to Anaximander as his personal invention, but it is incomplete, as though badly remembered or misconstrued. The infinite does not generate anything but all things exist through its potency to act upon them. There is reflection of its light through (apparent) self-polarisation. The infinite does not in itself produce anything at all but through 'essence' (*purusha*), 'substance' (*prakriti*) produces all things, for example. Nothing is really destroyed in its essence, it is that form can be transcended and no longer exists as such. The manifested worlds are not infinite but *indefinite*. The going out of the indefinitude of manifested worlds and their return to the primordial source or infinite is likened in the Hindu doctrine to the breath (*swara*), which has two phases, inhalation and exhalation (*hum-sa*). This applies from the greatest of the cosmic cycles to the smallest, so that physical breathing is an analogy for the principle, and is the basis of yoga practice as defined in the Upanishads.

---

[44] Cf. Heraclitus.

In spite of the scholastic insistence on individual invention, Anaximander had a teacher called Thales.[45] The ideas utilised Greek mythology, and is it not always the case that the universal tradition wears many different disguises as according to differing cultures? According to scholars, Anaximander was 'searching for a universal principle', which is absurd unless we suppose that he really was the first of the profane scientists, as is sometimes claimed. He retained the universal tradition of a cosmic order, which scholars think is 'religious', but which is very far from being the case.[46] According to historians he also 'tried to explain it rationally' but using the older mythological language that ascribed the power of divine ordinance to various modes of reality—something that for them awakens horror! We can now begin to see with what unrelenting prejudice these anti-metaphysical commentators have obfuscated all of the ancient or traditional doctrines. According to them, such a symbolic language was suitable for a society that 'could see gods everywhere'—which is a kind of unintentional truth, for ancient people had faculties that were considerably more extended than the people of today. The scholars always insist that metaphysical doctrines rest on 'belief', which is no more than a form of insult. It is also a reversal of the truth, for it is conventional science that rests on experiment and hypothesis, so that its 'truth' is always changing, for it lacks any principle whatsoever.

Again, we learn that the Greeks were supposed to have 'believed' that universal principles could also be applied to human societies. In fact, was it not always the case in any traditional civilisation that metaphysical doctrines applied through and through, ordering all of life, which is in fact where the word 'civilisation' originates in its true sense? The word *nomos* (law), for example, originally meant divinely ordered or natural law, but was used later to mean man-made law only. Similar words occur in all other languages for law or legislation. Sometimes this is confused with actual historical personages, as in the case of the ancient Egyptian King Narmer, whose name means 'Legislator', which is as according to the divine principle.[47]

---

[45] Thales is reckoned to have lived approximately from the 7th to the 6th century BC.
[46] Religion as such did not even exist at that time. 'Religion' is a term that can only properly be applied to the relatively modern streams of Judaism, Christiantiy and Islam.
[47] Cf. 'King Scorpion and the Royal Way', *Nu Hermetica*.

Thus we have here an example of the incomprehension of modern thinkers that aggressively promote their ignorance everywhere, and that will never be satisfied until all truth and real knowledge is totally suppressed. There are two words in the Vedanta that describe it exactly. The first is 'false knowledge'; the second is 'ignorance'. The false knowledge is *viparyaya*, which means, taken more or less literally, 'a motion removed from the [original] motion of any given object'. Movements or vibrations that are the means of knowledge (*pramâna*) coincide in nature with the same vibrations of the object of perception.[48] The vibrations of false knowledge, however, through the conditions of the mind, create a superimposition or imprint upon that which is perceived. That which is perceived is a mental image only, having no bearing on nature or any real knowledge. Thus, it is the condition of *viparyaya*, 'false knowledge'.

There is also a general field for all the modifications of the false knowledge, and this is called *avidya*, 'ignorance'. Whereas *vidya* means 'knowledge', *avidya* is to be entirely without knowledge in any real sense. In the etymological sense of the root *vid*, which means 'to know' but also 'to exist', to be without knowledge is no different from not existing at all, because the being is not what it sees or thinks, but what it truly knows. If it knows nothing, it cannot really exist at all and so *avidya* is also identified with the negative or inverse aspect of the tattva ('element') *akasha*, 'spirit', which is darkness, or otherwise the *guna* of *tamas*. It is as though the *tattvic* cycles, that weave the fabric of existence through the power of the Great Breath (*swara*), also give rise to appearances that can cause delusion to the mind that is not trained through rigorous discipline to never lose sight of the principle, or the Real. If false knowledge becomes a habitual state of mind, then descent into complete darkness or *avidya* may become permanent, leading ultimately to the dispersion of the being.

Most interestingly, Anaximander is reported as having said that the earth (or world) floats in space and is flat, as the top of a cylinder. This is naturally taken as though it were literal fact, not metaphysical symbolism. Those who ridicule what they think is a 'flat earth theory' are themselves ridiculous, for they are deluded by their own strictly limited point of view. The cylinder is used as a geometric analogy for the multiple and indefinite worlds of being. The surface of it (or the surfaces, indefinite) is 'flat' because it is conceived symbolically as a horizontal plane extended to a radius.[49]

---

[48] The shape of the inner ear, for example, mirrors the shape of sound itself.
[49] Cf. René Guénon, *The Multiple States of Being* [Sophia Perennis].

Furthermore, Anaximander is reported as having thought that the Sun and Moon are 'hollow rings of fire'. Naturally, this is thought by the profane to be the production of a scientific theory. From the metaphysical point of view, the Sun and the Moon appear to travel about the earth in circles, over time. From the point of view of the Eternal Present, simultaneity, or when the Manvantara withdraws from manifestation at the End of Time, the Sun and the Moon are 'circles of fire', continuous—because there is no more time.[50] This exists in both the Hindu and the Arabic traditions, as 'a thousand suns appearing in the sky', or a similar analogy for what happens at the end of time, in the moment of dissolution.

It is very possible that Anaximander learned a metaphysical doctrine from his teacher, or his travels, and was subsequently totally misunderstood by his contemporaries and other Greeks who came after him, which would not be surprising. He was then even further misunderstood, to what might even be termed an ultimate extent by modern scholars. The 'infinite' was reduced by the other Greeks, and even more now, to the 'indefinite', which is merely incalculable and not infinite or eternal at all. Modern scholars take what Anaximander said as being meant literally or materially, whereas in fact at the time of the 6th century BC the Greek word for 'material' did not even have the meaning it took on much later in modern Europe.

For a while the cosmology of Apeiron was accepted by Greek philosophers, a phase that the scholars think to be 'abstraction', since they cannot conceive of anything beyond the most basic level of physicality. They also think that the eventual shifting away from what they call 'mythology' to rationality, which they understand and so approve of, was caused by new political conditions. Notably, sociologists and historians like to suppose that society and politics governs all thought, as though ideas could be changed from below, which is something that can only be said of our world in the present times.

---

[50] Cf. *Nu Hermetica*, 'Cosmic Cycles'.

Andromeda

In the (Egyptian) Book of the Law, II: 27–29, reason, when that is regarded as the sole means of knowing reality or truth, is cursed to the ages in no uncertain terms, and is called 'Because and his kin'. Reason has 'kin' or family relations in the sense that it has products, as can be seen everywhere today through the applications of profane or conventional sciences.

> *There is great danger in me; for who doth not understand these runes shall make a great miss. He shall fall down into the pit called Because, and there he shall perish with the dogs of Reason.*
> *Now a curse upon Because and his kin!*
> *May Because be accursèd for ever!*

This is the oracle of Hadit as the Serpent of Knowledge. Hadit is the Egyptian equivalent of the Sanskrit Atma. Hadit is the pure and unconditioned Atma (Self) in the unmanifested state, which is free of all limitations. Hadit, in that case, is 'not extended' (II: 2). But Atma manifests in the individual and corporeal state as *jivatma*, which is as it were a reflection of pure Atma. From there, Atma is veiled in increasingly complex determinations. These include the inward sense (*manas*) and all the aspects of individual mind that include reason, memory and imagination. In this case Hadit becomes the Serpent of Knowledge and, through the ego (*ahankara*), he has the power to weave illusions and spells, deluding the individual self into believing in the strictly limited appearance of things, even its own products.

As we near the end of a Cosmic Cycle, the capacity for delusion among the human species is increased until spiritual reality becomes almost completely unknown.[51] One of the symptoms of such a vast increase in bewilderment is the confusion and inversion of spiritual symbolism that has taken place in relatively recent times. This even amounts to a counterfeit spirituality, one that has by now been completely absorbed into postmodern culture. In the Book of the Law, II: 58, it is declared,

> *Yea! deem not of change. Ye shall be as ye are and not other.*

---

[51] Cf. 'Cosmic Cycles', *Nu Hermetica*.

Hadit is here speaking as the principle (Atma). The True Self does not change in its essence, but the individuality comes about through determinations—which are the superimpositions upon the Real as constantly referred to in Advaitan texts. The individuality is therefore limited by definition. Furthermore, even a being whose nature has reached that of the supreme realisation, which is that of the pure, unconditioned Self, they will appear to others as no different than they ever were. And this is because the point of view of those 'others' is that of the corporeal state. Thus, at the transfiguration of Christ Jesus on Mount Hermon, the disciples that witnessed it were afraid, remaining in confusion.[52] Even after his crucifixion and death, when he appeared to Mary Magdalene in the midst of his transformation, she wanted to touch his body—which was at least a desire of greater intimacy than that of Thomas, who wanted to place his finger in the wounds merely to prove something as 'evidence'. Thus conventional science was born from doubt and uncertainty, and there it shall remain forever bound by the chains of ignorance.

Initiatic transmission has its source wholly outside of and beyond the human domain. This happens to strike to the very core of the postmodernist and New Age delusion, which has by now become accepted by most people as a kind of 'spirituality' in itself, though it is a counterfeit of the Antichrist or anti-spiritual force in man. The quest for self-improvement, self-perfection, is a vain and futile one. Analytical research, experimental research, quantitative evaluation, forms an iron cage for the soul. Reason alone cannot reason its way out of the cage of reason. We cannot do it by 'working through it' as though one could do work on the self, in the way of a mechanic that wants to improve the performance of a machine or engine. All that does is place more attention on the individuality (Sanskrit *ahankara*) that is causing the agitation—the consequence is only more agitation. That agitation is very much the abnormal condition that is the 'norm' of our times.

All arguments, reasoning, thesis and anti-thesis, even if aimed at 'liberation', as in the conventional and not the technical sense, keep the person chained to the rock as Andromeda. Andromeda could not free herself from herself and neither can anyone. To go about it any other way is to give all power to the reasoning ego, which loves to imagine it is in control of everything. So long as the state of ignorance (Sanskrit *avidya*) is maintained, everything is in the realm of the 'psychological' and it will stay that way.

---

[52] Cf. 'Dual Symbolism and Symbolic Inversion'.

In the Greek myth, Andromeda was the daughter of King Cepheus and Queen Cassiope of Joppa in Palestine.[53] Cassiope offended the Nereids, a species of nymph or water elemental, by boasting that Andromeda was more beautiful than they were. An enraged Poseidon then sent a sea monster to devastate the kingdom of King Cepheus. Andromeda was subsequently chained to a rock and left to be devoured by the sea monster, as a sacrifice. When Perseus flew by on the winged horse Pegasus he fell in love with Andromeda and asked Cepheus for her hand. Cepheus instantly agreed, and Perseus slew the monster. Unfortunately, however, Andromeda had previously been promised to her uncle Phineas, and he tried to claim her at the wedding feast. Perseus resolved the problem by swiftly turning him to stone with the power of Medusa's head. As the legend has it, Andromeda later bore Perseus six sons and a daughter.

Andromeda was chained to the rock by her community as a 'sacrifice' to the monstrous sea serpent or psychic force, which in this case is associated with the notion of vanity—vanity that devours or eats up the soul with pride. The 'community' may symbolise all the contingent matters arising within the individual domain. These are what chain us to our fate. We cannot obtain liberation by merely rearranging the elements of our self or attacking them in some way. Perseus, a mortal, was born of the God Zeus, and is the type of the avatar, Holy Guardian Angel or Saviour. Pegasus, the celestial horse, symbolises nobility and courage—the royal attributes. Originally, the kingly warrior caste required the divine ordinance of the priestly class.[54] Thus the *descent* of Perseus from on high was required before the monster could be slain, the evil psychic force neutralised and Andromeda reborn as the soul set free.

When the nobility is separated from the spiritual principle, evil is wrought in the world. In the present times this situation is further degraded—first the nobles separated themselves from the priesthood, to gain the power of ordinance that was not rightfully theirs. In modern times the merchant class then usurped the power of the nobles, setting up governance based purely on materialism and greed. Even truth is seen as an expediency that is owned and determined by the wealthy and powerful. Materialism admits to no possibility of truth beyond the self and rejects the path of initiation by putting the self in the way of the Self. Materialism rejects all real spirituality, even when it pretends to embrace something it calls 'spirituality', which is a counterfeit.

---

[53] Called 'Ethiopia' in the myth. [Encyclopaedia Britannica.]
[54] Sanskrit Kshatriyas and Brahmins.

The symbolism of the six sons and one daughter is worth looking into. This could as easily have been six daughters and one son, and in some ancient legends it is. The figure of 'six' is the hexagram of the macrocosm. When three lines form a three-dimensional cross then it has six radii to a given circumference. The principial point where the lines meet is the 'seventh ray', which is the invisible (formless) solar ray or spiritual influence.[55] However, when governance (or ego) is separated from the spiritual principle, upon which its very existence depends, disorder and disequilibrium is the only possible outcome.

While vanity is not what used to be called a 'mortal sin', it is allied to pride and that can in turn lead to the rejection of all spiritual possibilities outside of and beyond the individual modality—and that is the philosophy of rational atheist humanism, which has by now reached its apotheosis. In the (authentic) Christian tradition, for example, the rejection of the Holy Spirit is the only unforgivable sin, for it amounts to total rejection of Christ, the Word and the Way. That sin cannot be forgiven because Christ alone has the power to forgive sins. The rejection of spiritual reality, which is taken as a matter of fact by a great many persons today, means it is not possible to attain salvation, the exoteric or religious goal, let alone liberation (or deliverance), the esoteric goal.

It will be necessary to qualify some of these terms. 'Salvation' is the religious objective but not the initiated one. One may seek salvation, the continuation of the soul as individuality.[56] 'Liberation' is from the Sanskrit *moksha* and is the 'end of the path' in so far as it is the fulsome and complete translation from the finite world of the individuality to the infinite world of spirit and eternity. These are principles held in common to all paths that have a basis in initiation. At the further end, which departs from all exoteric considerations to embrace the purely esoteric, all ways are the same path.

There is a particular kind of purification that is necessary, though it has nothing to do with 'self improvement'. There is a 'heat' or 'fire' associated with the path of knowledge, usually in relation to practices such as yoga, though it is by no means exclusive to that. It is an interior fire, and when properly directed it consumes or destroys everything that opposes spiritual realisation. It is symbolised in the language of alchemy and is also referred to as the transmutation of the Qliphoth or shells, as termed in the Qabalistic texts.

---

[55] Cf. 'Metaphysical Basis of Love and Will', *Nu Hermetica*.
[56] Such a continuation of the individuality has nothing to do whatsoever with the Theosophical invention of 'reincarnation', which itself has nothing to do with any traditional knowledge.

This 'burning up' does not, in itself, constitute either initiation or spiritual realisation but it is a very necessary part of all preparations and practices that are directed towards that goal.[57] The preparations therefore, including even the study of theoretical knowledge, which is indispensible, are in themselves 'purification' in a very real sense. It would otherwise be difficult, if not impossible, for individuals to detach themselves from the limiting conditions, especially as those very conditions are in a sense part of that individuality.

If this was difficult in the time of Sri Ramakrishna, little more than a century ago, how much more so now, with all the hypnotic toys and devices of profane science, where continuous distraction to attention is built into their very nature? The cell phone was quickly utilised by the System of Antichrist to assert more and more control over the lives of individuals. The purifications, such as are necessary to the goal of initiation and spiritual realisation, may perhaps require more pain and effort than at any other time in history for the person that is hopelessly dependent on such technologies, especially if that dependency reaches into the core of their idea of 'self' or 'identity'.

There is thus no real difference between such purifications and that called 'sacrifice' on the path of knowledge, which is not a path to anywhere at all unless it involves the following out of a discipline. Sacrifice is thus a ritual act, in the proper sense of what ritual means, a 'rite', 'ordinance' or setting things in order. In all cases it is really the ego that is being sacrificed for a higher state, as is evident in the symbolism of all initiatic ways. The 'self' will always stand in the way of the Self or True Will, and it is for this reason, of self-identification, that it is impossible for the many to follow out the way of knowledge, for they will never give up or change what they believe, in their state of ignorance, to be a part of their self.

For the Initiate, the obstructions or contingencies are destroyed in the preparations, for in the growing light of knowledge they cease to exist and vanish away as the phantoms they truly are. Nothing that is real, however, is ever destroyed. And this brings us back to 'deem not of change', which can be understood on more than one level. In one sense, the individuality or apparent state of the being is not changed in its determinations, which is all that limits and so defines it as such, through attachment to a body. That which is real and lasting (Atma) is not changed by anything, and cannot be destroyed any more than it can be created or born.

---

[57] See 'Fiery Aspiration', *Metamorphosis*.

Sacred Magic of Abramelin

Some have thought *The Book of the Sacred Magic of Abramelin the Mage* to have been written by a German Talmudic Rabbi; other scholars, who love to argue over meaningless facts, refute this. Whether it is true or not, the division of the whole field of a traditional science into two, 'high magick' and 'low magick', probably owes to those who sought to make an apology for the perplexing contradictions in the fifteenth century manuscript.[58] The book makes a persuasive case for 'high and holy magic', said to be taught by the Egyptian master Abramelin to Abraham, who then wrote it down for the benefit of his son Lamech.

The first part of the book is autobiographical, and tells of Abraham's travels and achievements. It is also filled with much heavy condemnation of sorcerers, astrologers, diabolists and the like, who, according to the author are black magicians with no real knowledge, and who should be rigorously avoided along with their lying works. As frequently takes place throughout the book, stern warning is given against the deceits of the Devil and the hosts of Evil Spirits that follow him—most excellent advice! The second part of the book is focused on the operation of the Knowledge and Conversation of the Holy Guardian Angel, which requires careful preparations over a six-month period (or six moons), prayer, piety and various abstentions. It culminates with the vision of the Guardian Angel, classed as the 'Convocation of the Good Spirits'. It is very peculiar then, given all that has been said previously, that this is immediately followed in the next chapter by an evocation of the Four Evil Princes of the World: Lucifer, Leviathan, Satan and Belial, and Eight Sub-Princes.[59]

The book's third section is for the most part talismans consisting of Hebrew letter-squares for obtaining visions, wealth, invisibility, transforming men into asses (something that surely does not require a magic spell to accomplish) and much other diabolical nonsense typical of black grimoires. The talismans are under the governance of the aforementioned Evil Spirits, the Sub-Princes and their legions of hideous servitors. Strangely, some of these effects are supposed to be wrought by a combination of good and evil spirits.

---

[58] The earliest version dates from 1508 but the text states internally that it was originally written in 1458.
[59] The names of the Sub-Princes are frequently to be found in late-medieval grimoires and many more books concocted later so that publishers could profit from the morbid curiosity of a degenerate literary class.

If a person has truly realised God, one may well ask what need have they of gaining the favour of profane persons, flying through the air, walking under water and all the rest? Clearly the Knowledge and Conversation of the Holy Guardian Angel as recounted here is a very different class of operation from that which we have written of, or otherwise alluded to, in previous books. The *Sacred Magic* gained a great deal of respect and admiration among certain members of the Golden Dawn. It was later argued by Crowley that a magician might need to resort to 'low magick' to arrange things in his material circumstances to make a Great Work possible in the first place. This, however, puts the black magic before the high and holy magick; whichever way round it goes, the way to any God-realisation will certainly not be opened by resort to traffick with spirits of the most inferior kind imaginable.

Crowley actually abandoned the Abramelin Operation, persuaded by what appeared to be an opportunity to assume leadership of the by then failing Order of the Golden Dawn—an escapade that was to end in humiliation for him. By a strange twist, the book's instructions insist that one must first complete the holy magic so as to earn the right to perform the black magic with impunity! That of course, did not deter Crowley from making full use of the letter-squares to curse other members of the Golden Dawn. He later produced elaborate justifications for such actions. It is or should be obvious by now that black magic is not something that can assist towards the goal of yoga, or of any real knowledge. It automatically implies an unprincipled use of ordinary natural laws towards inferior aims and purposes. Furthermore, magick as such can never be high or holy in itself, as its operation is limited to the psychic realm of the individuality—though if it is reserved for rites and practices that are aimed at the goal of yoga then it becomes a useful means to that end.

In the wake of Crowley, others have wanted to divide magick into high and low categories, and some have even posited something called 'grey magick'.[60] None of this fulfils any other purpose than to cloak the real intentions of those souls who have no desire for real knowledge, and who only seek to use some secret means to gain advantage in completely ordinary affairs. To pretend that such a skewed rationalisation has something to do with a high and holy purpose is to become adept only at the art of self-deception.

---

[60] In the text we are referring to the term is 'gray magick'—the American spelling is used. This was the work of the author Donald Michael-Kraig, an enthusiastic Crowleyphile who was so deeply deluded as to think that astral vampirism can be a means of knowing the Holy Guardian Angel!

In the *Sacred Magic* it is instructed that a medium, a child, should produce some magical writing or characters on a silver plate. Whether this is understood as writing done in the usual way, by hand, with pen, ink or brush, or if it is seen as something appearing supernaturally, makes no real difference. The use of a silver plate would certainly imply that the writing begins at least in the same way that one may see images formed from clouds in the sky. The child medium—'intelligent, and not older than seven years of age'—could be seen as analogous, which the book's apologists have sometimes proposed. The divine 'child' (as well as 'king') is a correspondence of Tiphereth, the realm of the Angel-messenger. This child is in reality the symbol of the *boddhi* or higher intellectual intuition, formless in its nature and in that which it perceives.[61] It is extremely unlikely, however, that the intentions of this magical operation are so exalted. It is not stated that the 'sign' or characters spell the name of the Angel as such; it is only a kind of mark or proof as evidence of his visit. The importance of the 'name', called Nama in Sanskrit, is great nonetheless, and we will come to this later as it is a whole subject in itself. The writing of characters, or indeed, an oracle of some sort, has a validity that depends very much on the knowledge and level of initiation of the theurgist. A 'received' work (Sanskrit *shruti*) must not be confused either with psychism or 'creativity', and in any case the primary goal of the Great Work must always take first priority.[62]

Whether or not the book of *Sacred Magic* was literally given to 'Abraham' by an Egyptian mage is irrelevant. According to Jewish lore, Moses spent some time in Egypt, and as we know, Christianity really owes more to ancient Egyptian Alexandria than it does to the Middle Eastern or Judaic traditions. Similarly, while the writers of a past era suffered derisive criticism for supposing the book of Tarot to have originated in Egypt, the truth of this does not depend on the production of such a book being a literal fact. Much of our spiritual knowledge, science and civilisation was disseminated from ancient Egypt to the rest of the world; it is only in relatively recent times that the fact is met with incomprehension and quite often laughter, as is especially the case with Egyptologists.

---

[61] Cf. 'Sat-Chit-Ananda'.
[62] By 'primary goal' is meant here not the ultimate goal, but the first real initiation, which comes about through non-psychic *transmission*.

That being said, it becomes clear that the Abraham of this book regards magick as inferior to the true secrets of the Qabalah, which is of course perfectly true. He regards the operation of the book, and its evil works of sorcery—which are somehow exempt from the scorn and condemnation he has afforded all other sources for the same—as being in a class of 'natural magic', which he deems was something the Egyptians excelled in. This also is true, in that magick depends on natural laws and is no more than a manipulation of such. If it is done without knowledge of any true principle, then it becomes 'black', or otherwise it is simply degenerate. The view of the Egyptian tradition here is that it only reaches as far as natural magic, which shows prejudice that is unfortunately commonplace in exotericism. At the same time we must remember that if these magical arts were given to Abraham in Egypt in the fifteenth century, it is certain that they were in a much-degraded form.

The book has it that the true secrets of the Qabalah can only be given to the eldest son. The book was therefore given by Abraham to his second son, Lamech, out of compassion, a sort of compensation.[63] From this we can then begin to understand some of the seeming contradictions in the operation itself. It is really completely exoteric, requiring only belief in God, and indeed fear of God, to accomplish. The operation is strictly limited to the psychic realm, and does not imply, or require, any real knowledge at all. As such it is like a vision of the Sanskrit *jivatma* but without knowledge of the true principle, Atma.[64] At best it might convey the 'sense of eternity', but we have to then wonder that if Lamech went on to evoke the infernal spirits as recommended he would not be destroyed by those same powers with great rapidity?

It is not our intention here to comment on the introduction and notes to the book that were added by S.L. MacGregor Mathers, who translated it into English for the first time. It must suffice to say that he was clearly taken in completely by the book's pretensions, in spite of his disagreement with some of its extreme condemnations and prejudices, and that the glamour of the book and the reputation it would acquire obviously appealed to his vanity, as was the case with Crowley and others. It is quite odd that he seems not to have noticed the gigantic self-contradictions that litter the book throughout. On one page we are warned against the deceits of the Devil, on the next we are instructed in how to evoke him to obtain treasure!

---

[63] The name LMCh means 'mercy' or 'compassion' in Hebrew.
[64] See 'Sat-Chit-Ananda'.

It could be speculated that the almost seamless merging of the high and holy magic with works of outright black magic, even while such are being condemned, as well as the disorderly arrangement of the content, was done deliberately, and is a form of 'blind'.[65] Perhaps the entire book was an elaborate ploy to send the unworthy to hell—though that is something they are usually more than ready to do without assistance from anyone else.

The theory that this elevation of psychism to the 'high and holy', while simultaneously combining its dubious fruits with the evocation of Evil Spirits, is completely skewed in its basis. It rests on the supposition, quite correctly, that the proper place of man is between the angels and the devils, which is consistent with all traditions. It then follows that a man has a counterpart in the angelic realm and a counterpart in the demonic or infernal realm. This also is not wrong, and we shall explain later how that may be approached from the metaphysical point of view.[66] The little twist in the logic that brings down the pack of cards, leaving only the joker standing, is that we are asked to believe that a Holy Angel, of the celestial worlds or supra-human states, would want to give us instruction in commerce with foul demons to hopeless, vain and futile ends.

The book is nonetheless enigmatic and not in any way like other grimoires, even while carrying much of the same trappings in the way of the infernal hierarchy: the Four Evil Princes are not unique to this book by any means and may be found elsewhere, with some variations, as with the legions of servitors. If we compare the devout part of the operation with Laya Yoga, for example, where there is an ascent of chakras or centres of subtle force, we find that the 'magical powers' belonging to the demons, as according to Abramelin, are considered to be quite natural and even useful in so far as being an indicator of development. The Eastern doctrines nonetheless warn against the use of the powers or of attaching any great importance to them, let alone regarding them as a goal, sufficient in itself. There is also the fact that Laya Yoga, or any valid practice, always aims at the *moksha* liberation, the knowledge of God or of the Real being a preliminary step on the way—a step comparable to the 'Knowledge and Conversation' as we regard it. The peculiarity of this work of Abramelin is in its great attention to every detail of the infernal hierarchies, of which many of the 'devils' can be recognised as merely Gods from more ancient times, long forgotten and so demonised.

---

[65] Abraham tells us that he threw the content around in a haphazard fashion to force Lamech to read it over and over again until it was well learned.
[66] Cf. 'Name and Form: Nama-Rupa'.

While there are vague murmurs from Abraham through the book that along the way the Guardian Angel might teach the 'ways of God' to the unknowing but faithful practitioner, the overwhelming bias of the operational intent is towards getting a psychic 'proof' of the Angel along with a mystic sense of rapture every Saturday if Jewish or every Sunday if Christian, or at least a vague sense of contentment.[67] What is called 'mystical' depends on two things, firstly, religious belief, and secondly, an exaltation of the emotions. None of that is considered in any way useful to the goal of yoga, indeed, it is seen generally as a hindrance that might even bar the way permanently to initiation and spiritual realisation. After this vague, mystic rapture, the whole bent of the work is to obtain treasure, accumulate a fortune and perform miracles, aided by supernatural potencies of an infernal nature. Also, many of the intended results of the use of the talismans, such as how to get the love of a woman already married (every kind of adultery is catered for) would horrify any person obedient to the moral teaching of their religion. It is very hard to imagine then that a pious person would have the slightest interest in such obvious diabolism. And yet the very nature of the operation requires piety.

Who then is the book really intended for, unless we are to take it at face value and believe, as apparently Mathers did, that it was really written and composed especially for one man, Lamech? This young man Lamech would have had to be a highly extraordinary, unusual individual. In the fifteenth century, perception of the subtle realm was far more common than it is now, though we know that John Dee, for example, a generation later, still needed to employ a medium, Edward Kelly. The facility for prolonged and ardent aspiration is extremely rare now, but was probably quite uncommon at the time of Abraham, a fact that he makes quite plain. The sheer bravado that is required to evoke such horrible demons is not at all uncommon today, but those who do this have no belief in any God whatsoever, so they are completely ruled out from performing such an operation as this. The sheer reckless disregard required is no doubt what made this work appeal to the likes of Mathers and Crowley, but there is no evidence that either of these ever completed the operation, though the latter certainly made use of the squares. The fact that Crowley subsequently cursed and reviled Mathers, his benefactor, to whom he had once pledged undying loyalty, tells perhaps of the consequences of the arrogance of modernists who play a game of occultism.

---

[67] The book has it that the operator can be of any religion or denomination. Also, they must not renounce their faith and convert to another religion, as that would mean denying the truth of the religion they were born into.

Satanic Inversion of the Angel

A great deal of confusion has existed over the whole matter of the Holy Guardian Angel and the Bornless Ritual, which was adapted by the Golden Dawn from a Coptic papyrus for the purpose of invoking the said Angel. Some of this confusion owes to the version of the ritual produced by Aleister Crowley. While this was an improvement on the unwieldy procedures of the Golden Dawn, Crowley's point of view was entirely corporeal (and so profane), and this, added to his Satanic bias, means his instructions for performing the ritual easily mislead the unwary; and this is so whether they understand the 'blinds' he used to cover his real intentions or not.

This matter of confusion owing to Crowley's need to cover his real operational procedures, which were in many cases unlawful—and not only in the profane legal sense of that—is serious enough to justify a more detailed explanation than we have given before, some aspects of which are to this day still kept as 'secrets' by those who continue to profit from Crowley's somewhat dubious reputation. By the time Crowley wrote up his version of the ritual, *Liber Samekh*, he was supplying his motley assortment of 'disciples' with narcotic drugs. He eventually reduced his notion of the Holy Guardian Angel to a figure of Satan as a goat-headed god. This in itself requires an explanation. It was Eliphas Levi that first introduced the idea that the pentagram with point downwards symbolises the Sabbatic Goat, or Baphomet. It is from there that some members of the Golden Dawn began to view the downwards-pointing pentagram as something to be feared. Before Levi published his particular formulation of the pentagram (1856), there was no particular rule about which way up a pentagram might be. The notion of Baphomet is fantasy, and rests on a double confusion; firstly, the Knights Templar were accused of worshipping idols, among other things, by the court of King Phillip of France and were then tortured into giving false confessions before being burned at the stake.[68] Such idols included a 'head', presumably an oracular one. Later, those who believed the accusers (evidently Crowley was among these) deduced, by pure supposition, that the Templars must have revered an image of Baphomet, which they further supposed to be Satan or the Devil—these two things also not being exactly the same. According to the Bible, Satan is an angel of the Lord that was sent to test Jesus at the temptation, in which various magical powers were offered and rejected by the avatar.

---

[68] See 'Knights of the Cross'.

The Devil, on the other hand, is merely a general name for the selfish wants and desires of men. While this is sometimes elevated to the level of a supernatural being, there is no doctrinal or theological basis for making such a presumption. There has long been confusion between the ram-headed god of Mendes, called Ba-neb-djedet by the Egyptians, and the alleged worship of goats, and this also owes to sheer fantasy. The confusion originates with Herodotus, the Greek traveller. In a complicated account in his famed *Histories*, Herodotus incorrectly describes the Delta god of Mendes as goat-headed. Much popular fiction associating the worship or sacrifice of goats with devil worship arises solely from this tale. If Herodotus did indeed travel to Mendes, then the local Egyptians were pulling his leg. The goat is a creature that did not inhabit the Delta region of northern Egypt. The principal god there was ram-headed, not goat-headed.[69]

Having decided that his 'personal angel' must be none other than Satan, Crowley then further reduced this to the image of the male generative organs, or more often, the actual organs themselves. As this had always been his principle object of adoration as well as a means of invoking psychic apparitions, the notion was pleasing to him, and provided countless opportunities for concealing his real activities under the cloak of 'holy ritual'.[70] He portrayed this Devil in his *Thoth* Tarot Atu XV. What has escaped the notice of even many of his followers is that the trump also depicts what he called a 'ritual' of the XIth or 'highest' degree of the OTO. The rings of Saturn in this case symbolise the favoured 'candidate for initiation'.[71] It should not be necessary to go further than we have done here to explain what Crowley actually meant by the term 'initiation'. Crowley deliberately inverted all symbolism to the most inferior degree possible.

---

[69] Herodotus, *History*, Book II p. 42, Robin Waterfield translation.
[70] In spite of what is usually written, Aiwass was not the 'Holy Guardian Angel of Aleister Crowley'—unless we accept a total confusion of identities! Others, however, going to work on this, have supposed that Aiwass of the Book of the Law must therefore be a name of Satan, and have tried to prove it. To compound the confusion to an almost unbelievable level, Crowley later produced a pen and ink drawing, which he said was an extraterrestrial named 'Lam', and used it to illustrate his flattering commentary on the work of the fraudulent medium, Madame Blavatsky. He later gave the original to Kenneth Grant in return for doing some work, telling him that it was "Aiwass". Others have then thought that Crowley's Guardian Angel must have been a Tibetan monk (*lama*). Need we say more?
[71] That is, as pertaining to the posterior of the (male) candidate.

While there can be an analogous relation made between any part of the human body and a higher principle this cannot be reversed, so that the higher principle merely symbolises the bodily form, without destroying all possibilities of real initiation. Yet that is exactly what Crowley did, and in some ways to an even greater extent, Kenneth Grant—though the latter preferred voyeuristic fantasy to Crowley's sadomasochism.

Crowley, from the evidence of all that he wrote, saw no difference between the physical state and the subtle and even spiritual states. Through his bias, mentality and particular predispositions, he had no knowledge of spiritual states but faked them instead with poetised versification assisted by sexual activity and powerful narcotic and other drugs to bring about an effect. Such effects, though quite fascinating to the profane sensationalist and prurient onlooker, do not involve any real knowledge or initiation whatsoever. The Order that he set up to replace the Golden Dawn was merely a counterfeit of a counterfeit, a double deceit or deception. As with the founders of the pseudo-masonic group that he also took control of, his claim to the high degrees of Freemasonry was completely fraudulent. It was likewise with his claims to any kind of initiation whatsoever other than 'virtual' or symbolic, as was gained through the benevolence of the Order of the Golden Dawn—an Order that he sought to subvert and destroy for entirely political and therefore profane reasons.[72] His published version of the ritual of a Neophyte was a cover for another ritual that involves abduction and sadomasochism, and this is still used, though secretly, by some factions of the various organisations that claim a 'lineage'. The reasons for the secrecy become evident once it is known what the ritual actually involves.[73]

---

[72] When Crowley left Cambridge he spent a short time with a post in the Diplomatic Service. He continued to work for the intelligence services on an unofficial basis for much of his life. It was due to some of the dirtier work he was engaged in during the First World War that some thought him to be a traitor to his country. In fact, this was not true—though he betrayed almost every person he had dealings with (including his wife Rose Crowley), and very often for complex reasons connected with his spying activities both at home and abroad.

[73] The published version of this ritual is called *Liber Pyramidos*, some of which owes to the work of George Cecil Jones, a member of the Golden Dawn. The secret version of the ritual preferred by Crowley and his epigones is called *Liber 671* or ThROA. The title refers to the 'throat' of the candidate, which is seized by the initiating officer with both hands before the candidate is thrown violently to the ground. Other details of the ritual—including the preliminaries—are too sordid to go into here.

St. Matthew and the Angel, Guercino (1622)

Knowledge and Conversation

In *Nu Hermetica* we wrote two chapters that have direct relation to what is termed, the 'Knowledge and Conversation of the Holy Guardian Angel'.[74] In the light of what we have said here in the previous chapter, that did not go far enough. Confusion abounds on this subject. Visions of angels, spirits or anything else of that type can have little if anything to do with the 'Knowledge and Conversation' that we have referred to the work of Tiphereth. Such things are no more than psychic apparitions; while they may have a certain reality relative to their appearance, and under some rare circumstances can even act as a support to initiation, none of it constitutes initiation in itself. It makes no difference whether it is visual or audio phenomena that are involved, though the audio sense perception is the higher of the two.[75] All of this pertains to the class of sensorial perception. A great deal of attention has also been placed on the Holy Guardian Angel as a sort of personal guide or something that helps us through life, which amounts to a subversion of spiritual knowledge. Some have reduced this even further to the level of spirit-guide or elemental, or worse, a kind of 'imaginary friend' that can be artificially constructed through the use of visualisation techniques.[76]

A great deal of emphasis has been placed on learning the name of the Angel, which again, through reduction to a simplistic level of understanding, places further limitation and reinforces the notion of having a 'private angel' uniquely personal to oneself—an incredibly flattering notion. These are quite silly ideas, but they have become very popular among those who would have us believe that spiritual experience (itself often confused with mysticism) can be turned on and off like a tap, 'at will'. This is not to deny that names and letters form an important part of theoretical knowledge, and we shall return to this later, but taking it literally obfuscates the meaning entirely.

---

[74] 'The Holy Guardian Angel' and 'Hekate Soteira', *Nu Hermetica*.
[75] The visual faculty, whether it is functioning in the physical or the subtle realm, corresponds to the *manipura* chakra, whereas the audio corresponds to *vishuddha*.
[76] Steinbrecher did this in his *The Inner Guide Meditation*, but there are by now no doubt dozens of other New Age or 'psychological' writers that have duplicated the fraud.

One of the most insidious notions put about, which owes to a literal interpretation of the *Sacred Magic of Abramelin* grimoire, is that the Knowledge and Conversation of the Holy Guardian Angel can be got through a medium.[77] This reduces the knowledge of God or Reality to mere psychism, and second-hand psychism at that. The delusionary notion that spiritual knowledge or initiatic realisation can be obtained, hired or purchased through a medium, once again owes to other false notions, for instance, that some kind of formula is involved.[78]

There are some types of oracular or even scriptural writing that are not derived from the psychic level at all, though obviously they must be 'translated' into language or symbolism so long as they are written down. In Sanskrit, the directly received knowledge is called *shruti*. There is no precise equivalent to this term in the English language. It means 'hearing' or 'heard', which pertains to the higher intellectual intuition called *boddhi*. The attributes of the state of *boddhi*, as previously mentioned, are formless.[79] Discursive thought or any commentary on what is derived from *boddhi* is called *smriti*, which is 'reflected'. Such writing and comment cannot be a personal invention of someone; they must be learned in the doctrine of their tradition.

However, the production of such texts does not really concern us here, though it would be easy to supply examples. What kind of conversation are we then speaking of? Does it mean that a holy angel is going to visit us every night and whisper flattering words in our ear? Well if that should be the case, it would be a devil not an angel. The Sanskrit *boddhi* is in fact the most accurate term to describe the development of the individual that is required to reach the necessary level to receive the Knowledge and Conversation we have in mind. It is of the realm of the formless, so that anything that has form, image or sound is at best more than as a reflection of the Moon upon a pool of water. Concentration of the mind is absolutely necessary.

---

[77] See 'Sacred Magic of Abramelin'.
[78] Crowley and his followers used magical means to further a completely vain and futile quest to find an actual 'Word of an Aeon', a word that could be written down in the ordinary way and numbered Qabalistically, and that would exalt them to the level of a major avatar, conferring on them all the magical powers they desired! It should hardly be necessary to add that no individual being can effect any change in Cosmic Cycles as that individual is strictly limited, by definition, to the conditions of that individuality.
[79] Cf. 'Sat-Chit-Ananda'.

There is another aspect to this. We think of angels as being of the heavenly or celestial realm, perhaps reaching to the intermediary world, which is accessible to the human state. How much does a person really desire to know truth? In most cases a person desires to find a mate or to get enough money to buy a house and get on the 'ladder' to an improved worldly status. Or it may be they desire magick, to lift them out of the boredom of their mundane existence. How interesting it will be to fly through the air and to visit the inhabitants of other worlds, perhaps collecting some secret powers along the way. All of that involves in the first place the desires of completely ordinary men and women, and in the second place, the desires of completely ordinary men and women to find an escape from the boredom of leading a completely ordinary life in the first place. It all amounts to pretty much the same thing.

Now if we were to ask the question, 'Supposing you could have one of two things, which would you choose? Either you can know spiritual reality or you can get your mate, acquire properties or whatever it is that your heart desires. Which do you choose?' Most likely the person would prevaricate, saying, 'Well, if I know spiritual reality, will that help me get a mate and buy some real estate later?' And if we say 'No', then certainly they will not pursue the idea of seeking knowledge for its own sake. To them, spiritual reality is in any case a kind of abstraction, not a real thing in the same way that things of the sensorial world are. If it can't get them something they want, then why should they seek it? Or it may be that they have learned some strange things about 'spirituality' from books they have read or from other people. They imagine it is about being good and holy, which as well as solving all their problems would also place them far above other human beings. How flattering are such ideas of goodness and holiness!

There is an inversion of this notion, which mostly afflicts those who want a magical path and not a spiritual one. This often involves something dark and slightly sinister—'sorcery' will always carry the romance of sex and power; or otherwise it simply carries the rebellious notions of youth, in which things of the spirit were seen to be the domain of sallow-faced priests or doorstep evangelists of one kind or another, or perhaps the school teacher who made us learn lines from the Bible as a punishment. One way or another it becomes a cloaked means of taking revenge for some perceived injustice. When that bottle of wine is opened it turns out to be far more inferior than *vin ordinaire* and it is unlikely, is it not, that we will even be so foolish as to want to drink it? Yet he who has such 'conversation' in his heart drinks it every day of his life.

Did we mention 'high and holy magic'? How easy it is to say that and yet have no idea at all what it can mean! Likewise with 'dark sorcery': everyone knows the story of Faust but would we really want to suffer his awful fate?

> I have securely blocked the way by which the King of Death will come;
> Henceforward all my doubts and fears are set at naught for ever.
> Shiva Himself is standing guard at the nine doorways of my house,
> Which has one Pillar for support, and three ropes to secure it.
> The Lord has made His dwelling-place the thousand-petalled lotus flower within the head,
> And comforts me with never-ceasing care.

Those are the words of Sri Ramakrishna, as recorded by his faithful disciple on June 17th, 1883. The 'nine doorways' may be symbolised by the apertures of the body. The 'one pillar' is Brahma. The 'three ropes' are the three *gunas*, which are the fundamental conditions of all manifested beings. This is naturally in the context of the Hindu doctrines, but it has its equivalent in every path; when viewed from the 'centre' then all paths look the same; they are only wearing different disguises on the outside.

The real secrets are incommunicable, so the language of symbol and metaphor is used to convey something to those who will not mistake the symbol for that which it symbolises. So as not to lose sight of the universal nature of all spiritual knowledge, we can look at the symbolism most familiar to those of us that came in through the door marked 'magick', a door that has many strange symbols carved into it, from Rosicrucianism to alchemy and the Qabalah. Tiphereth is the solar centre of the Tree of Life and it is here that the realisation of the Guardian Angel takes place. It is only from this centre onward that the world of time and space can be transcended. The 'spiritual sun' is said to rise above the Waters of Space here, which may further be depicted within a holy hexagram symbolising the celestial planets and luminaries in a harmonised arrangement. It is here that man is able to come into contact with what, for want of better terms, can be called the Universal or Cosmic Man.[80]

---

[80] Cf. 'The Two Adams'.

This spiritual sun has its equivalent with the Hindu Atma. The full knowledge and realisation of Atma is no less than the knowledge of God and the knowledge of the Real, but there are gradations to such realisation. The reflection of the sun can be seen on the surface of water and it looks exactly like the sun but it is a reflection, not the sun itself. It is this reflection that is perceived when it is known that this sun or spiritual Self is the centre of what is called *jivatma*, the individuality. Jivatma could not exist without Atma, yet in the state of ignorance that is the usual state of human affairs, the individuality is thought to be separate and uniquely 'itself'. Yet, it is only Atma that can be said to be separately and uniquely Itself, in the sense that Atma cannot be limited or defined in any way. Atma is not subject to conditions or determinations. All conditioned, determined states are a reflection of the Real, of the Atma. The light of Atma is not Atma, but the reflection of Atma. The further stage of knowledge is when Atma is seen to 'shine but not give off light'. We are what we *know*, not what we see or perceive. When we truly know Atma—a term that is often translated as 'God' in English, for convenience, though it is far from exact—then in that knowledge we are *known*. And in that knowledge we are changed, permanently and forever. We are what we know and we *become* what we know. There can be a change of state in the being, and that is a 'death' in so far as we can never return to the previous states.

The unconditioned Atma, is the very life and existence of us, and without this 'centre' we simply could not be. In the normal state of affairs, this is not known or realised at all. Knowledge has at least two aspects: To truly know Atma is to undergo a change in the state of being, and as has been explained, that is a 'death'. There is also the knowledge of *jivatma* that is obtained through various faculties, also called the 'perceptible' or 'known' as opposed to the Intelligible. That kind of knowledge can never be more than the knowledge of dead things, as is always the case with conventional science, with its theories and measurements. The true knowledge is not perceived through the sensorial, neither the physical senses nor even the subtle senses. However, it is perfectly valid and very often necessary to develop the latter so long as that is not seen as an end in itself. The goal must always be paramount, which is no different than the goal of yoga.

It is for this reason that in yoga—which is not in any way separate from meditation—the physical senses are first withdrawn to the subtle, and then the subtle senses are withdrawn so that the chakras of the perceptible may be transcended. The mind that is able to perceive that which is formless, not having image, reflection or any sound, is the *boddhi*, as has previously been defined.[81] Now this higher intellectual faculty is latent in some and not at all in others, and that is why the degrees of knowledge and realisation are not open to all. Furthermore, when it exists in the latent state it must be brought to flower, so to speak.

For this reason, the symbolism of flowers, lotuses and so forth is frequently found in all traditions. The Buddha, in the earlier and more authentic doctrine, was said to have emerged from the flower of the *soma*, which symbolises the sum total of all knowledge. In Egypt, there is the child Harpocrates or Horus of Silence, depicted within a blue lotus—he is the 'child of silence' because there is no chance of real knowledge until the person is able to still the ceaseless internal dialogue, where we talk to ourselves as we have learned.

This brings us at last to another aspect of the Hindu doctrines that we have mentioned before, and shall return to later. The Sanskrit Om or AUM can symbolise three states of consciousness in man: Waking, Dreaming, and Dreamless Sleep. The wakeful state is the ordinary utilitarian function of perception and so there is a certain contradiction inherent in the term 'wakeful', because as the common state of awareness it constitutes ignorance. The dreaming state facilitates less restriction than the waking state but it is not too far apart from the mind as associated with the body. Everyone experiences dreamless sleep where only the pure Atma is aware but they are not conscious of the fact and neither do they recollect or have any knowledge of the Witness or Seer. Obviously no one attains initiation or spiritual realisation through the condition of deep sleep! The three states are both literal and analogous with the states of meditation, in which case the wakeful state corresponds to ordinary thought, the dreaming state with the subtle, and the dreamless with the realisation of Atma. With initiation, the person must pass through all the states in full consciousness and by analogy they also pass through the 'three worlds' as figured in all traditions. There is a natural order to manifestation; initiation reverses this by returning to the source.

---

[81] Cf. 'Sat-Chit-Ananda'.

Name and Form: Nama-Rupa

The Name has profound significance but as we have previously mentioned, the meaning has become greatly obscured through reduction to the most simple level of understanding possible. The Sanskrit Nama or 'name' is the nearest Hindu equivalent to the Holy Guardian Angel, a term used almost exclusively by a minority within that which might broadly be termed as the Western Mystery Tradition.[82] To compound the obscuration, that tradition in itself is scarcely known of at all by the average Westerner today. If it is said, for example, that a person writes books about the Western Mystery Tradition, many would raise their eyebrows and either enquire as to what is meant by this or otherwise assume (no matter what is said) that the subject matter is something to do with the fantastic or 'supernatural', such as ghosts, apparitions or what academics term 'paranormal phenomena'.

There is far more to Nama and Rupa than that which appears to be the case if we only know the conventional English translation, 'name and form'. The Name is that which produces or forms the individuality, and is therefore not itself formed by the individuality; its nature is of formless essence and it is of the supra-sensible realm. It is not identical to *purusha* or divine 'essence' but is a reflection of that. Individuality, however, does not only exist as attached to the corporeal or human state, or the formal state; an individuality can exist on the level of formless manifestation. As such, Nama can exist independently of Rupa, 'form', and can have direct correspondence with the supra-individual *devas*, the 'angels' of celestial or heavenly worlds (Paraloka).

The Name is no doubt that which was referred to in the Egyptian tradition as the *ren*; while it is not Ra, the solar principle itself, it is of the same essence in reality, as reflected on a lower arc. The Name is that which is able to continue to exist after physical mortality and even after psychic dispersion (the 'second death'). It thus has a direct relevance to the resurrection and immortalisation of the soul.

---

[82] The Western Mystery Tradition was essentially a *lost* tradition following the destruction of the Knights Templar (see 'Knights of the Cross'). It was continued secretly for a short time by the Rosicrucian fraternity but this soon withdrew. Later attempts to revive the current were almost entirely counterfeit. What remains is in the form of systemised symbolism, taken out from its traditional context and, through confused translation and populist over-simplification, reduced to virtually nothing.

We must carefully distinguish between the ordinary meaning of a 'name' and the Nama. If we take Nama literally, as some have done in the modern attempts to retrace the threads of the long lost Western Mystery Tradition, we make a considerable error. Even while there is an analogous relation between Nama and a name composed of letters and sounds that can be written down and uttered in the ordinary way, it is not an exact or true relation. As we have said, Narma is a reflection of 'essence' within the domain of the individuality. As such it is not of the sensible world, that is, all that can be apprehended by the corporeal senses. It does not even truly exist within the subtle realm, although from the corporeal point of view Nama and Rupa can be viewed as the subtle part of the individuality and the corporeal part—which is the least of all degrees of manifest being and the most strictly limited. Now having said this, there is an analogous relation to be drawn between Nama and letters and numbers, especially the Pythagorean numbers. Lamech, the second son of the patriarch in the Abramelin grimoire is a good example of this. The value of that name in Hebrew is 78, which is the sum of all the numbers between one and twelve. It therefore has a relation by correspondence with HVA, a name of Kether, the 'crown' or summit.[83]

As the nature of Nama is formless essence, though it is within manifestation, it is able to exist, as we have previously said, without Rupa altogether, even when Rupa is regarded as form on the subtle level and not body. We can then begin to see why, in what little has been written on the Holy Guardian Angel that is not merely a sort of mystical obfuscation, there is usually an insistence on the importance of the *name* of the Angel. In the book of St. John, 1: 1, it is famously written, 'In the beginning was the Word, and the Word was with God, and the Word was God'. This is consistent across all doctrines, including that of the ancient Egyptians. A manifested being is known by its 'true name', as in the legend of Isis and Ra, where Isis is able to rejuvenate Ra by tricking him into disclosing his secret name or *ren*. In biblical lore, Adam is said to have given names to all the creatures, and this is identical with their coming into being. The Adam before the fall is not man in any ordinary sense, but is Universal Man, and as the totality of being is beyond even the angels. The matter of the two Adams in the books of Genesis is an interesting one, and we will return to it later.[84]

---

[83] See 'Sacred Magic of Abramelin'.
[84] See 'The Two Adams'.

One most curious thing regarding Nama is that when it exists separately from Rupa, in the formless state, then through upward transposition it may inhabit the realm of the angels and archetypal worlds. This is the domain of the supra-individual Idea, a word that is related to the Greek *eidolon* or *eidos*, which is usually thought to mean 'image' but has more to do with formless 'essence'.[85] As René Guénon has mentioned, there is a certain comparison to be made with the sense of the idea of the artist, from which meaning is drawn, and finally the completed work.[86]

The *eidolon*, as with Nama, can exist on both sides, as it were, of the formless individual state and realm of angels. This means that while Nama can enter the supra-individual state it can do so and still have a name; otherwise it could not of course be 'Nama'. It is only when the being leaves the manifested state altogether, and enters the unconditioned state, that it can be said to be 'nameless', for it has entered eternity. We can begin to understand how the Knowledge and Conversation of the Guardian Angel works from a metaphysical point of view. On reaching the 'centre', which has its correspondence in the individuality, the reflection of Atma or the Real is perceived as a reflection of the sun shining upon water. This is *jivatma*, in terms of the Hindu doctrines.[87] There are, according to the same doctrines, two *jivatmas*, for from the spiritual or higher point of view there is no difference, the lower being merely a reflection of the higher. Naturally, if the sun stopped shining, its reflection in water would also disappear. When the true name or the seed 'essence' of the individual self is known, then by upward transposition the angelic or celestial counterpart may be known. This is one very good reason, however, for the renunciation of the 'magical powers' that is integral to traditional knowledge. If the person, on perceiving the reflected image, immediately stoops down as it were, to engage their attention on the infernal powers, the way to the true knowledge of Atma, the Real, is in serious jeopardy and may even be barred permanently so the person remains bound by the coils of Leviathan.[88]

---

[85] Cf. *Nu Hermetica*, p. 183.
[86] *Study of the Hindu Doctrines*, 'Narma and Rupa' [Sophia Perennis]. It might be added that art in the real sense is not at all 'whatever you make of it', as applies in postmodernism today. It must reflect the essence of its true type, and so it could be said that all non-traditional forms of art are not truly art as such. This is very particularly true of what is sometimes called 'conceptual art', as that has no reach at all beyond the commonplace.
[87] Cf. 'Sat-Chit-Ananda'.
[88] Cf. 'Sacred Magic of Abramelin'.

The Two Adams

In the book of Genesis there are two Adams named, a fact that has been frequently noted in various ways and from various points of view by biblical scholars and theologians as well as by occultists. In the book of Genesis, 1: 26, the Elohim—a plural form of 'God' that is both male and female and yet neuter at the same time—are said to create Adam. Here, Adam is plain 'Adam', spelled ADM in Hebrew. While some scholars, even Christian ones, will sometimes admit to the plural form of Elohim, they usually find ways of avoiding the implication; for example, by saying that it means 'God and the angels'. However, there is no such Order of Angels in Briah, the world of creation. As we have mentioned across various other writings, what we are really dealing with is an older 'creation' and a newer one that is in all probability a superimposition.[89] The Hebrew Tetragrammaton or Demiurge does not make an appearance until the second book of Genesis where, quite surprisingly, the whole creation of Adam and the world seems to take place for a second time.

Christian scholars and theologians always insist that the Bible is the work of God and not written by any man. This is true of all traditional doctrines but biblical texts were copied and recopied by scribes and made subject to alterations and rearrangements over time. Many of these changes and additions were doubtless made for political and social reasons, which means that the 'Word of God' is an adulterated one in the Judaeo Christian tradition. There is also the key question of translation. Once Hebrew vowel pointing was added to Aramaic texts the meaning was fixed and made determinate to a particular view. The original texts were always unpointed so that different levels of meaning could be construed from them, as according to the level of initiation. Some of the meanings are even seemingly quite opposite, which is perfectly normal in traditional metaphysics. Once the Hebrew scriptures were translated through Greek and Latin and finally made subject to the language of common people in England and Europe, one had to dig very deep to discover the esotericism that had been obscured if not destroyed altogether.

---

[89] The term 'creation' is frequently used in cosmological discussion but it is highly inaccurate as a thing cannot be brought into existence that does not already exist, at least latently. It inevitably anthropomorphises God or Ishvara.

Adam (ADM) of Genesis 1: 26 becomes *the* Adam (ATh H-ADM) in Genesis 1: 27, the next verse. The use of both definite article and the particle is as if to underline the difference with emphasis. The same grammatical context for Adam is used again in 2: 7. While there will always be some who will deny there are two Adams, there is an undeniable difference in the Hebrew. A typical scholastic line is that while 1: 26 is general cosmological creation and of man (or the race of men), 1: 27 and 2: 7 refer to a more specific creation of *the* man, as concerned with humanity. There is then continuity, for Christians at least, between the Old and New Testaments: the second Adam exists so that through generation from Adam and Eve, Christ is eventually born from the Virgin Mary to redeem humanity. This neatly avoids the matter of whether there are two Adams or even two races—the latter supposition being one that borders on heresy, of course.

The problem with the 'anticipation of Christ' theory is that, firstly, it all depends on generation in time and has no metaphysical basis at all. Neither does it take account of the virgin birth. Secondly, the Old Testament is not a Christian book; it is fundamental to the Jewish tradition. When Christianity was taken out of its Egyptian origin and reformulated into a religion there was apparently a need to merge it with Judaism so there could then be an 'Old Covenant' and a 'New Covenant'. Presumably there were political and social intentions to artificially form a 'universal tradition' where none previously existed in the exoteric sense, only the esoteric. As for the 'two races' point of view, while seeming on the face of it to be more imaginative than anything else, it is more plausible if we consider the Cosmic Cycles. In vastly ancient times there were races on the earth, not only in the subtle modalities or even 'heaven', that were non-human, even if they might have had some human characteristics.

What we propose is the complete reverse of the scholastic and the theological views of the two Adams. Metaphysically, the spiritual must come before the essential, the essential before the substantial and the substantial before the physical or end result. Therefore the Adam born of the Elohim, or 'God and the Angels' in the first book of Genesis, is Adam Kadmon, the 'Primordial Adam', a fact that is not contended by any but the most obtuse. As 'Universal Man', this Adam is androgynous and is not involved in manifestation. We should be careful not to anthropomorphise the term 'Universal Man', for the corporeal state is one of the defining requirements of the human, and Adam Kadmon is non-corporeal. We shall return to this later.

The race of Adam Kadmon, as in verse 1: 26 of Genesis, is 'of the starry heaven', and not of the earth at all.[90] In verse 1: 27, it is said that the Elohim then made woman—at this point she has not been named Eve. Adam is then called *the* Adam. The separation of male and female is the first step towards the human, although neither of the pair can truly be said to have a name or Nama until Genesis 3: 20 where it is said, 'And Adam called his wife's name Eve; because she was the mother of all living'. This is still not a man or a woman in any sense we can think of it from the corporeal point of view. Eve is the mother *of all living*, something that scholars will pass off with the simplistic notion that Eve was the 'first woman'. The name Eve in itself is often associated with 'sin', as though the sinful nature was already implicit in the nature of woman, which is absurd.

In fact the name Eve (ChVH) is derived from a root that is the feminine form of 'He' or 'Lord' (HVA), and which is also a title afforded Kether the Crown, the first emanation of the Tree of Life in the Qabalah—the Supernal Eden is implicit. There is a substitution in this name of Eve of a *vav* for a *yod*, since HIA means 'she', 'that'. The substitution changes the view of Eve as nature becoming visible to *chevah*, which means 'stumbling', an indication of the coming fall of Adam and Eve and their banishment from Eden.

As it was Adam that gave Eve her name here, we can make a comparison with the Sanskrit *purusha* and *prakriti*, 'essence' and 'substance'. When personified as Devas in the Hindu tradition this pair is always male essence and female substance. Neither are in manifestation in time and space even while nothing could manifest as such without them, as principles. In more ancient metaphysical traditions such as that of Egypt, the situation is sometimes reversed so that essence is the feminine and substance the male. We should remember that none of this implies sex; it is a matter of active and passive principles. In the most ancient traditions, the Goddess did not require a father to produce her son, as in the case of Hathoor and Horus, and Nuit and Set.

It is curious indeed that the original creation of Adam by the Elohim is echoed much later in the biblical texts when the story of the Nephilim is recounted, as being 'giants', the progeny of the Sons of Elohim and the daughters of earth—by which could equally be meant 'essence' and 'substance' or Nama and Rupa.[91]

---

[90] Cf. *Nu Hermetica*, p. 212.
[91] Cf. *Nu Hermetica*, 'Sons of Anak' and 'Sons of Gods'.

We must refute the standard scholastic line, which is that the race of Nephilim sought to destroy all the descendants of *the* Adam, or the second Adam, and that the Sons of the Elohim were 'fallen angels'. This rests on ignorance of the fact that all avatars descend, which is the very meaning of the name, in order to *reascend*. The Sons of the Elohim descended to earth from the top of Mount Hermon, where they swore an oath regarding the daughters of earth upon whom they wished to beget progeny, which would be divine or semi-divine. In the New Testament, Christ Jesus ascends Mount Hermon to visibly achieve transfiguration in the eyes of his disciples, thus recollecting the Sons of Gods—his true race. Thus Christ was not in any way descended from the second Adam or even the race of men as such. His descent is from the heavenly order, and that is in complete concordance with the Christian doctrine while happening to agree with the Gnostic one at the same time, which Christian scholars of course still condemn as heresy.

We can now see that the 'Guardian Angel' is not a supposition made from a medieval grimoire, or from a fragment of scripture or Jewish lore that rests on interpretation, but forms part of a coherent doctrine both metaphysical and cosmological. The Nama, as referred to earlier, is the 'signature' of the individual being.[92] The *boddhi* or the higher intellectual intuition is that which forms the individuality, and yet at the same time is able to know Atma or Reality directly, for in its own nature *boddhi* is formless and by upward transposition is one with the 'essence', which is in turn one with Atman or 'Atma Itself'. Adam Kadmon or the Universal Man is the principle of all manifestation, the sum totality of all states of being, and for this reason we reaffirm that it is an error to anthropomorphise this, for the human state is only one degree of all the indefinite degrees of manifestation. The human being, the second Adam, nonetheless has the possibility of attaining the realisation and so the actualisation of the existence of the Universal Man, through initiation. So long as Universal Man remains an ideal, he exists in the 'virtual' state, though this is the only place we can begin the Way that leads to the true realisation. Once fully realised, there is a permanent change in the state of the being. The two Adams are therefore descriptive of different states of being: the perfected or primordial state and the fallen state of man.[93]

---

[92] See 'Name and Form: Nama-Rupa'.
[93] Cf. Guénon, *The Symbolism of the Cross* [Sophia Perennis], in particular, 'Universal Man' pp. 12–15.

The Recording Angel

According to ancient Egyptian tradition, the scribe God Tahuti, in later times called the Recording Angel, records the names of all those who will attain to immortality in the Book of Life. They then become as Living Souls (*khus*). In more ancient times still, the work of recording the name of a Living Soul was an attribute of the goddess Sesheta, or Septet.[94] To understand the writing of the name, the Egyptian *ren*, in the Book of Life or Book of Thoth, one must know something of the Hindu doctrine concerning Nama and Rupa, Name and Form. We have discussed this elsewhere in some detail, so it will suffice to say here that this is far more than a moral test of aptitude, in which bad deeds are punished and good deeds are rewarded.[95] Such moral attributions are in any case an addition made by religious theologians in relatively recent times, and which rest on an anthropomorphic conception of God. Such ideas, though needed to suit the mentality of people at various times, inevitably distort the metaphysical doctrine. Unfortunately, it is these religious notions that Egyptologists and others have applied when trying to construe the meaning of ancient symbolism and scriptures that owe nothing at all to religious thought.

There is an occult notion of an Akashic Record that derives from the Theosophical Movement and that was taken up by the whole of the Western Mystery Tradition thereafter. This is a purely modern invention; the idea is that all deeds and actions whatsoever are inscribed or impressed into a subtle or dreaming repository. When this is likened to the Qabalistic Treasure House of Images (Yesod), then the confusions are further confounded.[96] It is possible that this invention rested on a misunderstanding of the Hindu doctrine of *apurva*, which so perplexed Nietzsche that he had to create his own imagined and erroneous version of it, called 'eternal recurrence'.[97] There are multiple confusions here; the subtle realm or Astral Plane, as it is sometimes termed, has nothing to do with *akasha* (Sanskrit) or the 'spirit', though like everything else it owes its existence to that which is immutable.

---

[94] Cf. *The Egyptian Tarot of Thelema,* Atu XXI.
[95] See 'Name and Form: Nama-Rupa'.
[96] A title of Yesod, the ninth sephira, number or emanation. While there is a repository or collective memory, in which resides the degraded remnants of former traditions such as folk lore, for example, and which is a reflection of cosmic memory, this has nothing to do with individual deeds and actions.
[97] See 'The Key of Magick'.

Deeds and actions are mutable or subject to change.[98] If these deeds and actions are in accordance with the True Will (Sanskrit *dharma*), then they may partake of a 'sense of eternity'. This is always the case with what Patanjali termed 'right action', which is typified as ritual action when the rite expresses true or universal principles. But that is not what is meant by the pervasive notion of the Akashic Record, which has also allowed occultists to indulge in endless entertaining diversions concerning 'past lives', another even more insidious modern invention.[99]

Tahuti and other Egyptian gods had an attribute related to the Book of Life, which is called the Net, the weave or fabric from which worlds are spun. Tahuti, whose temple was the House of the Net, is sometimes shown as wearing this weave in the form of a starry nemmys, and goddesses are sometimes shown wearing a lattice or diamond-shaped criss-cross pattern as a garment covering their bodies.[100] The simplest form of this symbolism is a cross, composed of a vertical and horizontal line, which becomes three-dimensional when another line passes through the centre at right angles to the others. This, the Cube of Space, is identical to the early Christian adoption of the Chi-Rho as the monogram of Christ Jesus. The symbolism can be understood, through the analogy of the weave of warp and weft, as depicting a universal cross that is able to replicate indefinitely, producing numerous worlds or states of being as well as countless individual creatures, which are a microcosmic reflection of the macrocosm.

Weaving, embroidery, music and dancing are traditionally crafts associated with women, though are not necessarily exclusive to them. In ancient times, long before the world religions were formed, these crafts formed the basis of the initiatic traditions in the same way that stone cutting and sculpture did. Only remnants of this traditional knowledge were able to survive, in the solely male province of Masonry, for example. We have to go back to times of great antiquity to find civilisations that fully supported the initiation of both men and women.

---

[98] Ibid.
[99] Cf. 'Karma and Sin', *Nu Hermetica*.
[100] See 'The House of the Net' [*ibid*].

In traditional Hindu dance and music, the metaphysical aspect has not been altered, whether modern practitioners understand that or not. Hindu sacred dance begins and ends, for example, with the salutation called *namashka*, 'naming or defining space', which is identical in form to the Hermetic Cube of Space of six directions.[101]

The thread of the spirit that invisibly weaves all things is called *sutra* in Sanskrit, of which the *Brahma Sutras* are the most well known example. The *sutra* or 'weave' is symbolised as a book in more than one ancient tradition. Sometimes the Holy Grail is likened to a sacred book, as the repository of all knowledge. The 'weaving' is also associated with the Hindu 'Tantra'. The book or *sutra* is not only concerned with production but also with travelling or journeying to the eternal source of all knowledge, which is the way of initiation. Some of the medieval spells for invisibility are precisely that, when properly understood; the 'cloak of invisibility' is of course symbolised by a woven garment. The well known word-spell from the Key of Solomon, 'Abracadabra', was meant to be recited or written eleven times, each time losing a letter, until only the initial 'A' remained; when this too is banished, the invisibility obtains. Zomar Levan is a Hebrew term that means 'white (or pure) weaving'; this is precisely the following of the golden thread that leads outside of space and time.[102] In an Egyptian spell, one of very many where such symbolism is used, it is said:

> Open thou the ways, that I may return through the wheels of thy spinning, that have established the throne of my becoming, that was my seat before my beginning.[103]

---

[101] Namashka is interpreted in various ways, sometimes as 'obedience', in so far as it is traditionally done to offer prayer and greetings to God, guru and audience. It is also used as a merely customary greeting, sometimes called *namaste*, and so the true meaning is frequently not known today.

[102] Transliterated: TzMR LBN (צמר לבן). The numerical value is 412, which, interestingly enough, is the equivalent of the letter *beth* (BITh) spelled in full, which means 'house' and refers to the first manifestation from primal unity projected into space, which is itself the 'abode' or House of God.

[103] See 'Spell 78', *Babalon Unveiled*.

All this would seem far removed from the practice of Keeping the Record, sometimes called the magical diary record, but as we shall see, a strong relation may be asserted. The method by which a daily practice with times, dates, solar and lunar courses, observations or insights gained, is written faithfully and methodically into a journal has been likened to a 'scientific record'. However, the methods of profane science are useless in terms of initiated, metaphysical or spiritual realisation. Our reasons for recording such data are quite different, as is the way in which it is recorded, if we look beyond the most outward appearance of this.

Although we will not coin the term, as that would give rise to confusion in a field where confusion already abounds, an Akashic Record comes closer to the real meaning and use of a diary record in spiritual practice or operative theurgy. Sound, including speech and language, corresponds to the *vishuddha* chakra in the Tantras.[104] The chakras are not physical locations as such; their attributions are analogous; the *vishuddha* chakra corresponds to the larynx and ears and the faculties of speech or utterance, and hearing. The *vishuddha* chakra corresponds to *akasha* or spirit, whereas the four chakras below correspond to elemental principles—air, fire, water and earth.

For this reason it is said that music is the most spiritual of art forms. In the Hindu doctrines there are two main classes of speech, called *para-vak* and *vak*. The former is 'beyond speech', which is sometimes termed 'primordial speech'. The latter is speech when that is understood as vocalisation made via the larynx.[105] Evolutionists misunderstand the import of this entirely as they are limited by the belief that things must improve or get better over time, which they call 'progress'. It is not that one modality is better than the other, as the modalities serve different purposes, but it is the primordial or 'beyond speech' that is superior in the natural order, or closer to spirit or metaphysical reality. Para-vak is sound vibration but is without vibration in any physical sense; it is beyond action and is instantaneous or simultaneous, owing to the formless state. As such, it is much closer than physical sound to the higher intellectual intuition (Sanskrit *boddhi*), and it is this alone that can touch upon the knowledge of the Real, or of Atma, the True Self.

---

[104] Cf. 'Kundalini Yoga'.
[105] See 'Brahmacharya'.

Ritual and meditation can have varying degrees of quality and we are not the same at any given moment even if knowledge itself remains unchanged. Effective meditation reaches further than the merely symbolic or virtual. In that case some 'unpacking' is required in the writing afterwards. Although the ritual is closed as such, the interior work continues. In unpacking or translating into what can be spoken or written, things will arise that did not seem to have been apparent at the time. When that happens it is perfectly valid to include them in the record and even to apply some development if that is the fruit of what was received as a seed. This is a discovered method in so far as it cannot be taught. It can be likened to the rapid growth and flowering of what seems like a very small seed or kernel when writing up the diary record after the practice—and we should note that it is for this reason that the record must always be written up immediately after the practice. There is then an expansion on any non-verbal transmission being 'vocalised', put into words or written down—and these really amount to the same thing, because of our mentality—something we shall return to later.

Now the seed, identical to the traditional symbol of the grain or mustard seed, as well as the centre of any cross or weaving, is universal; in that is the sum total of all knowledge. The seed principle is not particular or subject to determination in itself. A type or image of that seed is then produced, which is particular or relative—as it is subject to determination. It is that which is unpacked when writing, and which represents a transition from *para-vak*, 'beyond speech', to *vak*, 'speech'. The importance of this cannot be overestimated.

The observation of certain subtleties of the meditation or working itself is important when establishing the practice. There is a 'sense of eternity' perceptible in the symbolism, which is very ancient in the case of a true and proper rite. The knowledge of *ajna* or the third eye chakra is beyond the perceptible and so does not equate to sound, vision or any of the senses, whether they be of the subtle or physical realm. This knowledge really equates to what may be called the 'divine threshold', for it is characterised by the union of Shiva and Shakti no less than union with God, which is the goal of yoga as defined by Patanjali.[106]

---

[106] The goal of yoga as according to Advaita Vedanta does not stop at 'union with God', which equates to the first veil of Atma and is in the realm of Being. See 'The Star of Man'.

It is worth repeating that sound, speech and hearing correspond to the *vishuddha* chakra, which has an analogous location with the larynx and ears. Vishuddha and therefore sound also equates to spirit or *akasha*, and so subtle sound vibration is the highest of the senses in man. The inner perceptions of sound or vibration at the most developed level translate into oracular knowledge, received directly from deity by a devotee. Perhaps because it is the highest of the senses the subtle or inner audio perception is scarcely found in the records of practitioners now. However, as there is everywhere today an increasing degradation of even the physical senses this should not perhaps be surprising, and it is a matter we shall go into here in some detail. Noise is the infernal signature of the System of Antichrist. We have become subjected to increasing levels of noise over time, which is scarcely recognised as the environmental poison that it really is. As for the conversion of music, sound and visual images into the noise of digital representation, we shall come to that later.

The sense of touch equates to *anahatha*, the 'heart' chakra and air element (*vayu*). It is highly probable that the *anahatha* chakra has atrophied owing to the emphasis that the modern profane point of view has placed on the emotions, to the extent that what is no more than sentimentality, a characteristic of the modern age, is even thought to be somehow significant or meaningful in itself. We speak of being 'touched' by something, very often referring to the emotional response, but the response stands in the way of the super-sensible possibilities latent in the *anahatha* chakra, which is the metaphysical centre of the being.

The sense of vision equates to the *manipura* chakra, fire (*tejas*) and the solar plexus. Visual images, whether created in the mind deliberately or arising spontaneously, are more readily accessible to practitioners today. In ritual and in yoga it is necessary therefore to spend quite some time in the elaborate evocation of visual symbolic images and other constructions, which are designed to support an effective working. Unfortunately it is not uncommon nowadays to find practitioners that are detained, temporarily or even permanently in extreme cases, at the visual level. Where the images pertain to the concrete mentation (Qabalistic Hod of Assiah), this then creates a bar against any real initiation.

Nature is not at all systematic or mechanical; its manifestation is through the curve, the circular or spiralic means, and the waveform. It is no coincidence that the shape of the inner ear reflects the analogue shape of sound itself. It is no coincidence that the eye is like the sun, and it was for this reason that the Egyptians utilised the Eye of Horus as a symbol of knowledge as well as the transmission and reception of that knowledge. The fact that practitioners find it much easier in the main to work with visual images doubtless owes to the vast emphasis on images, as opposed to words and language, in our times. One of the real problems with this is that it owes to completely artificial or plastic products, films, photography and the like. When film images, as with sound and music, were translated into digital media, further degradation took place, putting even greater distance between the unreal and the real as that is relative to nature. The artifice of digital or virtual reality is one of the most destructive weapons in the technological armorium of the System of Antichrist, deadening the physical senses let alone their subtle counterparts, and so sealing off the ways that might otherwise lead upward through the veil of the senses to the true or metaphysical knowledge.

Taste equates to *svadhisthana* and the element of water, and the chakra is analogously located below the naval, somewhat above the *muladhara* at the base. Water is considered to be prehensile and sapid, for it moulds itself to any form it is poured into, cleaving to it, and is thus 'knowing' or 'wise' through discernment.[107] Thus the Holy Grail or vessel (Egyptian *ab* or *nu*) is in one aspect the repository of knowledge.[108] In the Qabalah, Hod is the Water Temple and at the same time is associated with thought or mentation, on the side of Form. In its higher sense, water is that which pours forth from the fount of life itself. Among the inverse aspects of the perception of taste is gluttony, the addiction to the sensation as separated entirely from its higher principle. All the physical senses have this power to lead the soul astray through the prehensile quality that is in them—in nature no elements exist separately, but in combination.

---

[107] 'Sapid' and 'sapient' share a common Latin root with *sapere*, 'wise'.
[108] This knowledge is not to be confused with mere 'information'.

Finally, the sense of smell equates to the *muladhara* chakra, the 'foundation', base of the spine and the earth element. The sense of smell is common to all, though the degree of sensitivity differs far more from one individual to the next than is usually realised. The corresponding subtle perception, however, is of the formless realm at its root, and for this reason 'fragrance' is something often counted as an attribute of deity, whether that is Isis of Egypt or Prakriti of the Hindus. The perfumes, incense or fragrance used in ritual magick are a symbolic means, through the analogy with the physical sense, of 'touching' upon deity itself; thus in Hermetic practice the vision of the Lord, or of Adonai, is closely associated with the 'perfume', as is the vision of Isis.

It thus becomes evident that all these senses, whether physical or subtle, are degrees or gradations of knowledge as subject to various modifications, and knowledge has as its ultimate source the principle itself, in which is total knowledge. The digression upon the matter of the senses was a necessary one, but having dealt with that in some detail we can now return to the metaphysical principle. Guénon has declared that,

> A principle obviously possesses proportionately less universality the greater degree of relativity; to use the language of mathematics, it may be said that a determinative 'plus' is equivalent to a metaphysical 'minus'.[109]

The principle itself (Atma) is the 'mover that is not moved'. The principle is undetermined and is not subject to any modification or change—otherwise it would not be the principial Atma. Atma cannot be determined, changed or affected in any way at all, but action and (subsequently) determination comes about as a consequence of the presence of Atma, without which, nothing could exist at all. Atma is not relative and nor is Atma subject to relativity, which is a type of determination. Thus Atma, undetermined, is the pure metaphysical reality. Below that (in a manner of speaking) in the worlds of being or of manifestation there are degrees of reality that are subject to conditions or determinations. The latter are the reflections upon the Real.

---

[109] See p. 105 of *Introduction to the Study of the Hindu Doctrines* [Sophia Perennis].

The more subject to determination are these degrees, the less metaphysical or real in any true sense they are. The determinations and relativity are the 'plus' factor. Thus, when the reflected seed of knowledge is unpacked, or translated into any language that can be spoken or written down, or conceptualised in any way, then from the mathematical (or quantitative) point of view there has been addition. The pure metaphysical reality is, in these terms, a subtraction, not an addition.

In that way, speech and writing, all discursive thought, is the reverse of meditation in the true sense, which is not even thought as such—thought owes particularly to the human corporeal state. But we need to travel in both directions so long as it is expedient to do so, and both directions have their use: the meditation practice is for touching the higher states of being and ultimately pure knowledge; the writing, speech or thought is to develop individual possibilities that in turn act as a support to effective initiation.

When all is concentrated to a 'single point' in yoga meditation (*dhyana*) then *ajna* is the symbolic 'location'. But it works much better to posit the point, seed or star as located vertically above the top of the head. That is to say, the consciousness awareness is placed upward above the crown altogether and fixed to a point with position but no dimensions. A beginner has to start by visualising a star, orb or point of light as though existing vertically above the head; the more advanced practice, on the other hand, requires visualisation as a preparation only. We have to get inside of the metaphysical 'point', not be viewing it as from outside. Ajna is beyond sight and even sound, so we have to get 'everything' in there. It is symbolised as being very, very small (the 'mustard seed') because really it has no dimension at all; it is not in space and time and is not a thing in itself. At first this is difficult, because we want some result, some sensation or experience, and most likely will get nothing at all, or at least it will seem like nothing because it is non-sensorial and formless in its nature. So we will be aware that we are breathing and that we are sitting. That is fine so long as we can resist the urge to have thoughts about it, as reflective, or see things or hear things concerning anything else. This requires an effort of concentration and if we get tense, either mentally or physically, we will fall down the ladder, so to speak, and will have to get back in again and resume from where we started. The trick then is to apply some considerable effort of concentration while remaining completely relaxed and unmoved by anything in any given direction. When it seems very hard to do this—and sometimes it is harder than at other times—then the mantra is very useful.

As previously mentioned, most people who do this are better at visualising things than anything else, and sometimes they get too comfortable with that, so it becomes very difficult to progress beyond the visual sense. The Veil of Paroketh or the threshold of a Dominus Liminis is not called a 'threshold' for nothing. The hearing sense, analogously located at *vishuddha* chakra, is a vital step before pure knowledge can really be attained. We need every step on the ladder. The *vishuddha* corresponds to *akasha*, spirit or sometimes space.[110] If we should hear some sound, like the tinkling of a bell, or a wind—it could be anything at all—then it is a sign that we are on the way to the destination and need to continue with quiet resolution, not to get detained there but to continue on and upward. Listening for the word of the Shakti Devi is then in many ways far more efficacious (whether anything is heard or not) than trying to see her, or to create images for her—even though that has its uses too; we need all the steps on the ladder.

Some flounder and lose their way in grades or degrees precisely for the reason they do not really understand the need to keep writing up records of rituals and yoga. They find it a task, a bit of boring work that is expected of them, and they rebel against it, whether they know this or not. It is extremely unlikely that someone like, say, Patanjali, would ever have written a record of his ritual or yoga. We know for certain that Ramakrishna would not have dreamed of it, he didn't write anything at all; he spoke to his disciples a great deal, but he wrote nothing, and neither did Pythagoras.[111]

We are by now near the very end of the Kali Yuga, whether people understand that or not. Our mentality is such that we think in words, in language, a great deal of the time. This is why attention must be paid to the modern corruptions of language, for we think according to language, and thought shapes our deeds and actions. When a person does not keep the record, their language does not develop internally. So by language here we are speaking about the written word, but we are also alluding to a great deal more than the written or the spoken word.

---

[110] In the ritual, it is this exactly that we are invoking or calling in when we make the pentagrams of spirit and sound their requisite names over the altar at the centre of the circle of all. The 'Spirits of Spirit' are not seen but can be heard with the inner ear.

[111] Fortunately, a devotee wrote down almost every word that Ramakrishna uttered during a period of some years. The remarkable record is preserved in *The Gospel according to Sri Ramakrishna*.

It may occur to us that we see people everywhere that are losing their grip on language. Language is fast degrading into jargon, 'key words', 'tools', and having 'choices' that can be reduced down to virtually clicking on one of two icons. There are many now that are not actually capable of keeping the kind of record of practice that we have described here, and that for reasons of that linguistic limitation are not capable of even doing the practices at all. Initiation is then impossible, and not because writing and language is initiation but because initiation is on a subtler level than language and writing.[112] If their state of being is below that of ordinary language, initiation is completely out of their reach. For the same reason, of that linguistic incomprehension, they will not understand this at all!

According to the *Katha Upanishad*, the true knowledge cannot be reached at all without the meditation practice. By 'meditation' here is meant *dhyana*, which involves first *dharana*, the concentration of the mind. That has to be learned over time, with prolonged practice and considerable effort put in.

> The wise, realising through meditation
> The timeless Self, beyond all perception,
> Hidden in the cave of the heart,
> Leave pain and pleasure far behind.
> Those who know they are neither body nor mind
> But the immemorial Self, the divine
> Principle of existence, find the source
> Of all joy and live in joy abiding.
> I see the gates of joy are opening
> For you, Nachiketa.[113]

The relation of guru and *chela*, or teacher and student, is also indispensible, as is also illustrated in the *Kena Upanishad*. It is not only that questions must be asked of the guru, as strictly relating to the path, but also these questions must be the 'right' questions. It is in the kind of question that is asked that a guru is able to know the potential and readiness of the *chela*; such questions act as a key to the unlocking of further progress, which is something held in common with all true and ancient traditions.

---

[112] Previously, an illiterate person could be initiated but there is almost no trace left today of the oral traditions and rites that made this possible.
[113] I.2.12—13. Translated by Eknath Easwaran [Penguin Arkana].

Oracle of Isis

ORACLE OF THE FOURTEENTH DAY OF THE MOON.[114]
Some say I am a Great Light;
Others a mote that cannot be seen,
Or imagined or dreamed.

Some say I am like a bird with soft feathers fanning
That one only feels as a coolness to the face,
Or a fragrance in the Night.

I am Pure Being,
And I shine by my own light;
I am not Reflection.

Even the light of the Sun is derived from mine,
Yet to some I am like one single drop of Dew.
And this I have given to you.
It is alike and the same
To the knowledge of my Name.

---

[114] Author's diary record of 13th May 2022, Sun in Taurus, Moon in Libra.

The Throne of Ra

We are indebted to the Egyptologists for their painstaking research, their indexing and cataloguing of artefacts and hieroglyphs. Without this we would have almost no chance of construing the meaning of the vast legacy of Egypt, which has survived miraculously over thousands of years through invasion, war and now, in modern times, the destruction of the human intellect through the suppression of all real knowledge. Unfortunately, the Egyptologists have never stayed within the strictly limited bounds of their profane science, and have always sought to extend beyond those limits to a domain that should properly be reserved for those few that that have any comprehension of ancient metaphysics. They either attempt to supply meaning based on speculation and their narrow view of even the physical world, or, as is now more fashionable, deny there is any meaning at all to the sacred texts. It is then very difficult to make recommendations concerning Egyptological works, even though we must rely on these for the facts that are the basis for any study.

E.A. Wallis Budge is by now very unfashionable with modern Egyptologists, something that is in his favour. For while the latter think themselves to have advanced considerably since the time of Budge, in fact their understanding has only degenerated further, and this corresponds to the increased level of their profane arrogance so far as all matters of the Sacred Science are concerned. While they will no doubt hesitate to derogate living traditions such as Islam, Judaism, Buddhism and Christianity, ancient Egypt is to them an open field where they can mock and parody all that they do not understand. While Budge did not go that far, he sometimes seemed to be in two minds as to whether the lost Egyptian tradition was in some ways superior to those which survive in modern times or an attempt by the 'primitive' Egyptians, which Budge thought to be a simple-minded race, to produce theories about the universe much like the theories produced by profane sciences. Budge, as with all Egyptologists, was an evolutionist and so he was ipso facto excluded from gaining any real comprehension of the ancient civilisations. Evolutionist theories deny the natural order and are essentially anti-metaphysical.

We would not do without the works of Budge but when it comes to meaning supplied to the facts we cannot rely on Budge or any Egyptologist. We must apply rigorous discrimination in separating what are truly 'the facts' and what is merely supposition. We will take as an example Chapter IV of *The Gods of the Egyptians Volume One*.[115] This follows a chapter called 'Egyptian Religion', which by its title is already a distortion, for the Egyptian tradition vastly precedes anything that can in any way be called a religion. After these general remarks, composed from assumptions that are based on a digest of theological notions, Budge proceeds to an examination of what he imagines to be the ancient Egyptian idea of heaven.

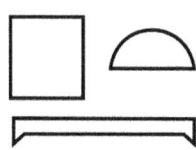

Left: hieroglyph for pt (pet), 'heaven'

Firstly, Budge imagines that heaven must have a place in relation to the earth, that it is a physical location. This is absurd; all traditions agree that heaven as such is not a physical place and does not even exist in the subtle realm. It may be symbolised as being above the earth or above the sky but the symbol is not a measurable object or thing as its meaning is metaphysical.

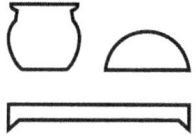

He then discerns a difference between *pet*, which he says means 'heaven' and *nut* (left), of which he says means 'sky'. He thinks that heaven must be above the sky, as indeed it is depicted in the hieroglyphs, for the *djet* sky determinative shows the sky resting upon the eastern and western horizons, as does the goddess Nuit, its personification. But the sky itself is a natural symbol, and its hieroglyphs are not exclusively used to indicate what is merely visible to the senses. As the 'roof' of the world it may equally symbolise the *way* to heaven—a word that literally means 'lift up'—and very often the terms 'sky' and 'heaven' are interchangeable in ancient languages.[116] Although the hieroglyphs drawn above the sky determinative in both cases are phonetic, *p-t* in the former case, *n-t* in the latter, they have their own meaning and their use here is not arbitrary. It escapes Budge's attention entirely that the difference between them is that 'p' is a rectangle and 'n' is a vase, because he is looking at this in the most grossly simplistic way imaginable.

---

[115] Pp. 156–169, Dover Publications, New York.
[116] 'Heaven' is from Old English *heofen*, related to German *himmel* and Dutch *hemel*.

Later, Budge will declare that it is the Egyptians, in fact, that are 'primitive', and that their conceptions, as he terms it, are 'simple'. The rectangular shape used for the *pt* is identical to that used to determine *het*, a house, abode or shrine, usually an abode of a God or the symbol of a God. The vase or urn used for *nut* is the primary symbol of Nuit, the goddess of the night sky. The vase or urn is circular looking at it one way, or roughly spherical, for it is the span of All, which is at the most primordial level the sum total of all possibilities held within the unmanifest principle. As similar to the hieroglyph for the 'heart' (*ab*), it is a form of the Holy Grail, which is a kind of secondary reflection of the supreme principle.

Now we can properly see a clear difference between the two hieroglyphs. On the one hand we have the shrine, house or abode of a God, and on the other hand we have the sum total of all possibilities. This is far more than merely 'space', as some would have it, as even space is subject to determination and limitation and belongs strictly to the physical or corporeal domain. It may help to recollect that *pt* was personified as the God Ptah and that the name of his house, Hut Ka Ptah, is the origin of the name Egypt as heard by the Greeks. Heaven naturally embraces the earth, and the link between these is supplied by the shrine, temple or abode, lest man should forget. Thus Nuit is also heaven, as expressed by her reach across the two horizons where the sun rises in the morning and sets in the evening. Unless man worships at the lotus feet of the Goddess in the Dark Age of Kali Yuga, he is counted among the legions of the damned—a subject we shall return to. However, according to Budge,

> The hieroglyphic for heaven and sky represents a slab [sic.], each end of which rests on a support, and we may assume that the primitive Egyptians believed that each end of heaven rested upon a support (i.e., two mountains); out of one mountain came the sun every morning, and into the other he entered every night.[117]

Some scholars hold the opinion that the Pythagorean tetractys was an arithmetical device to assist 'early learners'. The Egyptological view of the hieroglyph for heaven is clearly on a par with such wilful ignorance. That same attitude is now pursued everywhere and with relentless aggression for, unlike Budge's generation, the latest brood of scientistic dogmatists will not rest until all real knowledge is erased from human minds. Dogma, whether religious or scientific, is based on emotional prejudice and belief. And yet we are told here, as we are told time and time again, that 'primitive' Egyptians *believed*.

---

[117] P. 156 [*ibid*].

Commentators on ancient knowledge, who will attack anything they do not understand, will constantly assert the word 'belief', which for them makes an identification with modern religion; and that, in their opinion, whether they declare it or not, is mere superstition. Metaphysics is an exact science and its nature is axiomatic as it declares demonstrable truth with certainty, not belief. Such truth is known only to those who have the innate capacity for knowledge beyond the reach of the human sense perceptions and so beyond the reach of modern sciences, which only admit to the existence of physical 'matter'. Metaphysics is incompatible with either dogma or belief, and these two really amount to the same thing.

There is sometimes an association made with the 'roof' of the sky or heaven, and iron. Budge thought that this was another example of Egyptian beliefs, that the sky was thought literally to be made of iron, a notion so absurd as to be unworthy of further comment. Iron ore is commonly found in the earth but it requires very intense industrial processes to make the metal from it. The real reason that the ancient Egyptians made nothing from iron until, as reckoned by historians, about 3000–2500 BC, is because such metals were regarded by the sages as poisonous, as indeed they are, and on more than one level. Altars were made from stone and ritual artefacts were made from wood, bone or clay. The Egyptians are not known for iron production until as relatively late as 600 BC but they made use of iron from meteorites, which is the main source of iron on the earth's surface. They called meteoric iron the 'metal of heaven' (*bia-n-pt*) from at least the time of the Pyramid Texts.[118] There is a further explanation for the 'metal of heaven', which is that fire, lightning and stones that fall from heaven symbolise initiatic transmission and in some cases, oracles. Another matter of interest is that the use of even meteoric iron may have come about during the cyclical period of time that the Hindu doctrine terms the Kali Yuga or 'Age of Iron', approximately 6,000 years ago.[119] This Age of Darkness, which naturally occurs at the end of a greater Cosmic Cycle, comes about in the same way that a flower blooms, throws off seeds and then decays, returning to its elements. Mankind is increasingly forgetful of the eternal principle that sustains all of life, without which nothing can exist. Towards the end of the Dark Age, the way to heaven is effectively sealed shut by ignorance and by the machinations of anti-spiritual forces, which we have referred to as the 'System of Antichrist'. The 'doors to heaven' are as though sealed shut by iron bars.

---

[118] Thought to date from around 2375 BC.
[119] Cf. 'Cosmic Cycles', *Nu Hermetica*.

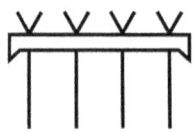 Budge goes on to mention the fourfold division of the heavens into four cardinal quarters, as though this was something unique to the Egyptians, or even their invention, whereas it accords with all ancient traditions. The canopy of heaven was then depicted as upon pillars, or supports. We see such a canopy in some of the Tarot decks where it is shown above a chariot, which is the vessel or sunboat of heaven, the means of going forth, though in reality that means is the principle itself, the 'mover that is not moved'. According to Budge,

> That this is a very ancient view concerning the sky is proved by the hieroglyphic, which is used in texts to determine words for rain, storm, and the like; here we have a picture of the sky falling [sic.] and being pierced by the four pillars of heaven.

The similarity of words for rain, storm and lightning owes to the origin of all language in non-verbal utterance. Before words became proper nouns they were descriptive of actions, such as 'lightening the darkness of earth' in Hindu (*indratama*), which later became the proper noun, Indra.[120] In fact Budge has here reversed the meaning, for 'heaven' quite literally means 'lifting up' or 'raising', as we have explained, and it must be clearly understood that the supports, as we might call them, are not in fact holding up the sky; they are in no way separate from the principle itself, though in a different modality.

When the canopy of heaven is shown as a rectangle, a central pillar makes up the fifth point, though it is really the first as it corresponds to the vertical axis or divine ordinance. According to Budge this arose at a relatively late period in Egypt, but this seems very unlikely considering its universal import. A pyramid or any sacred building generally has four corners and a founding stone, whether visible or not, which marks the central axis from roof to floor, which is the unitive principle and sacred will-ordinance. It marks the height and the depth, and together with the cardinal directions forms the Cube of Space or three-dimensional cross.[121]

Budge has noted that the central prop was sometimes personified as a God, Heh, though he does not mention that this name has an etymological link with 'eternity'.[122] In fact, the God is typically shown as a figure holding two branches, in which case he is identical with the middle pillar of the Qabalistic Tree of Life.

---

[120] Cf. 'Brahmacharya'.
[121] Cf. 'Metaphysical Basis of Thelema', *Nu Hermetica*.
[122] See the hieroglyphic illustration on p. 169.

Another example of universal symbolism is that the heavens were sometimes shown as the head of a man, resembling a vase or chalice, another form of the Holy Grail or King of the World. That this is no human person but what is sometimes called Cosmic or Universal Man is made clear by the fact that the sun and the moon were said to be his eyes, while the four supports were made of his long, flowing hair. It seems almost impossible that Budge could never have heard of the analogy of hair used for the solar radiance, or influence of the solar principle itself, for it occurs in almost all ancient traditions including the Hindu, Hebrew, Arabic and Native American Indian. The solar symbolism is reinforced by the fact that the Four Children of Horus, who were also identified with the cardinal quarters, were the embodiments of the four sceptres or supports, and that they 'bring forth the boat of the Eye of Tum, which is on the Lake of Kha'. Tum is a form of Ra, particular to Aunnu (Greek Heliopolis). The Lake of Kha is related to the Egyptian Akh: pure light radiance, not to be confused with visible light itself. Sometimes this is identified with the solar 'breath', which again is not the physical breath but has close affinity with the Hindu *prana*, which is the life-giving modality of Atma Itself or the supreme principle.

Budge next turns to look at the Company of Heaven, or the Companions of the Gods in Heaven, which is the title of the chapter in question. Budge points out that Ra was chief among the dwellers in heaven.[123] According to Budge, Ra sits on an iron throne that has sides ornamented with the faces of lions and the feet of bulls. Round about him are the other Gods in his retinue, which form the 'nucleus of the inhabitants of heaven'. Now, whether the throne of Ra was made of iron or not is difficult to know with any certainty, as Budge does not give the hieroglyphs and there is some Egyptological confusion regarding metals other than gold or silver. It might have been copper, for example, but what is more important is that Ra is the supreme principle, Atma Itself, as it is put in Sanskrit, and so is far more than being a mere representation of the visible sun.

The face of the lion has always symbolised the supreme principle in its solar aspect; it is the face of the Sun, or the face of God. The bull's feet symbolise the foundation of manifestation, extending to the terrestrial domain. The Throne of Ra thus links heaven and earth and is of the type of the Sphinx. It is quite right that Ra would then occupy the most central position, as is shown geometrically by the metaphysical point in the circle, and that the circle of other Gods would surround him.

---

[123] P. 158, *The Gods of the Egyptians* [ibid].

As the Egyptians, in common with the Hindus and others, made a division of three worlds, there were many Gods assigned to the various degrees of manifestation. These are attributes of the first appearance of God, 'the Lord' or Ishvara (Sanskrit), which is Pure Being, not subject to determination. First and foremost of these 'classes of beings', were the Shemsu-Heru, the followers in the way of Horus. The name is quite easy to construe from the hieroglyphs as these consist in the first place of a bundle tied to a reed. This signifies journeying, going forth or 'following'. There then follows the hawk determinative for Horus himself, and finally there are three other hawks perched on standards, which denote the plural. These are, as Budge points out, 'almost equal to the gods'. A text from Pepi I is cited, where it is said that such a company are the ones that bathed and anointed Pepi, and that recited the chapter of 'those who come forth' on his behalf, and also the chapter of 'those who rise up', viz., to heaven, a clear indication of what would be termed in Sanskrit yogins, or otherwise the initiates. Pepi I was a sixth Dynasty Egyptian king or pharaoh; as at that time the kings were still initiated by the priesthood, his friends on earth were initiates that would also be his company in heaven—that is to say, after they had achieved full resurrection.

Next is mentioned a company called Ashemu, of which Budge says are a class of beings whose characteristics are unknown, but that are referred to in connection with the *sekhemu*.[124] Strangely, Budge does not mention here that *sekhemu* means 'powerful ones', from *sekhem*, usually translated as 'power' and associated with the vertical axis of any cross, the will-ordinance. The symbol of *sekhem* is a sceptre that clearly denotes the principle itself, at the pole, and its axial extension. At the centre or midpoint is the head of a horned creature, which is always a symbol of the primordial tradition and sacerdotal power.

According to Budge, *ashem* is usually translated as 'form in which a god is visible', but that it must have another and an older meaning. It would have been useful to know if Budge had some idea of what that might be. However, he gives the hieroglyphs for the Company of Ashemu and this gives us some indications at least. The *ashem* (or possibly *ishim*) is composed of the sign of 'reach' (or of evocation), the rolled scroll of ordinance and the owl of seeing or beholding. The rest denotes the plural in exactly the same way as the retinue of Horus, as hawks perched on standards.

---

[124] Teta I. 327.

The sense of visibility or form is thus derived from the presence of the owl (*m*). Horus is also very particularly associated with the 'all-seeing eye'. There is an almost identical Order of Angels in the Qabalah called the Ashim or sometimes Ishim. Similarly, very little seems to be known of the Ashim other than speculation over whether the name means 'flames' or 'men', because the Hebrew root *ash* can mean either. However, the Sanskrit Ishvara does not denote a man, but God or 'Lord' as the first manifestation or the first appearance, that also causes the appearance of all things through his divine presence (Ishvara can be male or female, we should note). The accurate sense of the name is Pure Being, for it is not subject to determination. Fire is also a quality attributed to the Shakti power, which is identical to Egyptian *sekhem* and is at the same time corresponded to the power of seeing or of forming images. On a higher arc, fire is identical with spirit, especially when associated with the lightning or 'fire from heaven', as symbolised in the name Zelbarachith.[125] The Order of Ashim corresponds to Malkuth or to Yesod, both of which are the throne, seat or foundation of Shakti power in the microcosm. We can ascertain that the Ashemu are similar to the Devas of the Hindu doctrines, which are the attributes of Ishvara, the Devas being a personification of the same powers. These are here helpful agencies that protect the initiate and confer powers,

In the third case, of these obviously very specialised inhabitants of various regions of heaven or the sky, we have the Hamemet, or Henmemet. Of these, Budge says that they 'appear to be a class of beings who either were to become, or had already been, human beings, but the Egyptians had no clear idea of their attributes...' We think, on the contrary, that when Budge adds that they 'have been understood in different ways by different scholars', it is the scholars that have no clear idea, not the ancient Egyptians.

The Egyptians, as becomes evident from even a light study such as this one, had an exact and complete metaphysical, cosmological and magical doctrine. Fortunately, Budge thought to include both the hieroglyphs and his translation of a hymn from the *Theban Book of the Dead* (so-called):

---

[125] Zelbarachith is a Hebrew noun (זלברחית) that has similar forms in Arabic, composed of *zel*, 'fire' and *barach*, 'blessing', implying transmission from heaven to earth. Note the value, 657, is equal to 210 by multiplication of the integers.

Akh or Crested Ibis; also called Khu or 'Spirit'—a celestial being

In a hymn it is said of Ra, 'when he riseth the *rekhit* (i.e., 'rational beings') live, and the *hamemet* exult in him; Osiris is called [lord of] the *hamemet* in Kher-aha; and the deceased says in Chapter xlii of the Book of the Dead, 'And shall do me hurt neither men, nor gods, nor spirits, nor the dead (or damned), nor the *pat,* nor the *rhekit,* nor the *hamemet.*' Elsewhere the deceased prays 'that the company of the gods may hold their peace whilst the *hamemet* talk with me'; and it seems from a passage in an inscription of Hatshepsut as if in the latter part of the dynastic period the word had come to mean a class of men and women, especially as is determined by the signs [man and woman], which usually indicate a number of human beings ... finally, that the *hamemet* were believed [sic.] to live upon grain is proved by the passage in a hymn to Amen-Ra wherein this god is said to be the 'maker of the green herb which giveth life to the beasts and cattle, and of the plant of life, of the *hamemet'.*

What transpires is that the Hamemet are a type of solar *devas,* as with the Ashemu, that are best understood as luminous or radiant, whose abode is the subtle realm. They are neither good nor evil but perform a dual function, which is to protect the initiate and drive away inimical or profane influences. Among these profane ones are the damned, which we have previously noted here, for they are the ones, legion in our times, that absolutely reject the eternal principle, whether it is for salvation or deliverance. It is most interesting to see how exact the Egyptian depiction of the damned is. The hieroglyph shows a man in the act of driving an axe through his own head. The axe is a symbol of the divine principle itself, the Neter, for nothing, not even the damned, could exist at all without it. As man's very existence depends on the eternal principle, the ever-living, then his total rejection of that is an act of self-destruction. It is not about 'divine retribution', as is sometimes proclaimed by religious zealots as well as those who seek to attack any religion or spiritual science whatsoever, but is self-invoked, self-willed annihilation, whether through ignorance or sheer malice.

Grain or seed is always, in all traditions, a symbol of *paramatma,* the principle of the Real, undetermined; the fact that the Hamemet are said to live upon this means they require no other sustenance than pure spirit. They are therefore much beyond the inferior gods of the *duat,* for example. The 'plant of life' is of course the Tree of Life, another symbol found in most if not all traditions, and is the entirety of a 'world' or state of being, including the formal and the formless aspects.

That the Hamemet may take the form of men and women is beyond any doubt from the hieroglyphs. The fact they live on nothing but spirit might conceivably place them in a class of avatars, which would also account for their ability to help and guard the initiate even at relatively lower degrees. Their hieroglyph depicts the solar circle and point, from which issues rays or emanations, threefold, and it is this they adore. Their realm is thus equivalent to the centre of Yetzirah, the subtle World of Formation in the Qabalah, so they are similar to angels, or Greek daemons.

In the text of Pepi II two further classes of beings are mentioned, the Afa and Utennu, and two divisions of followers of Set. Of the former, Budge says that 'we know nothing'. However the Af is the 'word', the Logos principle that is the equivalent of the Hindu *vak* and Latin *vox*; in its higher aspect, *para-vak* is the non-verbal or primordial speech.[126] It is by this power that things are named, something given high esteem in the Egyptian tradition as it is the means of passing beyond the lower states. The Utennu, as is perfectly clear from their hieroglyphs, are likened to 'vessels', as the *nu* termination also indicates. The Ut is the primal utterance, the power of speech itself, and so it becomes very clear why these classes of being are linked. We have the higher or more primordial type of non-verbal utterance, which derives from direct knowledge, and the secondary or lower type of verbal utterance, by which things are named. Both are needed in the journey of the soul.

It is also clear from the text of Pepi II that this, as with most so-called spells, is not a simple prayer or petition but a precise mapping out of the path of initiation, comparable to the detailed and sensuous descriptions of the Tantrik texts.[127] From the hieroglyphs it is clear that the upper and lower class of the followers of Set, or Setians, correspond to the Cosmic or Universal Man at the centre of a state of being on the one hand, and the foundation for this, which is the priestly way.[128] Pepi firstly announces that he is himself the divine hawk, the type of the Horus king, and thus he is able to rise up to heaven as Horus does. It is notable that Horus is described not as the son of Isis but as the son of Nuit, an earlier and more metaphysical designation in that Horus born of Nuit did not require a father.

---

[126] Cf. 'Brahmacharya'.
[127] Cf. Sir John Woodroffe, *The Serpent Power*.
[128] P. 160, *The Gods of the Egyptians* [ibid].

Pepi II achieves the ascendancy through the power of meditation or silence, embodied as Harpocrates. Then, by the double power of the *wadjet* eye, which has been established for him, he rises to 'smite the crowns', which is no different than to 'strike at the worship of Nu', as it is declared in the Book of the Law, III: 45. The Serpent Power or Kundalini Shakti has thus risen to the crown chakra or *brahmarandra*, for the purpose of liberation. Having accomplished all these things, the king is able to command the gods named Utennu and Afa. In other words he has full command of the Logoidal powers and has nothing to fear from 'the two uraei guides, and the jackals, and the spirits (*khus*), and the Set beings, both the Upper and the Lower'.

After a passage describing something of the Gods that watch over cities, and the souls of cities, Budge then leaves the subject of the innumerable dwellers in the heaven worlds and passes on to the subject of the spirits and souls of 'the righteous men and women who once lived upon this earth'. Consideration of these initiates that have transformed into divine beings, or 'living ones', is vital to the whole matter of the soul's journey, or of initiation, from the human point of view. Line 206 from King Unas reads,

> Hail Unas, behold thou hast not departed dead but as living thou hast gone to take up thy seat upon the throne of Osiris. Thy sceptre *āb* is in thy hand, and thou givest commands unto the living ones; thy sceptre *mekes* and thy sceptre *nekhebet* are in thy hands, and thou givest thine orders to those whose habitations are hidden.

The sceptre called *āb* is a form of the *sekhem*, described previously. The sceptres called *mekes* and *nekhebet* are presumably names for the 'crook and flail' carried by the pharaohs, and as these are not the usual names for them it is interesting to learn that the former is the power of *seeing* or beholding while the latter is the attribute of the 'essential honey', or of eternity itself. The governance of the king continues in this abode, which is much like the paradise or terrestrial Eden of other traditions.

Whereas the passage quoted from King Pepi II has ultimate liberation (Sanskrit *moksha*) as the goal, the lines from King Unas are confined to the lesser mysteries, of salvation, which perpetuates an existence that resembles the earthly one in certain ways. The former way is that of eternity while the latter is that of perpetuity.[129]

---

[129] Egyptian texts or 'spells' often include both ways, which is derived from the metaphysical perspective of *simultaneity*.

Comparing this with a text from King Teta, of whom 'the seat of his heart is declared to be among the living ones on earth forever', Budge adds a very confused note that, according to the Egyptians, a man could 'attain all the attributes of a divine being, or let us say, of an angel, and at the same time enjoy an existence upon earth as well as in heaven'. That is the goal of the yogin, to attain liberation while still alive on earth, but it is not what Budge intends here. The confusion owes to an inability to discern a difference between the terrestrial paradise and heaven or eternity. The existence 'upon earth' is in no way to be thought of as the earth itself, or the human world as we know it; its existence is in the subtle domain on the threshold of the formal and formless states.[130] He goes from bad to worse when he supposes that this idea arose—as though it were an invention in historical terms—because the Egyptians wished to provide a future for the dead body! The dead body is, by definition, dead, and has no past, no present and no future; to suggest that the Egyptians thought otherwise is, at the very least, to misunderstand symbolism.

Budge's errors then become too numerous to list as they are formed from misunderstood theological and philosophical notions. As a consequence he then comes to the conclusion that the continued existence of the king was literally 'in some region on this earth'. He confuses initiatic 'grades' or degrees with civic or social elevation. Very strangely, as it is inconsistent with what he concludes the chapter with, he reverses the order of the earlier knowledge of the predynastic times with the more degraded knowledge of later times, so the predynastic period is shown to be more 'primitive' than the dynastic one. The inconsistency serves to show how far evolutionists are prepared to twist facts to fit into their notions of 'progress'. Budge's confusion unfortunately deepens when he touches on the subject of the Ka or 'vital body' as it is often described:

> In his dreams the Egyptian saw a figure of himself or a duplicate, engaged in various occupations, and to this figure he gave the name *ka*; it was born with a man, it remained within him, usually inoperative [!] and survived him at death. It never left the body in the grave or tomb, and the offerings that were made in the halls of the tombs of all periods were intended to maintain its existence.

---

[130] There are rare exceptions, but it would involve a lengthy digression from our subject to go into this in any great detail.

This is not only supposition but is also sheer fantasy. The Ka is often likened to a 'body' or 'double' of some sort but it is really comparable with the Chinese *chi* and Hindu *prana* or 'vital breath', though the correspondence is not an exact one. If the Ka were 'inoperative' in the man, as Budge suggests, the man would be dead. As for not leaving the body in the grave or tomb, this is an entirely outward view based on folk customs where offerings were made to the Ka of the deceased. Once the physical body is dead it is dead, it has no future. Offerings to the Ka form part of the shamanistic traditions, where it is desired to join the ancestors in a kind of perpetual existence, comparable in some ways to salvation (or Amentet), a return to an earthly paradise or terrestrial Eden. Budge makes no distinction here between the practices of initiation and the practices of folk traditions.

> Nevertheless, the *ka* of Horus is in heaven, and also the *ka* of Teta, which is adjured to bring that which the king might eat with it; and as the *kau* of men and gods lived in heaven so there lived also the *kau* of cities ... and the 'lords of *kau* praised Ra both in the dominions of Horus and in the dominions of Set'.[131]

Budge here confuses simultaneity, which is the perfect unification of different degrees of existence within the principle itself (or Throne of Ra), with temporal time and space—so it would seem that all that is in heaven or the highest degrees of existence were merely a kind of double or duplicate of that which is on the earth. As King Unas is said to be the chief of *kau* [viz., *ka* in the plural form] then it is clear that the 'lords of *kau*' are risen kings, or otherwise their abode is at the same degree of existence. The line concerning King Unas, that he is 'chief of *kau*' is interpreted by Budge as 'chief of the doubles', but it is notable that the hieroglyphs simply depict a human face that is at the same time a chalice or vase, symbol of the 'heart' or later, the Holy Grail and Cosmic Man or the King of the World. This indicates an exact metaphysics, for the king is then said to 'gather together hearts for the great wise chief', as interpreted by Budge.[132] In other words, it is the function of the king to 'gather the light that is scattered', which is to return all to the unmanifest principle.

> When Unas had eaten the bodies of the gods, and had absorbed all their souls and spirits, it is said that the 'flame of Unas is in their bones, for their soul [*ba*] is with Unas, and their shadows [*khaibet*] are with their forms.'[133]

---

[131] Teta I. 192
[132] Unas, line 395.
[133] Unas, line 523, Teta, line 330.

The simplistic interpretation makes the formula of ascent sound bizarre, but it is in fact completely normal and in accordance with other metaphysical traditions—all of which are truly one primordial or universal truth. According to the Hindu doctrines, when all the faculties and functions have been withdrawn into the vital breath so that they subsist as possibilities or latency, the vital breath along with all its functions is in turn subsumed into the *jivatma*, the 'living soul'. Jivatma is the most central principle of the individuality and is itself a reflection of the Atma or True Self.[134]

The king or initiate must assimilate the manifestations of the being at each level, or in different states of being. The 'flame of Unas is in their bones', for there can be flames, but each flame is one fire or 'flame of flames', which is the principial source of all flames. Budge goes on to mention other parts or faculties of the being: the soul or *ba*, the spirit or *khu* and the power called *sekhem*, which corresponds to the Shakti of the Hindu Tantras. What is important here is that all these parts were unified in the Sahu, which is akin to the 'divine breath' and no different than the breath of Ra himself that gives life to all things. Sahu is a condensation of Sia, vision, perception, and Hu, will and command, or ordinance. These, together with Heka, the magical power, are elsewhere described as companions of Ra in the sun boat.

Budge, however, thinks the Sahu to be a 'spiritual body', which is a metaphysical impossibility as the spirit cannot be limited or confined in any way. If the spirit could be a body then it would not be spirit, for it would then naturally be subject to all the limits and determinations that govern formal states. This unfortunately gets worse, as Budge goes on to declare, as though it were a matter of fact, that the spiritual body 'grew out of the dead body', as if anything could grow from something that is already dead!

After saying something about the complex orders of being, easily comparable to the almost countless Devas and Kalās of the Tantras, Budge describes some very sensuous poetic lines from King Teta. This concerns the great lake of Sekhet-hotep—the 'power at peace' that is comparable to Brahma, or otherwise the Shakti, the 'resting place' of the spirit, of which action is a consequence but is in no way vital to the spirit itself. The description includes a beautiful fertile region of white wheat and red barley, growing to a great height, and numerous 'canals' or waterways, and the bread and beer of eternity, or of that which is incorruptible.

---

[134] See 'The Star of Man'.

There is a heavenly fig tree, a form of the Tree of Life, and a vine upon which feed the beatified ones. The bread is in fact that which the Eye of Horus 'shed upon the branches of the olive-tree', another form of the Tree of Life. We know then that bread is an analogy for pure radiance, and it is this that nurtures the risen souls. The symbolism of red and white is not confined to the Egyptian tradition but extends into all other traditions including that of alchemy, where it is the red and the white tinctures or Lion and Eagle. These are respectively the equivalent of *purusha*, 'essence' or Atma Itself, and *prakriti*, the 'substance' that produces all things, as we have frequently mentioned.

The 'bread of heaven' is the *manna*, referred to in the Bible, which is that upon which the beatified souls are nurtured, it being no less than the pure knowledge of Brahma, the supreme principle. The canals or waterways of this heavenly region are directly comparable to the *nadis* or 'channels' of the Tantras, especially if we think of those described as being located in the upper chakras, between *ajna* and *sahasrara*.[135] The beatitude is directly comparable to *sat-chit-ananda*.[136] Those who partake of Brahma as the supreme principle may also partake of the attributes of Brahma, and this corresponds to the *anandamaya kosha* or first envelope of being.[137] It will be helpful to quote here from the Brahma-Sūtras, as given by Guénon:[138]

> The intellect, the inward sense, and also the faculties of sensation and action, are developed and reabsorbed in a similar sequence, and this sequence always follows that of the elements from which these faculties proceed as regards their constitution. As to *Purusha*, its emanation is not a birth, neither is it a production. One cannot in fact, assign to it any limitation, since, being identified with the Supreme *Brahma*, it partakes of its infinite essence. It is active, but only in principle, for this activity is not essential to it nor inherent to it, but is simply eventual and contingent. As the carpenter, grasping in his hand his axe and his other tools and then laying them aside, enjoys tranquility and repose, so this *Ātmā* in its union with its instruments, is active, and, in relinquishing them, enjoys repose and tranquility.[139]

---

[135] Cf. Woodroffe, *The Serpent Power*.
[136] See 'Sat-Chit-Ananda'.
[137] See 'The Star of Man'.
[138] *Man and His Becoming according to the Vedānta*, pp. 63–64 [Sophia Perennis].
[139] Brahma-Sūtras, 11.3.14–17 and 33–40.

The ancient Egyptian texts that Budge has quoted portray a complex metaphysical and cosmological understanding, especially in relation to initiation or ascent. It seems quite extraordinary that Budge goes on to say of all this,

> All these details show the simple character of the heavens which the primitive Egyptians imagined, and prove that it was at first intended to be nothing but the celestial complement of a terrestrial farm or estate.

The 'simple character' is purely within Budges total incomprehension of the import of what he is dealing with, and his desire to prove that the Egyptian sacred texts are the mere product of imagining, as of a 'primitive' people, as yet uniformed by the superior knowledge of material science! He goes on to make an unfavourable comparison between that which he calls the 'simple material heaven' of the Egyptians and the paradisical worlds described by the Hebrew and Islamic poets. He is unable to see that all such scriptures are in exact agreement, and the only difference is in the symbolism used, and even there the symbolism is quite often identical. He continues to give his fantastical notion of an 'Egyptian gentleman', which in fact sounds more like a description of a man of the English aristocracy of the times that Budge lived in, with all its vain pretensions.

> The above mentioned facts will show that in his conception of heaven the Egyptian never succeeded in freeing himself wholly from material ideas and the wish to make sure of eternal life and happiness by means of his own acts.

It has not occurred to Budge, nor almost any other Egyptologist, to think for one moment that it might be they that are unable to free themselves from material conceptions! There is much more but it is best we leave it there other than to mention that Budge thinks that 'ladders to heaven', which include the Tree of Life in all traditions, was a literal belief to the extent that without a model of a ladder being placed in the tomb, the Egyptian could not hope to achieve his passage to heaven.

The evidence we have given here is enough to prove that which we have always insisted on: that Egypt not only enjoyed a complete metaphysics and unified doctrine, far superior to that of any modern religion or science, but also was the source of all learning and civilisation. When the Egyptian language was superseded by first the Greek, then the Latin and finally the Arabic tongue, its knowledge was not in fact lost. It was disseminated outwardly to all the nations of the world, there to be clothed in the various forms as appropriate to those civilisations. It is our task now to 'gather the light that was scattered' as we prepare for the ending of an entire Cosmic Cycle.

Postmodern Shamanism

We must now examine some of the commonplace delusions of postmodern or New Age shamanism. There is a fixation that can easily amount to an obsession with what is termed in New Age language 'letting go of attachments'. This is a distortion, even subversion, of spiritual knowledge. Let us look at the doctrine in its pure form. If the ego (*ahankara* or individual thought) should work through the faculty that is able to give form to ideas (*chitta*) and then identifies with a perceived object, the self is led to fall into delusion through becoming bound up with that object. This is exactly what is called 'attachment' in the New Age counterfeit spirituality. However, postmodern shamanism then goes to work on this without any real knowledge, doctrine or principial basis. It produces 'positive affirmations' that are no more than self-hypnosis, increasing the levels of delusion still further. It recommends various 'therapies' that only increase self-obsession and dependency, even transferring such a dependency from the ground of real relationships to that of merely professional or counterfeit relationships. Self-created 'rituals' are encouraged, which involve ridding oneself of 'personal demons', a theory that insists all other persons are merely projections of the ego, thus reinforcing isolationism.

We should remember that a ritual in the true sense is a *rite*; it means 'ordinance', and that means it must depend from a spiritual or higher principle. If it is separated from its higher principle it can only manifest in the most negative and degraded form possible within the human domain, even the sub-human level.

The individual self is contained within Atma as a possibility (unmanifested) but the individual self or person cannot contain the Atma—the Atma cannot be contained or limited by anything. With postmodernism, the doctrine is inverted so that the therapist or analyst's victims are encouraged to believe that a divine or spiritual nature exists exclusively within the self. One then only needs to 'free oneself from attachments' to realise such a possibility—a possibility that is once again inverted so that it only represents completely ordinary goals, desires and personal objectives. All other traditional doctrine has been inverted similarly. For example, there is a state of the 'child' (*balya*) in the *sannyasin* in Hinduism, which has nothing to do with infantilism and is a very advanced level where there is no interest in anything but God (Ishvara). New Age anti-initiatic and psychological fake spirituality has made this the 'inner child'.

Confusing personal or romantic relationships with a desire for real knowledge, even a 'path' of knowledge, is another error of no small magnitude but this has been encouraged through countless books and courses. The self-appointed gurus use the notion of a 'soul twin' as a lure to capitalise on the alienation that many experience in the postmodern world. Romantic relationships can only be what they are because (by definition) they are exclusively determined and therefore limited not only to the domain of the human individuality but also what amounts to a tiny fraction of what that is in reality. All such relations function strictly on the horizontal plane, to use a geometric analogy, and are necessarily limited to that plane.

One of the most subversive notions of the postmodern fake spirituality is that a person should be guided by their 'intuition'. This conveniently rules out completely any need for study and learning of wisdom texts, affiliating with orthodoxy or initiatic organisations, or the performance of any devotional rites and observances other than devotion to the ego-self, which is always the primary objective. That has been disguised to a certain extent through the Human Potential movement. This produced an inverse hierarchy where 'self-esteem' and 'self-worth' are placed at the top of the mountain of hubris. This same creed successfully managed to translate the sin of pride into a virtue, so that various supposedly oppressed minorities commonly hold public celebrations to display their pride in whatever thing is supposed to make them different, with a view to becoming the same as everyone else!

Real intuition has nothing to do whatsoever with instinct or emotion, or with anything received from the psychic realm—this last of which must again be emphasised. The term 'guru', taken from the Hindu tradition although all initiatic paths have various words for one who is able to teach others, is often used now in a derogatory sense. By following their 'intuition' the person is supposed to have no need of anyone else unless that person happens to be a professional. No genuine guru, in the original sense of that word, would ever claim professional status; in fact that automatically disqualifies anyone from such a vocation.

We should consider then what a real guru does: The kind of knowledge we are speaking of here is incommunicable. It cannot be conveyed personally, or through any discursive thought or writing. Symbolism is the best we have but symbolism cannot convey such knowledge directly either; writing is also symbolism but is a step further removed from primordial symbolism.

We can say that the guru, who has reached the stage called in Sanskrit *pandita*, is a possessor of knowledge that is able to awaken corresponding possibilities in others, as the knowledge in itself is incommunicable. There are gradations and so certain limits to the knowledge that a guru may have attained. According to the level of knowledge, a guru may awaken possibilities in others but that is all. This must always involve transmitting a spiritual influence—though the teacher must speak and act on behalf of an initiatic organisation or body of tradition before that can take place. However, if the apprentice or *chela* is not able to reach beyond the abode of the individuality, or even the human psyche (which is much closer to the corporeal state than many people imagine), and if they are (in their ego *ahankara*) in some way opposed to or resistant to such truth, unknowing of the principle, then that resistance will manifest in their humanity in an evil and degraded form, a sort of parody of what it really is. And that is what is sometimes called 'personal demons' in the New Age counter-initiatic movement. However, no 'getting rid of demons', no 'working on the self', psychological analysis and objectification, no altered states or self-created ceremonies can do anything but deepen the delusion. It is only in the clear light of knowledge, in the special sense we mean it here, and the spiritual realisation that requires initiation, where all such demons vanish away in an instant. They simply cease to exist.

An even more insidious and very damaging form of postmodern shamanism has emerged in relatively recent times. The taking of hallucinogenic 'plant medicines', which have by now been given the euphemistic name 'entheogenic', is now utilised by psychologically based 'healing groups' that have no knowledge of spiritual realities or any doctrinal framework other than the 'cult of the self' and the study of modern social sciences. Even the word 'entheogen' is a lie. Divinity cannot be produced through any plant matter or chemical, neither can it be produced or realised from any psychic state, even if it is called 'non-ordinary' or 'non-conventional'. Experiments with plant and tree shades, even magick, when that is separated from any principle, can result in an entity being formed. Such an entity, for want of a better term, is a kind of semblance of the individuality or an intrusion into that individuality from a sub-infra level (below manifestation as such). Such entities are sub-human, or to put it another way, they have a relative existence on a sub-infra level, the lowest of the subtle regions. Such entities can to a certain extent act autonomously. In another sense, like the genie in a bottle, they will appear to carry out a person's wishes and commands (even if the host does not know it).

The obsessing entity will always tighten its grip until it eventually destroys the host—unless the latter abandons the practices that facilitated this in the first place, and even then, it may be too late. While the entity remains in possession the host has no possibility of ever touching any spiritual knowledge; the entity will have placed a barrier or shield that prevents any spiritual influence from entering the host's domain. The entity can know nothing of any spiritual reality other than in the sense where that is perceived as a threat to its own apparent (or strictly relative) existence; it therefore works primarily to 'protect' the person from all spiritual influences so the condition of ignorance is perpetuated.

To a certain extent that is exactly how the System of Antichrist is working in the world today. That System can and does work in the psychic realm as well as the material. This is all the more so now, with highly 'persuasive' hypnotic technologies combined with the intravenous injection of toxins on a massive scale. The System is thus able to modify the minds and the bodies of a slave population to suit its own purely destructive ends.

The Key of Magick

It is sometimes said that 'there are no authorities in occultism'.[140] This is a curious thing to say as, firstly, it is only true regarding individual persons. The rites are infallible, not the priest or teacher. Secondly, 'occultism' is a term descriptive of a broad body of speculative knowledge taken out from diverse sources and separated entirely from its doctrinal context. In that sense, the saying is true in so far as it concerns a state of disorder and disequilibrium. The occult movement produced countless pseudo-initiatic organisations. The statement is of course popular with the postmodernists who resent all hierarchies, even the spiritual or natural ones, other than the inverse hierarchy of the System of Antichrist to which they are enslaved. Such a profane mentality always denies the existence of any reliable or authoritative tradition, which is of course absurd. What follows is authoritative in that sense, and happens to be almost completely unknown in the modern world.

The Sanskrit term *karma*, as we have previously mentioned, is nearly always misconstrued through confusion with another term, *apurva*. It has suffered yet more confusion through certain moral attachments that were purely an invention of the Theosophists.[141]

In reality there is no cause and effect, only simultaneity, but we perceive things as a linear succession or sequence in time. Strictly from the temporal point of view, any action (*karma*) must have consequences or a perceived result or 'effect'.[142] Carried in the action is the seed of its effect or result, called *apurva* in Sanskrit. Apurva is not perceptible and therefore is not known. It is only known by its magical effect, result, or perceivable consequence. An effect cannot be the result of something that no longer exists. In another way, something that does not already exist cannot come into existence from 'nothing'. As it would be absurd to think that a cause and effect could be two singular, separated or discontinuous events, *apurva*, existing both inside and outside of time, is their common principle.

---

[140] This may have originated with Dion Fortune, who wrote that 'Occultism has no Pope' in her book *Psychic Self-Defense*.
[141] Cf. 'Karma and Sin', *Nu Hermetica*.
[142] Cf. 'Lapis Philosophorum', *Babalon Unveiled*.

Lugh of Three Faces (altar stone)—yesterday, today and tomorrow.

By *apurva* there is then uninterrupted relation and continuance through all worlds of manifestation—and we should remember that all manifestation is in reality cyclical in nature, not linear. Cyclical Manifestation includes all states of Being, and these are an indefinite multitude.[143] While the result that occurs must carry the same seed (*apurva*) as the cause or action, the effect is in no way identical or a mere replica of the action as there is change in the state of being. The action (*karma*) must travel along the horizontal, to use the geometric analogy, until it reaches its limit. It then returns. Likewise, the Cosmic Cycles or the multiple states of being can never replicate themselves but neither are they ever completely separate one from another. According to René Guénon, who has expounded on the complexities of this *darshana* or 'point of view' within the Hindu doctrines:

> Every action, and also, in a more general sense, every manifestation, marks a rupture of equilibrium ... a corresponding reaction is demanded in order to restore that equilibrium, since the sum of all differentiations must in the last instance be equivalent to the total indifferentiation.[144]

The human and cosmic orders are thus able to meet through the imperceptible 'thread of light' by which all the states or orders are connected. It is what is meant in the Gnostic texts when the Master says, of the five words that he found concealed in the seamless robe or garment that was given him,

> O Mystery, which is without in the world, for whose sake the universe hath arisen, this is the total outgoing and the total ascent, which hath emanated all emanations and all that is.[145]

In the Egyptian metaphysics, Horus is the 'one that returns', which is to say he returns to his identity with Ra as source of all life and manifestation. Horus is in no way separate from Ra but he is also the Universal Man (or Cosmic Man) who descends, 'goes out', and then reascends, is withdrawn.[146] In the practice of yoga it is the inward and the outward breath: Aum, the return (in-breath) through three states of consciousness, and the outgoing (out-breath) that brings about a new state of being or manifestation: Aum Mah.

---

[143] Indefinite as opposed to infinite, for manifestation cannot be infinite as that can only pertain to the realm of the eternal.
[144] 'Mimansa', *Introduction to the Study of the Hindu Doctrines*, p. 196 [Sophia Perennis].
[145] The Master Christ-Jesus or Emmanuel, *Pistis Sophia*. The five words have the value of 527, for which see *The Flaming Sword Sepher Sephiroth* Vol 2.
[146] Cf. 'The Two Adams'.

To paraphrase what Guénon said in his exposition on Mimansa *darshana*, this knowledge has an almost unlimited range of practical applications.[147] He preferred not to say it but the applications belong to the realm of traditional sciences, more especially the art of magick. However, anyone that is not able to comprehend what we have given here would best not enter into experimentation with a science they do not understand. The one that has sufficient knowledge will readily be able to work out and possibly put into practice the almost endless and vast implications of what is involved here.

---

[147] *Introduction to the Study of the Hindu Doctrines* [ibid].

I Am That

It is needful to at least touch on some of the metaphysical ground that supports what we are putting forward in regard to the Way of the Shakta as essential to the time we live in, close to the end of the Manvantara.[148] What is sometimes described as 'smaller than a seed that is in a grain of millet' is Atma Itself, which is not limited or contained by anything, or changed by anything. It has no location, as it is not in time and space. As such, it is the goal of yoga to realise this to the fullest extent possible.

We first need to examine the centre or the 'heart of the world' considered as a reflection in the microcosm of the metaphysical point, which expresses in analogous geometric terms the primordial state of unity that is Atma Itself. The Hebrew word Luz (LVZ) means 'almond, hazel', and is at the same time the name of a fabled Hittite city.[149] It is said that an almond-tree with a hole in it stood before the entrance to a cave that was near Luz. It was possible to pass through the hole, enter the cave and so discover the hidden city. The cave is analogous with the heart in which dwells the *avatara* or immortal principle; it is cognate with the Heart Girt with a Serpent or the *omphalos*. There are many similarities between the symbolism of the city of Luz and that found in other cultures. To name but one, there is the round megalith at Men-an Tol in Cornwall, of which folk-lore has it that if one passes naked through the hole in the stone three times, or nine times, bowing to the moon, a cure will be affected for diverse ills and wants. According to René Guénon, *The King of the World*:

> Luz, being imperishable, is the 'kernel of immortality' in the human being, just as the city that is designated by the same name is the 'abode of immortality': this is where the power of the 'Angel of Death' stops in both cases.

Guénon links Luz to the 'cult of the caverns', in which subterranean vaults or caves are used as centres or locations for initiatic rites, whether the places are actual or purely symbolic. In any case, it is for symbolic reasons that such places are chosen. The name Luz itself implies something covered or hidden, secret and silent, which is an attribute of the Egyptian goddess Neïth—some of whose rites were also enacted in a subterranean vault.

---

[148] Cf. 'Cosmic Cycles', *Nu Hermetica*.
[149] Cf. *Symbols of Sacred Science* Chapter 32 and *The King of the World* Chapter 7, René Guénon [Sophia Perennis].

In all cases, the roof or ceiling of the cave, directly above its central point, designates the 'sky' or 'heaven', which accounts for the starry ceilings that may be found in ancient Egyptian temples as well as Masonic ones. There is a further link with the hollow place and the colour blue or the sapphire stone. As the kernel of immortality, the almond or almond tree—the tree or fruit that is latent in the seed or nut—*luz* is considered to be indestructible and so is linked to resurrection. It contains all elements needed for the restoration of the soul, or if this is applied to the Cosmic Cycles, the restoration of the world or Kingdom following dissolution.

As a type of oval, egg or embryo, the Sanskrit *pinda* in which something of great value is hidden, *luz* is sometimes associated with the small hard bone of the coccyx at the base of the spine. According to the Tantras, the serpent Kundalini is coiled near the base of the spine in the subtle anatomy and by this Shakti dreams the world into existence. It is the condition of the 'fallen' or unawakened man. It is the practice of yoga that awakens the Kundalini from the sleeping state so that it passes upward through various chakras or centres. In *ajna* ('knowledge'), associated with the third eye chakra, resides the primordial state or the sense of eternity in man. When the serpent Kundalini is raised all the way to the crown chakra (*sahasrara*) then *moksha* liberation becomes possible, through a thread or solar ray that passes out beyond the human state to the higher states of being. It should be added, however, that even the lower states of Samadhi or yogic union are not attained through effort or practice alone but are a gift of Mahadevi Shakti Herself. According to *The Hebraic Tongue Restored*, the root form LV carries the following ideas:

> Every idea of liaison, cohesion, tendency of objects toward each other. The universal bond. The abstract line which *is conceived* going from one point to another and which is represented by the relations, *oh if! oh that! would to God that!*[150]

And on the root LZ:

> Every movement directed toward an object to show it, and expressed in an abstract sense by the relations *this, that*.

The word heard by Moses, 'I Am That I Am' (Eheieh Asher Eheieh), is traditionally ascribed to Kether the Crown, the first number or sephira of the Qabalistic Tree of Life. It might also be noted that the three Hebrew words each begin with the letter *aleph*, denoting the perfected threefold expression of unity; when the letter *aleph* is spelled in full (ALP) it has the value of 111.

---

[150] *The Hebraic Tongue Restored*, 'Index of Roots', Antoine Fabre d'Olivet.

Kether is symbolised geometrically as the metaphysical point within a circle. It is primordial unity, of which the number one is an analogy. The word of Moses is more precisely translated as 'Being is Being'.[151] There is Pure Being and there is Being perceiving Itself. The 'point' is thus able to replicate itself as a reflection. We may also understand this as the extension of the point into the line, which has two ends or poles. Through self-polarisation, for example, the spirit (Atma) is able, by extension, to be realised as *purusha* and *prakriti*, 'essence' (male) and 'substance' (female), which we have previously explained.[152] A line must be understood as the distance between two metaphysical points and as these points have no dimension, the distance between them can be as small as it possibly could be. When this is projected into time and space, the line that connects the two points is the *copula*; this 'linking together' has a further symbolism in the arc or dome of the sky, which is the symbol of the Egyptian goddess Nuit.

We sound Asherah (AShRH) instead of Eheieh (AHIH) to invoke the crown in practice. The Egyptians knew the name of the Canaanite Goddess Asherah as Qutesh, and these are both very similar to the Hindu forms of the Shakti such as Parvati, Kali and Durga. The name Asherah is derived from the root meaning 'that' (AShR) as well as 'woman'. An identical meaning and root is carried across feminine nouns in several languages, Eve being no exception. The use of Asherah does not contradict the Eheieh, which is an expression of Pure Being, but is complementary as it is inclusive of two possible points of view through invoking the *copula* by which they are united. It thus resolves all difficulties produced through monotheism. Asher is the *copula*, which is the relation between the 'two' (though they are a unity) as projected in space. Love is the domain of the Shakti.

The change from 'Being is Being', the word of Moses, to 'That', a name of the Shakti, was not an arbitrary one. In short, Mahadevi Shakti is 'That' as the line between the two points, which is able to know them. Although the word of Moses is Ishvara ('Lord'), the first envelope of being and so once removed from Atma Itself, Mahadevi Shakti is all of that and all it can be, but is also beyond even that![153]

---

[151] See René Guénon, 'Ontology of the Burning Bush', *The Symbolism of the Cross* [Sophia Perennis].
[152] See 'The Ass and the Ark' and 'The Two Adams'.
[153] Cf. *Hymns to the Goddess*, John Woodroffe.

Pure Being is gender neutral but in the Hindu doctrines there are the followers of the Trimurti (Brahmā, Shiva and Vishnu) and there are the Shaktas, who posit the Shakti as before all other Gods and creation. For this reason the Shakti is considered as a fourth aspect of Trimurti, so there is no doctrinal conflict. To the Brahmā devotees, all proceed from the heart of Brahmā, and the Shakti is conceived there in a certain sense as *purusha* 'essence', or otherwise Maya. But to the Shaktas, even Brahmā himself was actually born from the navel of the Shakti. The navel is a further symbolism of the heart or centre, and quite an obvious one. All churches at one time were built with a nave, which was the area from the entrance (*narthex*) to the transepts in front of the sanctuary as in the case of a cruciform church.[154] The nave is thus the exact equivalent of the 'Gate of Men' or summer solstice.

It is an error to assume, as most commentators have, that Nuit is only 'appearance' in her manifestation. Her manifestation is formless and she is more than that too. She is also the means of knowing—only God can know God. There is the Knower, there is the Known and there is Knowledge itself. The Knower is a term used frequently by the Advaitans, as well as in the yoga of Patanjali. Nuit is also indentified with space, as her hieroglyphs clearly indicate the sky, or the 'reach' of heaven. However, space cannot be infinite for it only exists in manifestation, and even more, it is particular to the state of the human being. Space and time is a particular modality or condition of the primordial state and is not in any way the primordial state itself. It has been the error of all modernist thinkers to try to prove in various ways that the universe (or space) is infinite, which is a reduction of the metaphysical supreme principle to conventional materialism. It is a metaphysical impossibility and contradicts all traditional knowledge.

Friedrich Nietzsche thus invented the term 'Eternal recurrence' to describe the universe as infinite and therefore infinitely recurring—that no thing or event can truly be singular in time and space. It seems that Nietzsche failed to develop the idea—which was intended to be a replacement for the Christian doctrine of salvation—even though it was the triumphant cadence in what is generally considered to be his seminal work *Thus Spake Zarathustra*.[155]

---

[154] In other cases there is a chancel area in front of the altar. Early churches were based on the Roman Catholic and Greek Orthodox Basilica.
[155] See Aaron Ridley, pp. 102–108, *Nietzsche on Art* [Routledge].

In trying to reinvent doctrine that he clearly did not understand in the first place, Nietzsche was influenced by the Hindu term *apurva*.[156] However, the *apurva* is based on traditional logic that in no way contradicts the unified Hindu doctrines. It is a key to understanding how Nuit is identified with space through her Egyoptian name, and yet this is no way implies that space is infinite, which is impossible. This will now be explained further:

As an action cannot be separate from its consequence in time, removed from it as it were by a line or measure of space, *apurva* is the line, or 'that', which is the relation between stars or points in space and time. Apurva necessarily exists both inside and outside of space and time. As related to the microcosm, *apurva* then has a correspondence with the *pinda* or embryonic latency. The Shakti Herself is thus able to produce *apurva*, and she is in truth the *apurva* itself. This means that Nuit or Mahadevi Shakti is not only the 'cause' that is in itself causeless, and unaffected by anything, but is also *present in the resultant*. This has considerable import and is something that can only be fully understood by way of thought and profound meditation.

---

[156] See 'The Key of Magick'.

Mysteria Magica Sexualis

We should never underestimate the contagious influence of Sigmund Freud upon occultists of the twentieth century. Freud first posited an 'unconscious', and that everything not pertaining directly to the individual can be relegated there. This entirely rules out any spiritual or non-human influence other than that which comes from an infra-human level. He then formulated his notion of the 'will', which he called 'libido', as existing in this infra-human or unconscious level. Libido naturally includes what others would then describe as the 'sex-force'. Since psychoanalysis began at least with the theory that all the ills of man are due to 'repression', or the inhibition of the libido, it naturally followed that it would be supposed that the sex-force was a 'key to it all', and was even the way to freedom or liberation—terms that were borrowed from the Eastern doctrines but taken out of their original context entirely. Later, this influence was to degenerate even further when a general acceptance of the theories of Carl Gustav Jung paved the way for a completely counterfeit 'spirituality' that has exerted a great evil on all modern culture.[157]

The writings of Aleister Crowley do not differ as much from the theories of Freud as he wished to have it known. His interpretation of symbolism was almost entirely 'phallic', where we must understand that to his mentality this was no longer a symbol as is revealed in the etymological sense of the word, but a material fact—which is typical of the 'naturalistic' thinking of our time. The Greek *phallos* means 'image', or better, 'substance', and bears a certain relationship with *idyll* and *eidolon*. Both terms have suffered degradation in modern usage; 'idyll' now carries a sentimental idea, while 'eidolon' carries a superficial notion of 'idealised person or thing' or even 'apparition or phantom', as though it were completely non-existent. All these words originally conveyed 'essence', which is *purusha* in the Sanskrit, a metaphysical term that has no relation with matter at all as *purusha* is not within manifestation. And similarly, the Sanskrit *lingam* has very similar meanings as the Greek *phallos*, meanings that entirely transcend that of the physical organ.

---

[157] Cf. 'Initiation', *Nu Hermetica*. For a very exacting explanation of the damage that has been wrought by Jung's psychoanalytical theories, see also René Guénon, 'Tradition and the Unconscious', *Symbols of Sacred Science* [Sophia Perennis].

Crowley borrowed his so-called 'sexual magick secret' either from the Hermetic Brotherhood of Luxor or Beverley Paschal Randoph, who was a member of the said organisation. As we shall see, this 'secret' was always in the ancient *Bhagavad Gita*, but that would not prevent occultists from claming it as their own invention. Crowley took what he would subseqently claim to be a mysterious revelation through to a level of actual obsession with deviant forms of sexual activity. The orientalist Kenneth Grant degraded this even further—further in the sense of the inversion of all symbolism to carry its grossest possible level of interpretation. Grant produced writings of a more fantastical nature than those of Crowley, essentially in the postmodern vein, saturated with his own particular obsession with sadomasochistic voyeurism. While neither of these two men were particularly unique or original in their selling of sex as a panacea to a public already persuaded by sexualised advertising, we mention them here as perhaps extreme examples of what has been a popular trend of our times. Crowley always aimed at popularism, and he achieved it by the same means as used by advertisers, film-makers, modern literature and by now, 'official' academia. In more recent times, some men with academic qualifications, usually psychological, have greatly exaggerated the importance of Crowley's work, claiming for example that some of it was on a level comparable to that of St. John's Revelation!

When sexual activity is isolated from any higher principle then evil comes about in the world as a consequence. The very notion of a higher principle is so misunderstood by now that it is commonly thought of as something to do with morality, whereas morality is of the lowest order, a mere social convention that is subject to constant change and modification in the modern world. Deviant possibilities of sex arise from a disequilibrium or confusion that can reach even to the spiritual level, and that is the real reason for using the word 'evil' in the first place. There are consequences for deviation, and these are by no means limited to particular forms of behaviour or mentality; they owe more to the degradation of the mentality of an entire civilisation. This has been greatly accelerated by the more general kind of deviation we are alluding to here, which owes to a widespread ignorance of spiritual law and now even natural principles, and this has come about through the very inversion of spiritual symbolism that has already been frequently mentioned here and elsewhere.[158]

---

[158] Cf. *Babalon Unveiled*, Lapis Philosophorum, on the 'universal talisman'.

It must be said that all those occultists who pretended that they had discovered a 'great secret' veiled it with a misappropriation of ancient symbolism, including that of alchemy, which only served to obfuscate the foulness of their activities and real intentions. It was entrusted to 'high officers' and the like, supposed adepts of magick. It was only a matter of time before others came along that did not hesitate to put it across in language that the profane could easily understand.

Even these others, apart from the postmodernists who will deny the very existence of any principle whatsoever, have tended to convey the elemental aspect of sex as though it were the supreme goal. They will speak of the 'Great Rite' and so forth. In fact, the use of sex in the Tantras was never very widespread and when it was used, then in most cases it was there for beginners, intermediate practitioners at the most. A great deal of what has been passed off for initiated knowledge in relatively quite recent times, including some practices lately supposed to be a traditional aspect of modern witchcraft and neo-paganism as well as hermeticism, are no more than complete fantasy, of a type that reveals nothing more than a profane mentality typical of the counterfeit initiatic movement. The real secrets are incommunicable and as such cannot be written down or conveyed directly.

The relation between Tantra, which means 'weaving', as in a tapestry or fabric, and sex, has been vastly amplified by the minds of profane occultists. The idea of what Tantra even is has suffered gross degradation; 'sexual magick', often inspired by instructions given by Crowley, is an experimental creation of Western minds, used for profane purposes. The principles were, as usual, inverted, and an attempt was made to reduce Tantra to a kind of mechanical science that could render results in the most inferior of the subtle regions. Later, as these invented secrets became more widely known, the counterfeit initiatic movement reduced Tantra to no more than an attempt to increase and prolong physical pleasure, and, as is usual with this degenerate mentality, to bring benefits to the corporeal state such as 'healing' and enhanced 'wellbeing'. Such goals are by now even thought by many persons to be spiritual yet they admit to nothing at all existing beyond the emotions and the body. In fact, such beneficial outcomes, if they even obtain, are due to little more than self-hypnotism and carry at the same time pitfalls and dangers that are seldom understood by the practitioners.

We commonly think of sexual activity as a physical phenomenon. But no activity is an isolated thing in reality. A dictionary will tell us that 'sex' is derived from the Latin *sexus*, 'six', which is related to 'hex' and 'hexagram', the geometric form of the number six. The curious correspondence between sex and the number six occurs in many tongues. For example, in Greek we have the *digamma*, which is simply 'two threes'. There is in Greek the *stigma*, which has the value of six and denotes literally a mark or point as made with an instrument (such as a burin), but also carries the idea of 'sin', in that its action leaves a residue or trace.

A 'hex' is a word for a magical spell—the capturing of a moment in time. There is no profane explanation for the numerical equation, only an esoteric one. The supreme principle is depicted by the metaphysical point in the circle. This is usually identified with the sun, though it means far more as metaphysical unity beyond any numerical, geometric or quantitative evaluation. The symbol of the 'three' or ternary is the most perfect expression of such inexpressible unity, a term for which in the present context we could substitute 'eternity'. This can easily be explained:

> If two lines extend from the point, through its self-polarisation, the base formed from their extremities brings forth three, which is the unity of one—and note that 'one' cannot truly be a unity if it is regarded as singular.[159]

It is notable that when 'sex' refers to an intimacy or conjunction between male and female, it is symbolic not only of 'three', as described above, but also of the hexagram if we consider that both male and female find a completion in the other, in exactly the same way that the hexagram symbolises this. This is nowhere more perfectly depicted, in the geometric form, by the various *yantras* of the Hindu Tantras. The *Sri Yantra* is a further and more complex form of the feminine triangle, and we will return to this later.[160]

---

[159] *Nu Hermetica*, p. 7.
[160] See 'The Sacred Heart'.

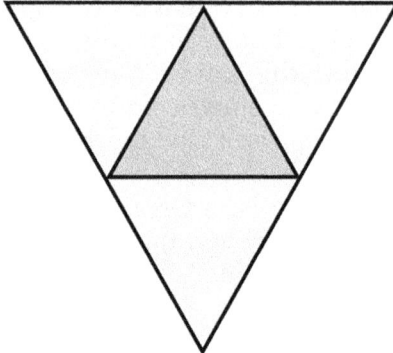

The *yantra* (above) depicts two equilateral triangles, an upright triangle within a down-pointing triangle. The triangles, as with the hexagram, are commonly explained as symbolising fire and water, or male and female, though that is only a particular aspect; in the same way, to explain the Chinese *yang* and *yin* in this way also limits it.

In the Tantras, the *yantra* shown here is most often coloured blue (larger triangle) and red (smaller triangle), though these can also be reversed. Generally, blue signifies the passive or receptive elements and red the active or transmissive, which is easy enough to understand. However, the downward pointing triangle is commonly misunderstood and thought to be inferior or even evil in some way, whereas in fact it denotes the supreme principle. Depicted in the way we have shown it here, the *yantra* may symbolise the principle of manifestation contained within the unmanifest—for the unmanifest must contain all possibilities latent within it. The feminine triad is therefore the supreme principle of the unmanifest. There are even some forms of Masonry where this is given as a symbol of the highest grade—though naturally this has led some into considerable error and confusion![161]

The dangers of taking yoga out from its doctrinal context and discipline will become obvious from the following: The *prana* or vital breath is experienced as sexual arousal when it is concentrated in the physical body at the level corresponding to the base chakra. When the 'electromagnetic' Serpent Power ascends to the heart chakra, then intense feelings of love can come about. In the higher chakras, intellectual exaltation can be experienced. The *shakti* can leave the chakras, passing through the *brahmarandra* chakra, analogously located at the top of the skull, and that is the legitimate aim of yoga.

---

[161] The 33rd degree, which once again conveys the idea of 'six'.

'Sacred sex', a term that has been used as a veil for demonic or otherwise completely ordinary activities, can only properly refer to the incorporation of sex in the practice of yoga. It obviously cannot be concerned at all with the production of physical progeny, as with the common outcome of sexual activity when carried to its natural conclusion. Nonetheless, the principle of generation is not limited to the physical abode alone. In the Tantras, generation corresponds to the elemental *tattva* or principle of *vayu*, 'air', and this is in turn placed with the *anahatha* or heart chakra. This also corresponds to the sense of touch, in so far as each of the five elemental *tattvas* has a correspondence with the senses, both physical and subtle.

That which is born from the palace of Shakti Devi, conceived through the combining and reabsorption of male (sun) and female (moon) essence, reflects the subtle image, so that it is given substance. From the point of view of the practitioner, the image is held and fixed in the mind so as to open a window, or 'point of view' (*darshana*), which is that of the *yantra* or symbol itself.

The above is an application or traditional science with a basis that is clearly set forth in the Hindu doctrines. It is put very concisely in the *Bhagavad Gita*, called the *Essence of the Upanishads*, Chapter Eight 'The Imperishable Brahma', verses 5, 6 and 7:

> And whoso, at the time of death, leaves his body, remembering Me alone and goes forth—he attains My being; considering this there is no doubt.
>
> For whatever object a man thinks of at the final moment, when he leaves his body—that alone does he attain, O son of Kunti, being ever absorbed in the thought thereof.
>
> Therefore, at all times, constantly remember Me and fight. With your mind and understanding absorbed in Me, you will surely come to Me.

The doctrine is echoed in the (Egyptian) Book of the Law, I: 61, the oracle of Nuit, albeit cryptically:

> *For one kiss wilt thou then be willing to give all; but whoso gives one particle of dust shall lose all in that hour.*

And in the oracle of Mentu, III: 62:

> *To Me do ye reverence! to me come ye through tribulation of ordeal, which is bliss.*

The nature of the sacrifice is referred to in the giving of 'one particle of dust', which is a determined or particular wish or desire. In that case, one may get what one wishes for, but the consequence is of partial or strictly limited knowledge, or even *avidya*, 'ignorance'.[162] This is set forth without obfuscation in the Tantras:[163]

> O Iśāni, as the old Lotus Born and others have said,
> The rule is that if others than Thyself art worshipped,
> Only the particular fruit desired is gained;
> But Thou giveth more even than is asked for.
> Make me then ever attached to Thee, by day and night.

Viewed technically, the production of a non-human child or flower of the *boddhi*, born in silence, has been inverted by black magicians so that it is exclusively reserved for the creation of artificial elementals. This is in effect no different than the formula of any talisman, but the use of it has now become widespread among profane occultists and experimentalists, owing to the publication of explicit instructions in books designed to be accessible by the average person. Owing to the inversion of symbolism that is always present and the particular bias and mindset of the commentators and practitioners, the talisman itself, in such cases, bears an inverse signature that is destructive to the soul and to all possibilities of real initiation. The writers, often using and re-using the works of Crowley as a basis, will claim to be 'high adepts', while listing their organisations and their academic psychological qualifications—which are no qualifications at all so far as initiation is concerned. It is clear from their works that none of them has the slightest idea of what initiation really is.

It remains to be said that there will be those who, seeing that we have fenced this around with caveats, will not heed the warnings and will plunder what is given here, if they are able to, for their own ends. It makes little odds, for what has been said here equally applies to all magical practices, and it is too late now to stop the tide turning back in the wrong direction. For persons such as these the gates of hell are already flung wide open in any case, and the doors of heaven are sealed shut forever.

---

[162] Literally, 'no knowledge': to be without knowledge at all in any real sense.
[163] *Hymns to the Goddess*, Sir John Woodroffe, 'Waves of Bliss' verse 13, translated from the hymn of Shankaracharya.

The Sacred Heart

The symbolism of the Grail, the Sacred Heart, owes to antiquity and it is hardly necessary to demonstrate in historical terms how this vastly preceded Christianity even while forming an essential part of that religion. If we take this as accepted, that the Grail symbolism is derived directly from a primordial tradition that existed long before there was any need for religion, then we can look at its meaning without too much digression. Let it suffice to say that what is now called 'religion', which is commonly used as descriptive of all ancient practices, even pre-religious ones such as that of Egypt, can only properly be applied to the relatively modern streams of Judaism, Christianity and Islam.[164]

The Egyptian *ab* (or *ib*) vessel has meanings that extend far beyond that of the physical organ, which is itself a symbol of the 'centre' of the world and of man. It is the heart, will, intelligence, wisdom and desire, and in combination with other hieroglyphics it covers all the complexities arising from such ideas. The symbolism of the 'city' or 'palace' is cognate when the heart is at the centre of what is usually a fourfold or eightfold structure. In biblical lore it is said there are four rivers flowing out of Eden. Eden is itself a dual symbol since there is a supernal and a terrestrial Eden or earthly paradise. The stream of water and the stream of blood are also terms for celestial fire or dew that drops down from heaven to bring forth a bloom, which may be a lotus in Egypt or the East, or a rose in the Western tradition. The flower is itself a symbol of the heart, especially the calyx or 'chalice'. The chakras or lotuses of Hindu and Tibetan Tantras have such a calyx, which is the eternal abode of the Shakti Devi, to whom is given the life-giving power of producing or manifesting creatures and forms and of withdrawing their life into that of the great unmanifest.

---

[164] Pre-religious traditions, which all derive from the one ancient primordial tradition, were previously called pagan, which was of course meant in the derogatory sense as used by Christian and other polemicists. However, to call all such traditions 'religious' is not an improvement, especially when we consider that the conventional notion of religion includes 'belief', which is almost as derogatory as 'paganism'—implying that ancient people were somehow inferior, that their doctrines were founded on superstition—yet another term that has had the meaning inverted so that it implies ignorance instead of higher intuition.

It is necessary to explain further two Sanskrit terms, *purusha* and *prakriti*, for these have no equivalent in any modern languages. To repeat what was said earlier,

> Of *purusha*, 'essence' (sometimes 'spirit'), it is said in the Upanishads that it resides in the pure heart of Brahma, and that heart is concave or hollow.[165]

This is sometimes supposed to mean 'nothing' or 'emptiness', but that is mistaken, for the unmanifest must contain all possibilities of manifestation.

> Through self-polarisation, *purusha* divides, or at least appears to do so, and becomes *prakriti*, 'substance'. In fact, *purusha* and *prakriti* are not really separate and can be understood as the northern and southern extremities of a vertical axis.

This primal division is shown in all ancient traditions, for example, in the symbolism of Tiamat, the Great Sea Dragon whose body is divided into pieces by Marduk to create the world, and also that of Osiris. These are cosmological as well as metaphysical realities, as in the case of Osiris who is divided into fourteen parts, the number not only of a lunar cycle but also of the greater Cosmic Cycles.

> Neither *purusha* nor *prakriti* are within manifestation in any degree, but *prakriti*, through the action of *purusha* upon her, is able to produce living forms and creatures. Prakriti is thus personified as a goddess, who, like Maya, weaves the tapestry of life and of all living forms.[166]

We can then see that those who have thought the heart to contain no more than emptiness only reflect the sterility of their thought, even while 'emptiness' and 'void' are used to indicate the cave of the heart, or the urn or vessel that is the hieroglyph for the Egyptian goddess Nuit.

The more detailed form of the *ab* or heart vessel hieroglyph shows symbolism identical in meaning to that of the Sanskrit AUM, where the *bindu* or point principle is embraced by a lunar crescent. In this case the point is extended to a mound so we have an image cognate with the Shiva-lingam and Shakti-yoni. We then have here the concave nature of the heart and its seed principle, *purusha*, as both primal mound and *prakriti* as the means of production, all contained within the Sacred Heart.

---

[165] Cf. 'Sat-Chit-Ananda'.
[166] The name 'Maya' means 'artist' or 'producer'. See 'Sat-Chit-Ananda'.

Comparisons may be made with the Graeco Egyptian Heart Girt with a Serpent.[167] A further interpretation of the *ab*, or *ab-heti*, when it is strongly identified with the 'house' or 'abode' of spirit, rests on its visual identification with the human skull. It is then emblematic of the way to the supernal Eden via the crown chakra when it is perceived as an opening and the skull itself as a 'cave'. In this case the handles of the jar are the ears and the lid is the doorway to heaven or the sky. The ears denote the ability to hear or receive, which is at the same time the means of initiatic transmission and reception. A word must be heard before it can be uttered. And finally—although the meanings of the heart are almost inexhaustible in scope—it must be said that the face of Hathoor, the House of Horus, is always drawn with this same heart-shape and pronounced ears. At Iunet, the Goddess is known as the Divine Pillar and so she encompasses the entire range of the symbolism of primal mound and the reach of the sky or eternity.

The ignorance of the modern mentality insists that all ancient civilisations must have had beliefs, comparable to the requirements of religion, or at least as that is conceived in the most retarded sense imaginable. We may then find it said, for example, that the ancient Egyptians believed that a child was formed from 'one drop of blood from its mother's heart', at the time of conception. How easy it is for those blind to all spiritual reality to see 'superstition' where there is only pure metaphysical symbolism that greatly exceeds their capacity for understanding! It is by this one drop, the *purusha* that resides in the Sacred Heart, that a 'child' or intelligence may flower—the flower itself being a universal symbol for the *prakriti* or substance. Here we have not only the means of the production of a life-form but also that of initiation and of spiritual realisation, for it is said that the child of Silence, called Harpocrates, is born from the lotus flower. That is in turn the symbol of the higher intellectual intuition or *boddhi*, arising from latency to effective activity. This, it will be realised, has been confused by the profane as an allusion to the production of elemental progeny—a typical inversion of symbolism.[168] A further symbol of the heart is found in Tantrism as a simple downward-pointing triangle and *bindu* mark in the centre, a form of *yantra*.

---

[167] Cf. 'Liber Zain', *The Phoenix and other Stellar Rites of Initiation*.
[168] See 'Mysteria Magica Sexualis'.

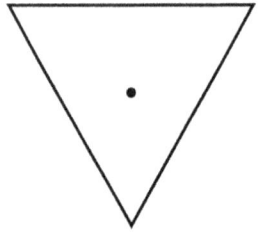 Guénon, who has gone into this subject in some depth, has mentioned that sometimes the heart is simplified by triangulation, so that the *yantra*, as well as being a depiction of the feminine or Shakti power, includes all of the ideas put forward thus far.[169] The triangle is the perfect expression of metaphysical unity, and the central point is its supreme principle, not expressible as either one or even zero or by any number. The triangle is also the root idea of form as expressed geometrically, though manifestation does not come about until the quaternary is invoked.

The symbolism of blood is intimately woven into that of the Holy Grail and Christian mysteries, which were originally a continuation of the earlier knowledge of the Celts, Druids and others. The Mass is, or once was, vital to Christianity, its central core of communion. It is modelled on the scene of the Last Supper, where Christ Jesus served bread and wine to his disciples after the manner of the high priest Melchizedek. After blessing the bread he broke it, gave it to the disciples, and said,

> Take, eat; this is my body.

He then took the chalice of wine, gave thanks and then passed it to them, saying,

> Drink from it, all of you; for this is my blood of the covenant, which is poured out for many for the forgiveness of sins.

This was repeated later at the crucifixion, where water and blood pouring from the wound made in his side from a centurian's lance were collected in a cup. As the legend goes, Joseph of Arimathea and Nicodemus took the Grail to the Knights of the Round Table in England, and from there to Brittany.

Prostestantism was an irreversible step towards the creation of a uniform pseudo-Christianity. Changes were made to the tenets of the faith, doctrine and rituals. This included a theological interpretation of the meaning of the Eucharist, which amounts to a formal rejection of the Catholic doctrine of transubstantiation. At least for a while, many people were not blind to the fact that their religion had been destroyed and a counterfeit put in its place. The heart had been torn out of the religion and Christianity left without a soul.

---

[169] Cf. Guénon, *Symbols of Sacred Science* [Sophia Perennis].

The Anglican Church Communion is by now mainly an 'option' for its ministers but in a denatured form. The Mass is now seen by many as 'only symbolic' and has been routinely denigrated even from within the Church's own ranks. According to Catholic doctrine, the miracle of the Mass is a literal fact. While the wine, if tested, would be found to be wine, not blood, any such tests only obtain to the materiality, which is no more than the appearance of a thing, not the reality. Thus it is said that the taste, smell and colour of the wine, after the transformation, is no more than a mere semblance, which is a metaphysical truth. There is a change in the actual substance of the wine, which is comparable to the *prakriti* of the Hindu tradition, and which is able to effect productions in the subtle domain. Thus, when the Mass was either discontinued or replaced by a neutered form of it, even the sacrament was removed from the religion and it became no more than a lifeless husk, a semblance or an appearance of what it once was. It was only a matter of time before the Church would lose all spiritual authority, having no more power to influence social or other matters. At the present time we see this as a fait accompli; Church authorities have bowed to pressure to make changes to their ethical and moral precepts from outside the Church, changes made on entirely profane grounds.

The Mass was by no means unique to Christianity, although that is sometimes falsely claimed in the same way that even the Cross is sometimes thought not to have existed longer than 2,000 years ago! There are entirely esoteric, non-religious forms of the Mass, and we have gone some way previously to explaining one of these.[170] It is said in one esoteric Mass, when raising the chalice upward to heaven,

> In the name of Isis, may this wine be transformed by the power of love and sacrifice.

In this case, the wine is not seen as changing into the blood of any particular prophet or avatar, but rather it is transformed into the universal essence, the *mezla* or 'starry dew' of Nuit. As this is a non-religious rite, it is performed effectively by a priest or a priestess, or both, so long as they are properly qualified. As with the true Catholic Mass, it would be ignorant to suppose that what takes place is 'only symbolic'. Anyone believing that to be the case would simply render their selves ineffectual and incapable of either receiving or conveying any spiritual influence—which is also the view of Catholicism.

---

[170] See 'The Whole World', *Nu Hermetica*.

Having said that, and to avoid any possible misunderstanding, the Christian church has never in any way supported initiation, and in the rare cases when initiated writings have clearly been produced, this was not as a result of any initiatic presence within the church. It must have once been initiatic, but there is no 'historical' evidence, and the whole matter is veiled in obscurity, perhaps deliberately.[171] As we have frequently stated, or made allusion to across various texts, the true origin of Christianity, which includes the pre-Christian Grail tradition, was in Egypt. Furthermore, this would have had almost no resemblance to what Christianity became later, and would not even have included an exoteric or religious function.

Having gone this far into explaining some of the technicalities of the Mass, it is fitting to look at a few aspects of how the subtle anatomy of the female plays a special part in this, in the same way that the subtle anatomy of the male was at one time at least essential to the effective performance of the Christian Mass, though we cannot go into that here.[172] What can at least be said is that even when a Mass is properly done, and the presiding minister fully capable, that is no guarantee that celebrants will truly receive what is being given. A seed may fall by the wayside, or on stony ground, and it is not the fault of the seed that no flower or fruit comes forth.

The *Sri Yantra* (facing page) has an analogous counterpart in the physical body of the female, linking it with the subtle states. The interlaced triangles subdivide into smaller triangles, and this forms a complex network of paths. The *yantra* is both a cosmological image of the emanations or radiations from the seed (*bindu*) principle, which exist both inside and outside of space and time, and of the microcosm. It is most often placed within the 'palace' of the Shakti Lolita, a fourfold representation of the centre of the world.

---

[171] Cf. René Guénon, *Christian Esoterism* [Sophia Perennis].
[172] It would necessitate a lengthy digression, in the present context, to go into matters related to the effectiveness of a priest, such as celibacy.

There are five major 'female' triangles, or six if we count the centre one enclosing the *bindu*, which does not have lines of its own and therefore only appears by virtue of the other triangles. There are four major 'male' triangles, making nine in all, ten including the centre and innermost, which therefore symbolises the unmanifest aspect— the centre can only be known by its surrounding space. Taking the geometrical triangles as a whole, a 'star', there are fourteen points, indicating the lunar cycle and also an entire Manvantara cycle as two septenaries, one facing forwards and one facing backwards. The first (or inner) circle has the eight petals typical of the Indian lotus, and symbolises space. The second circle has sixteen petals and therefore symbolises time. The third and outermost circle is surrounded by the fourfold walls of the City or Palace of the Shakti Lolita, and therefore represents the earth, or an entire world. This arrangement of lotus petals corresponds to the *anahatha* or heart chakra, and is the centre cavity or 'cave' where the divine *purusha* (spirit) makes a seal or impression upon *prakriti* (substance) to give form to all life and creatures. If we count the numbers the result is either 51 or 52, the number of letters in the Sanskrit sacred alphabet including the letter that is not sounded (it forms a part of AUM).

The symbol shows, by proportion and sacred geometry, the subtle interplay of Cosmic Cycles.[173] Making a comparison with the ancient Egyptian wisdom, every evening Ra the solar *principle* is swallowed into the mouth of Nuit, the body of stars and of space. He passes through her body, undergoing transformations. At dawn he is born afresh from her womb and ascends into exterior space in the winged form of the beetle Khephra, the principle of Ever-Becoming, which is descriptive of manifestation. The cycle of death, transformation and regeneration is thus symbolised in the *yantra* as simultaneity, which is only perceived as taking place through events or the passage of time from the corporeal point of view.

Horus, who is identical both with Ra as the solar principle and with the King, Perfected or Universal Man, is the manifester of the divine Word in flesh and the means of return to the stars, or to the source that is beyond all manifestation.[174] He is thus the Lord of the Two Horizons (Hormaku or Hrumachis), uniting all the dualities. As such he is not only the Lord of Initiation but also the goal itself, for as the head of the Sphinx he is wisdom and as the body of the lion he is the strength needed to bear the knowledge of the ineffable source. In true knowledge, we become what we know and we are thus changed forever.

---

[173] Cf. 'Cosmic Cycles', *Nu Hermetica*.
[174] Cf. 'The Two Adams'.

Don Juan

In some previous writings we referred to the works of Carlos Castaneda (1925–1998). He conveys the 'teachings of don Juan' through a cleverly crafted mixture of imagination and elements of traditional knowledge, possibly taken from diverse sources. It is impossible to know if it was derived directly from Yaqui sorcerers, as claimed by the author, or Navaho Indians, as some have speculated. Castaneda recollects, pieces together and tries to make sense of his experiences and encounters with don Juan through each book in the series. The works are highly entertaining, concentrating on 'altered states', outrageous magical tricks and a range of bizarre phenomena. And that is not to say that some of the things described cannot ever take place, or cannot be experienced.

There has been a great deal of speculation on Castaneda himself, and he has been subjected to much criticism and even personal attacks, which may account for his retirement from public life about five years after the first book was published until his death in Los Angeles at the age of 73 years. Whether the author was taken in by his own subterfuge, as some say, or otherwise kept up the pretence for so long that it was too late to back out—even acquiring disciples along the way—makes little or no difference so far as the value of what he wrote is concerned. It is certainly enigmatic, and bears no resemblance to the postmodern shamanism we discussed earlier. Castaneda was, or claimed to be, an anthropologist.[175] One wholly consistent factor in the many books he wrote is that his character never drops the methods of profane science, endlessly categorising and listing. However, he might have intentionally adopted the rôle as a kind of disguise, which is completely in accordance with one of the methods of the sorcerers, called *stalking*—which we will return to later. It may also have simply been a clever literary device to play off the rationalism of the ordinary man against the non-rational means of the sorcerers, which allows for a great deal of hilarious uproar.

---

[175] Some anthropologists dispute that Castaneda's PhD at UCLA was valid and are pointedly critical of his works on ethnological grounds. However, no anthropologist is qualified to interpret traditional sciences, whether that is thought to be sorcery or pure knowledge (*jnana*). Anthropology, ethnology, sociology and all other conventional sciences are profane by definition as they depend on research, data, 'historical facts' and individual speculative analysis. It is theoretical knowledge derived from personal invention.

In these books, Castaneda—or at least, the character he created—never seems to escape the limits of his ego (*ahankara*), no matter what experiences he is subjected to. It should be noted he also takes a completely passive stance through every series of adventures. Don Juan and Genaro, the principle sorcerers or *seers* (as they are later described) constantly use illusionary tricks and plant substances to shift Castaneda's awareness from one side to the other (left and right, *nagual* and *tonal*). Even after apparently spending years on the path of a seer and warrior, Castaneda remains helpless; he is completely unable to do this for himself, it seems. He consistently maintains the profane outlook, so that even when he has been turned into a crow his overriding concern is to know whether he 'really' turned into a crow physically, or whether he only imagined it.[176] After many years of being remorselessly blasted by sorcery and hallucinogenics he remains unconvinced and is prone to attacks of paranoia.

Much of this revolves around illusionary magick, setting people up and gaining an advantage, which is all part of the method called *stalking*. At first this seems to be no more than games of power, but it later transpires it is all part of the training, that there could be no other way to produce an impeccable warrior from such unpromising material. Until the end Castaneda remains in the same condition that he was in when he started; he is excessively emotional, subject to frequent bouts of melancholia and is in a constant state of abject fear and panic when confronted with 'non-conventional reality'. While don Juan gives much time to patiently explaining the unknown, no coherent doctrine emerges until the 'emanations of the Eagle' are demonstrated and explained, a subject we shall also return to later.

We are plunged into a highly ambiguous world. For example, in some discussions it seems as if the Abyss, instead of marking a departure, becomes the limit beyond which is only an eternity of vast solitude and loneliness. To increase the horror, don Juan says this can only be alleviated by the comfort of psychic 'pets', allies or spirit familiars. However, many of such very strange teachings delivered to Castaneda later turn out to be a false trail, deliberately planted as part of the *stalking* method. Castaneda's fears are played against him to the extent that the real reasons for so doing are not disclosed until years later—which is indeed the nature of spiritual realisation. Later in the same book that position is contradicted when it is recollected that the goal of seers is to attain total awareness and liberation—terms that seem more in keeping with the Advaitans than with native traditions, which usually centre on the cult of ancestors.

---

[176] *The Fire from Within* [Black Swan 1985].

When don Juan conveys a typically anthropological view of how the knowledge of the seers 'began', we must doubt either the teaching or at least the accuracy of Castaneda's account.[177] It is all supposed to have originated from experimentation with hallucinogenic plants.[178] We learn that the 'new seers' are better than the 'old seers' from the time before and during the Spanish conquest in which most of the seers were wiped out. The old seers favoured evil sorcery whereas the new seers were warriors on the path of knowledge. It is asserted that the old seers brought about their own destruction in some way, as if the conquest by the Spanish conquistadors was their own fault. It is difficult then not to suppose that such a historical and sociological interpretation, where notions of evolution and progress are taken as a matter of fact, is derived from academia. On the other hand, it has always been the case that after cyclical change the old knowledge is forgotten and condemned by subsequent generations.

The knowledge that concerns us has nothing to do with psychic visions or phenomena as such, and so a further disclaimer must be made. The writings of Castaneda endlessly circle around phenomena, and so never reach beyond the realm of the psyche. Anyone can drink cactus juice and obtain the vision of the 'Big Blue Man' or some such, but it means nothing and no change in the state of the being will take place. Real knowledge can never be attained through altered states, psychism, mediumism or experimentalism of any kind. It will not be gained by questions and answers, reading a book or through any discursive thought and analysis. It cannot be bestowed by individuals from their own side—and it must also be said that all of that is often fully supported by the teachings of don Juan, whoever that may have been. In the closing chapters of *The Fire from Within*, don Juan tells Castaneda that recollecting, putting it all back together and coming to realisation and full knowledge takes years, and ultimately the apprentice must make all such realisations himself. That certainly has nothing at all in common with the postmodern shamanism that was developed long after most of Castaneda's books were written, though some, who falsely claim to be 'traditionalists', have sought to place the writings in that category.

The teachings on the value of mysticism, which is often somewhat overrated as well as confused with non-religious paths, and on the 'personal God' or Ishvara, are completely in accordance with the path of *moksha* ('liberation') as revealed in the Vedanta.

---

[177] 'The New Seers' [*ibid*].
[178] Mescaline, peyote, jimson weed and psilocybin or Mexican mushrooms.

What don Juan calls the 'mold of man' is none other than the personal God or God-reflection. It is in reality nothing more than a kind of stamp, seal or impression by which man is defined and limited. This is in accordance with much of the Hermetic and Gnostic texts, as well as to a certain extent with Qabalistic doctrine. Don Juan explains it here with vigorous symbolism that happens to be in perfect agreement with ancient metaphysics:

> He said that I had to go beyond the mold, that the mold was merely a stage, a stopover that brought temporary peace and serenity to those who journey into the unknown, but that it was sterile, static. It was at the same time a flat reflected image in a mirror and the mirror itself. And the image was a man's image ...
>
> He assured me that even if I was able to *see*, I was bound to make the same misjudgment that mystics have made. Anyone who *sees* the mold of man automatically assumes that it is God.

To help Castaneda understand this better, don Juan remarks on the fact that the personal God is always anthropomorphised in the form of a male.

> 'Very cozy, eh', don Juan added, smiling. 'God is a male. What a relief!'

Castaneda, who had a Catholic upbringing, then has a further vision of the 'mold of man', which brings him to his knees in spite of what he has just learned. Don Juan chastises him:

> He called me pious and careless and said I would make a great priest; now I could even pass for a spiritual leader who had a chance *seeing* of God. He urged me, in a jocular way, to start preaching and describe what I had seen to everyone.

This chance *seeing* of God draws attention to the shortcomings of mysticism, which is that, apart from depending on emotionalism, it is usually unsupported by any real knowledge. And on the subject of emotionalism, don Juan puts this very succinctly:

> Beware of those who weep with realisation for they have realised nothing.

The world of don Juan's sorcerers, real or imagined, places an emphasis on the earth as central to existence, the source of all. That much is consistent with Native American Indian teaching, for what is called the 'earth' in that language also includes the 'sky'. In the Qabalah, Malkuth, the earth or kingdom, is said to be Kether the Crown, but after another fashion. The earth and heaven are not separate in reality but owe to a unitive principle, without which neither could exist. It is not the earth that is an illusion as such; it is the narrow view by which we habitually perceive it.

Oracle of Nuit

ORACLE OF THE FIRST DAY OF THE MOON.[179]
I am the Sun and the Moon.
I am all things and you.

I am the Star and the one who worships.
I am the fragrance and he who tastes it.
I am the lover and the one who is loved.

Know me!

For when you are below me, I am above you.
And when you are above, I am below.
I am height and depth, and infinite reach.
I am the one who learns, and the one who can teach.
I am the seeker, and that which he seeks.

ORACLE OF THE FOURTEENTH DAY.[180]
All of that [activity] is because of me, but I am not *of* any of that.
Neither am I in it.
Where am I?
Do you think I am here?
Am I there?
You see me here, you see me up there [the star] but I am your *seeing*, not what you see or know.

> Then let me know thee, instead of that or these things!

All such activity, if it is to know me, is of me, and so I am that activity in you, that desires to *know*.

---

[179] Author's diary record of 4th November 2021, dark Moon meditation.
[180] 17th December, full Moon meditation [*ibid*].

Dual and Non-Dual

The Advaitans have set forth that the Real can only be described in negative terms, what it is not, as all positive terms are necessarily dualistic. Thus the Non-dual reality is best thought of as a positive-negative statement, for that which is unmanifest is not in any way 'nothing', emptiness or void. That is in any case an impossibility since the unmanifest, as preceding manifestation and Being, must contain all possibilities within itself. The notion that a creator God or Demiurge could make a universe out of nothing, as if from outside itself, is a metaphysical absurdity. Nothing can be created (or produced) that does not in some way already exist, even as latency.

Following out the way of the 'personal God', called Ishvara in the Hindu doctrines, does not need to be in any way opposed to the Way of Knowledge and can take a person quite a long way. It is often the case, though, that orthodoxy, which always includes moral teaching, tends towards setting its face against the path of Knowledge. The historical persecution of the Gnostics is well known. They were called heretics for not accepting religious dogma, and yet some forms of Gnosticism predate the mandatory Christianity as contrived at the Imperial Council of Constantinople (AD 381), so can hardly be called heretical. That was not the first time in history, of course, when new legislative powers would be 'backdated' so that what was once not a sin was declared as sinful for all of time by the new self-appointed governance.[181] History does not really concern us much here; it is only necessary to recollect these matters so that we can look at how such blind obedience to dogma continues to afflict the profane, who are yet completely sincere in their motives and would certainly not think of themselves as profane.[182]

The supreme principial reality, the Real, is the 'mover that will not be moved'. Those who are swayed by the reasoning of theology will often point out that we cannot produce God from our activities, that any realisation of God can only be gained as a gift of God, 'in His Mercy', and so forth. This is not wrong as such.

---

[181] And that is not to say that governance appointed by 'the people', through voting for example, would be any less a contrivance or abberation.
[182] Dogmatic fanaticism is, today, hardly confined to religion. Scientism, for example, has now succeeded, through technological and legislative means, to persuade whole populations of the 'truth' of purely theoretical inventions that have no basis at all in reality.

However, the same reasoning is often used by the pious to dismiss as heretical any practices that they do not like or approve of, even if those practices are for the sole purpose of knowing God or Reality. Exotericism is 'outward' by definition and that automatically brings in all the contingencies of the individual state, including its dualistic tendency to see evil everywhere but in the one place it really exists, which is in the heart of man. We can look at this question another way. The Real is the 'mover that will not be moved'. While it is indeed the 'mover', it does not cause or produce anything in itself. All activity is only an appearance that is relative to the temporal conditions we inhabit in the corporeal state. No such activity can exist without the principle but the principle is not within the activity. Likewise, no realisation can come forth from activity; it will not be produced by activity, as before stated. The Real only provokes or stirs up activity from the temporal point of view. Thus when the personal God appears as a punishing tyrant or beneficent provider it can only be a reflection of man, made in the image of man. We can ask the question, 'Where is God? Is God here? Is God over there?' It is the question that is absurd, not the notion of God. Some, thinking themselves wiser than this, have posited God as an Empty Throne. But when they then posited that man sits upon that Throne, they made a mistake worse than that of the theologians. They glimpsed the emptiness of the personal God but were unable to transcend it and simply retreated into their shells. According to the oracle,

> You see me here, you see me up there (as a star), but I am your *seeing*, not what you see or know.[183]

If we do not truly desire to know God, then what is our purpose? We will take up certain practices to assist us, even if such knowledge will not be produced by such practices in themselves. The dogmatist, perhaps in his shame, in the pain of not knowing God, tries to place God out of reach for others. Even religion is then reduced to a kind of celebration of emptiness and sterility. All practices on the Way of Knowledge are condemned as vanity, all practices but that which is very narrowly prescribed are condemned as heresy.

We already said that it is quite correct to say that no realisation of God or Reality can be produced from any activity, 'altered states', phenomenal perception, or from any rite or ceremony as such. The realisation of God is God-given, as it must be. However, the faithful obedience to the personal God rests on incomplete knowledge, and necessarily so, for the Real is not within manifestation itself.

---

[183] Cf. 'Oracle of Nuit'.

The Real cannot by its very nature be limited or contained by anything. When activity is done out of the desire to know the Real, that desire to know is in itself the knowledge of God, even when not realised. To continue with the oracular voicing of the Shakti, a divine feminine personification of the principle:

> All such activity, if it is to *know* me, is of me, and so I am that activity in you, that desires *to know*.[184]

This is the mystery of will-ordinance. If it is put away from the self entirely, so separated by dualistic thought and reason, only the personal God that is a mirror of man can be known. When the desire to know God is a true desire—which is a very different thing from mere sincerity, as we know that can lead men to unthinkable evil—then that desire carries something of the very nature of that which is desired. The personal will then aligns with the divine Will, which is what is called *dharma* in Sanskrit—though the word has no exact equivalent in any modern language.

There is a reciprocal relation between that which we perceive and our selves, which perceive it. Whatever we perceive, through the act of perception, perceives *us*. If it is possible to know God then most certainly God knows us in that knowledge. This applies equally through all the possibilities of manifestation that are available to the human individuality, even non-human possibilities. It applies to any creature or thing, sentient or organic, whether of form or formless. In knowing any thing, we are known. It is knowledge that determines being, what we are and what we become. We are what we *know*, not what we see or think.

Nothing exists in separation in reality, nothing exists in isolation, which would be a complete impossibility. We may invoke Nuit while we are under her stars, but in transcending the stars there is nothing to invoke—not because there *is* nothing, but because from the point of view of the Real there is difference but no separation.

---

[184] Ibid.

The Eagle

In a previous chapter we referred to the teachings of don Juan, as relayed through the thoughts and writing of Carlos Castaneda. Whether or not these teachings came from a Mexican Indian or not is a moot point, as we cannot even know that now. As those teachings are clearly derived from diverse sources and sometimes the imagination of the author, it was necessary to dispel any false notions arising from these popular works. However, that is not to say there is nothing of value in any of it so long as we use rigorous discrimination to resolve the many contradictions and ambiguities therein, and to do what Castaneda seemed unable to do, which is to place it in the context of doctrinal knowledge that is already complete and requires no evidence of research or experimentation to support it—for such evidence is in any case worthless to the Way of Knowledge.

One of the most useful ideas to emerge from the texts is that of the emanations of the Eagle. This can easily be summarised: All we see in the world of objects and beings is in reality a type of construct composed from the emanations of the Eagle. The emanations are, to use our own description, 'threads of light-borne consciousness':

> The alignments between the stars or 'space-marks' are as tenuous threads of light-borne consciousness, not fixed, not still and not mobile either in the sense that we know this. We are what we know, not what we think or see. The soul 'becomes' through knowledge.[185]

The emanations are intelligent. It is through them that we are able to perceive. The emanations exist both macrocosmically and in man, the microcosm. All creature-life is also made up of the emanations, which are bundled or packaged together in a sphere of sensation, enclosed and to a certain extent sealed off from the emanations 'out there', as it is put in the language of don Juan. At the supra-mundane level, the Eagle is cognate with Atma or Hadit, and all worlds and beings are made of the Eagle's emanations, which can be otherwise symbolised as radiations from the 'centre' to any circumference.

There is a glowing band that runs vertically through the cocoon or egg of the emanations and this, through power of will or command of the Eagle, assembles a very small fraction of the total emanations. This creates 'our world', which is there by power of magical 'effect'. This is determined by ancestors, body, generation, parents, teachers and our environment, and is what is known as 'conventional reality'.

---

[185] 'Until the Stars be Numbered', p. 9 *Nu Hermetica*.

The power of will or ordinance is with the Eagle, but that which we perceive within our 'shell' or light-cocoon is shaped by where we place our attention. In the normal state of affairs that point of awareness is predetermined by such influences already mentioned. The ignorant person has no idea that either the emanations exist, or of the fact that our world is only real relative to what has already been determined—that what we see is only a minute fraction of the possibilities existing even within our own abode in the microcosm. Outside of this world, which is in reality a very narrow band of awareness of selected emanations, there are countless other worlds. These form part of a great unknown so far as ordinary consciousness is concerned.

A seer on the path of knowledge intends to shift awareness out of the narrow band of common perception, called the First Attention, and out into the unknown, which is called the Second Attention. While the methods for so doing are numerous, the most important of these is the power of Silence—that is, in the first instance, the stilling of the internal dialogue, the incessant commentary where we speak to ourselves, as we have learned from everyone else since the day we were born. For the intention of all that 'teaching' is to keep us within the confines of the First Attention and to constantly reinforce one particular and very limited perception of reality.

Some correspondence with matters already familiar might be helpful at this stage. The Eagle is not of course a being as such, unless considered as a form of the Demiurge, in which case the Eagle can be equally perceived as evil and tyrannical or good and merciful. We are not really concerned with that as the Demiurge only has an existence relative to human perceptions and is therefore a particular selection of emanations that vanishes away to nothing no sooner do we leave that strictly limited world. The Eagle can be likened to Ra in the Egyptian scheme, or Horus his reflection or son. He is the Atma of the Vedanta, and the emanations the radiance of Atma upon the universe. There is also a collation between the Eagle and all devouring Gods such as Mut, Sekhmet and Tawret. From the corporeal point of view, the soul faces destruction when passing through the Eagle's beak. To the Initiate, it is the way to ultimate freedom and eternal Deliverance.

The purpose of training on the path of knowledge—for example, the rites and practices, the observations, the discipline of Keeping the Record, the control of breath and of thought in yoga—is so that it is possible to effectively shift awareness and then move it back at will.

Through the power of Silence, the emanations within are stilled from their constant motion. It is then possible for some of them to become realigned with the emanations of the Eagle that are 'without'. In fact, all other creatures but man do this naturally. Man has long forgotten the knowledge of replenishing energy through alignment with this fountain of living waters, and so attempts to compensate through seeking vitality on the same plane, which binds awareness to objects of identification and perpetuates ignorance of the Real.[186]

There are applications of the knowledge of how awareness works, and how the point of attention can move. This was used once by the shamans but it is hardly in evidence today unless in an extremely degraded and inferior form. Nonetheless, even in the most degraded form imaginable, the power of this on human beings is devastating, it can drive them insane with fear or kill them. And this is because it is easily possible, for anyone that has the knowledge, to shift the point of awareness in another person even when the person has no idea anything is happening or being done at all.

Of course it is not our intention to use this knowledge for such evil and negative ends, and neither do we intend to disclose how it is accomplished in any great detail, for obvious reasons. However, we now inhabit a world where the conventional reality is completely manipulated by that which we term the 'System of Antichrist'. As a consequence, that reality is becoming increasingly confined. It is a certain fact, as it is a matter of ancient doctrines and not something that has been made up or imagined by any individual, that we will soon arrive at a point where all of space will be entirely consumed. The knowledge of how awareness can be moved is then vital to our survival or continuation so long as our world endures. We can then pass beyond that, across the rainbow bridge or arch of the heavens, to that which wholly transcends the physical, psychic and human conditions, ultimately leading to the Deliverance and total freedom. This is not a matter of personal salvation, for in so doing we take the whole essence of our world with us, to be perfectly restored. It is a matter of utmost expedience then, that we should become supremely accomplished at shifting our point of awareness at will.

---

[186] Cf. 'Postmodern Shamanism'.

Dreaming Attention

There are some further aspects of the 'teachings of don Juan' that are worthy of consideration, no matter what the source of those teachings might have been. There is a kind of trinity of precepts that are constantly referred to in those writings: *intention*, *stalking* and *dreaming*—and that is the order we are going to place them in here. Intention is not the same as will, which is ordinance. Intention is the personal aspect of will and unless it is exclusively concerned with the goals of the Way of Knowledge, it dissipates to nothing, for it amounts to no more than the desires of ordinary men and women—desires predetermined by the 'conventional reality' that shapes them. When intention is directed towards the vital concerns of the path, such as shifting the point of awareness, the emanations within the shell or cocoon line up with the emanations of the Eagle and only *then* become will, ordinance—which is invincible.

A slight digression is justified at this point. In our tradition we have something called the Four Powers of the Sphinx: to Know, to Dare, to Will and to keep Silence. One must first *dare to know*, for it requires great courage to step out of the narrow margin of perception we are encouraged to inhabit by other people, let alone the System of Antichrist, which is narrowing the margin down to virtual nothing. We have already said something about the nature of the will. It needs to be added that will and *intention* cannot be exercised without the help of the power of silence. It is only through silence, the cessation of the internal dialogue, that the Second Attention can be gained.

We are not going to enter into the matter of *stalking* here, beyond what was said previously (p. 126). Stalking requires close interaction with other people over a lengthy period of time—something that has become difficult if not completely impossible now we have entered the era of the Reign of Antichrist. The constantly shifting parameters of new regulations are frequently aimed at keeping people away from other people; the 'workforce' is increasingly driven to reach new 'targets', with restrictions on time for other activities, including social ones in any real or meaningful sense.

Dreaming has been misunderstood by readers of the teachings of don Juan. It is part of the essential conservation of energy (for the Great Work), which is something also misunderstood by generations that have been taught to pursue their every wish and whim, so that even temporary abstinence is seen as harmful to the being, whereas it may in fact be a vital means to the goal.

The art of *dreaming* involves tapping a vital natural resource that is wasted in the normal state of affairs. The chief misunderstanding of this—which has worked its way into becoming a kind of popular myth or folk-lore—is that it involves trying to remain aware while in the dreaming state so that dreams can be controlled. It follows that many people who have tried this failed to fulfil its true purpose, for they have supposed it is only about conjuring dreams and fantasies 'at will', to direct their dreams towards the satisfaction of ordinary desires and goals. It is not so, and the truth of the art of *dreaming* is almost the complete opposite of that. Any attempt to manipulate the content of dreams can only result in regaining the First Attention. Although the dreaming content can sometimes be manipulated to a certain extent, through various methods, that is a complete waste of energy. The content of dreams is for the most part irrelevant.

In dreaming, it is easily possible for the point of awareness to shift alignment so that other worlds or states of being are glimpsed, and this happens naturally. The purpose of the dreaming attention is to *fix the new points of alignment* so they become part of the total awareness of the being. According to René Guénon,

> Whatever may be the interior or exterior starting-point (which may vary according to the case) that gives a dream a certain direction, the events that unfold therein can only result from a combination of elements contained at least potentially and as if capable of a certain kind of realisation, within the integral comprehension of the individual; and if these elements, which are modifications of the individual, are indefinite in number, the variety of such possible combinations is equally so. A dream should be regarded as a mode of realisation for possibilities that, while belonging to the domain of human individuality, are for one reason or another not susceptible of realisation in a corporeal mode; such are, for example, the forms of beings belonging to the same world but other than man, forms that the latter possesses virtually in himself by reason of the central position he occupies in that world. These forms obviously cannot be realised by the human being except in the subtle state, and the dream is the most ordinary—one could also say the most normal—of all the means by which he is able to identify himself with other such beings, without in any way ceasing to be himself...[187]

It should perhaps go without saying, given what has been said elsewhere, that some factions have placed too much emphasis on the wakeful and dreaming states, thereby confining and strictly limiting themselves to the realm of the individuality; also that the three states (summarised in AUM) are both literal and analogous terms.

---

[187] 'Analogies Drawn from the Dream State', p. 36 *The Multiple States of Being* [Sophia Perennis].

Bearing the above in mind one must never be forgetful of the goal, which is to increase the power of awareness, strengthen the power of silence and at all times to exercise *intention*. That being understood, it can be seen how *dreaming attention* is a powerful and natural means of developing the full range of individual possibilities, not as an end in itself but as a means towards the attainment of final liberation.

The eye of *seeing* is to fix the alignments or emanations in the astrosome. The will-ordinance is that of Ra. In that, the intention of the warrior (or Horus) on the path of knowledge becomes the Will, which we call Thelema. The will to shift the alignments brings about, through knowledge, permanent change in the state of being through realisation. It can take years, however, for such realisation to come about, even when direct knowledge has been received. The interior work must be done; there is no 'instant enlightenment'.

In the Egyptian symbolism the eye of *seeing* is called Wadjet. It is a mistake to think that the right eye of Ra and the left eye of the Moon are separate independent functions, the wakeful consciousness and the dreaming state. The power of Ra fixes the perception of the eye of the Moon or 'left side'. In terms of the Eagle or Horus-hawk, one becomes the Eagle when Total Awareness is gained.

Ordinary and 'non-ordinary' events should not, as they are events as such, be regarded as extraordinary, for they are really completely normal but involve a shift of alignment away from the common or conventional one and towards the 'left side' of awareness. These can even pass unnoticed as they might so closely resemble ordinary events as to be almost completely indistinguishable from them. Only the seer with *intention* is able to perceive them for what they truly are and make use of them.

Having gone thus far, it would seem appropriate to give a few hints as to how this can be accomplished in practice. One must first have learned silence and the concentration of mind (*dharana*), and have developed the power of *intent*. A 'home' abode must be created artificially, before sleep. For example, one might prefer a forest glade or mountain top. One then places a simple symbol, an ancient one, upon a tree or a rock, taking care to see it perfectly. Enter silent meditation upon the symbol and the place. Dreams usually take place in sequences, one after another. At the end of each dream sequence one must place or impress the symbol somewhere on this location before the next begins. That is the beginning of the *art of dreaming*.

The Grail Castle Revisited

More than half a century ago now, W.E. Butler, with the assistance of Gareth Knight (Basil Wilby), created a course in practical Qabalah. One had to work through 50 lessons, one instalment per month. There was also a six-month preliminary module plus various supplementary papers, so it took about five years to complete. Very few persons, we were told, ever worked the course to its completion. By now it is no more than a historical archive. The eventual abandoning of the course after a few decades is not to be lamented for it is extremely unlikely that any student could either understand or work it now, and certainly not over such an extended period of time.

The nature of the course and how it came to be written is very curious. Butler always maintained that he did not compose it in the ordinary way but it was 'received' from one who stood behind him, as it were, and who immensely overshadowed him. What we shall describe here is how it is not the written content of the course that was relayed from the Master, but rather the metaphysical basis of its internal structure.

Butler spent some time in India while still young, and learned something of the *Yoga-Sutras* and Tantras. He made good use also of the books of Tantras translated and commented on by Arthur Avalon (Sir John Woodroffe) in *The Serpent Power*. Upon meeting Dion Fortune (Violet Firth) in London, he was persuaded that working in the Western Mystery Tradition, more suited to the disposition of a modern Westerner, could alleviate some of the 'difficulties' he had got into through practicing Laya Yoga. He thus took up the study of the Qabalah. In later life he was commissioned to write his course, which used the Tree of Life schema and the symbol of the Grail Castle as a sort of cunning disguise for what was effectively Kundalini Yoga, albeit with safety devices or 'cushioning'.[188]

---

[188] It is very unlikely that Butler would have read René Guénon's excellent study on Kundalini Yoga in relation to the Tree of Life, included in *Studies in Hinduism* (1966), which was not translated into English until long after Butler died. If he had done, he might have resolved some of the difficulties with integrating the sephiroth into a chakra system. The aforementioned difficulties have by now been resolved in our preliminary Egyptian Yoga method. See the following chapters.

Butler's course followed the traditional method by which a Great Symbol of the Universe is imagined and used as the basis for Tantra-yoga. We have described this previously, and it is worth quoting here at length.[189]

> The idea of using a composite symbol of the Great Work is a very ancient one. In the East there is the holy mountain called Meru, which has its counterpart in the Abiegnus of the Rosicrucians. In times of remote antiquity, cities and gods were interchangeable terms. In all traditions one begins by cleansing oneself of everything that is not essential to the Great Work. One must study the sacred scriptures and meditate profoundly upon them. Having cultivated fiery aspiration and acceptance of the path, the powers of the mind and imagination are then directed towards constructing a suitable symbol of the universe, be that Goddess, City or Man. Consciousness is placed imaginatively at the centre of the symbol while physically adopting the meditative posture or mudra. All distractions of body and mind must be overcome and concentration perfected through use of the sacred symbol. Once the Great Symbol has been properly constructed, the consciousness current is then circulated in the subtle body along with the breath in the physical body; the various centres, chakras or sephiroth are activated.

Butler and his colleagues preferred to use the symbolism of the Grail Castle. This consisted for the most part of a simple tower with a turret, but once the practitioner ventured inside, a very complex schema emerged, of which the full extent could not be realised until the course was completed. Inside the castle were various chambers that symbolised the sephiroth of the Tree of Life. At the centre was the Round Table, divided into twelve segments, each of which corresponds to a sign of the Zodiac. It requires an Oath of Dedication to find a seat at the Round Table. Negotiating the different levels vertically was achieved by the means of two spiral staircases, which those familiar with Laya Yoga will understand as the equivalent of the Ida and Pingala, the dual solar and lunar currents of the Serpent Power that must be equilibrated in the Tantras. The practitioner would climb up and down these stairways imaginatively and as the course developed they would fly up and down them more rapidly in their body of light or astrosome. They would also discover various wonders hidden among the different levels, such as a shrine to Black Isis in a secret chamber behind Yesod. Some of the Tarot trumps would be used as images, carefully placed to evoke certain potencies.

---

[189] *Hermetic Qabalah Foundation—Complete Course*, p. 70.

Meditation was the core of this discipline and this involved a unique approach. It involved a method of contemplation by which ideas or symbols are placed in the mind and held. Only thoughts related to the subject are allowed; all else is dismissed.

Towards the end of the course it became evident that a kind of astral double was being formed, something that also agrees with Woodroffe's commentary on the Tantras in relation to Kundalini Shakti. Butler seemed to identify the double with the analogy of the Golem as mentioned at the beginning of the *Sepher Yetzirah* source text. This is interesting enough in itself, for most people associate the Golem with the classic novel of the same name by Gustav Meyrink. However, the novel based on the Prague Ghetto only bears a passing resemblance to the metaphysics of the source texts, which accord with the three-dimensional cross symbolism and doctrine of Cosmic Cycles to be found in other traditions. The six directions of space, as we have explained elsewhere, are formed from the three lines of the three-dimensional cross or Cube of Space.[190] These are formed from the three Mother letters of the Hebrew alphabet.

According to the *Sepher Yetzirah*, it is these three Mother letters, Aleph, Mem and Shin, that are the primal means by which Cosmic Being is woven and given life and form. The Tree of Life springs forth from the interactions of these three primary elements, or principles. It should be noted that this ternary has no exact correspondence with the classical quaternary of air, fire, water and earth; the operation of the three Mother letters is on a higher arc. Meyrink's Golem was composed of Aleph, Mem and Tav. Thus, he had a semblance of life and a body of clay but lacked any Spirit (Shin). He was a kind of artificial elementar. When the letter Aleph was removed, his name spelled 'death', and his life was ended. It was (presumably) not the intention of Butler's course to create any such elementar; we must suppose that the double was composed of the whole Tree of Life as realised through five years of continuous meditation, a microcosm of the macrocosm, 'as above and so below'.

It seems that Butler and his colleagues in one sense wanted to reunite Christianity, or perhaps to put this in a broader sense, the 'Matter of Britain', with an esotericism, something that was long ago lost. The Grail symbolism predates even early Christianity but both the Celtic and Christian traditions carry elements of the universal or primordial knowledge.

---

[190] See 'Metaphysical Basis of Love and Will', *Nu Hermetica*.

Stained glass window from the Quimper Cathédrale, Saint Corentin

The ten sephiroth (each) of the Tree of Life and Tree of Knowledge are here depicted, surrounding the central and upper cross, which depicts both square and circle, as well as having twelve points (the Zodiac). The Grail rests upon corn for the bread and grapes for the wine of communion. Two birds are at the top of the chalice; one feeds upon the fruits of the tree while the other simply gazes upward at the solar glory. These are the two ways, Salvation (or Egyptian Amentet) and Deliverance (or the Egyptian Sahu).

The Holy Grail symbol is synonymous with the 'heart' and 'world centre'. The earliest and most exact symbol of this is found in the Egyptian hieroglyph of the heart-shaped *ab* vessel.[191] There is also a profound resonance with the Rosicrucian symbol of the cross with a rose at the central meeting point of the vertical and horizontal axes—the calyx of a flower is in itself a type of cup. The purpose of practices that are either initiatic or designed to support initiation is always one and the same: to journey through the labyrinth, in which is hidden the trials and obstructions to the way, and to find the centre. It is only from the central position that it is possible to make contact with cosmic intermediaries. These are able to assist further development and upward transposition through the different states of being—as opposed to traversing the horizontal plane that only represents an indefinitude of individual possibilities in one and the same state.[192]

There were intentional 'blinds' written into this course, as was the way of the occultists of Butler's time.[193] Most found it hard to follow, confusing, and at times inconsistent or even contradictory. However, the many devious twists and turns of the course, not to mention the apparent impossibility of some of the projections, owed not to the irritability, ill-health and advancing years of the author, as was frequently claimed even by those who administrated the course, but owed to the fact that the veiled metaphysical symbolism was truly a 'received' work. That is to say, a real spiritual influence was involved, which is at the same time the real goal of all such study and practice.

The dual spiral stairways, although thought by some to be capable of diagrammatic representation or at least a three-dimensional one, transcend what can be made or constructed whether on paper or with wood and glue (and some have even tried the latter). One was meant to conceive the symbol imaginatively but, as with all true metaphysical symbolism, its design was such that it would not yield to geometry or architecture without being greatly simplified and so necessarily reduced.

---

[191] Cf. 'The Sacred Heart'.
[192] All magical practices, for example, are confined to such horizontal development, for the realisation of modalities accessible through the subtle domain. Yoga is quite different as it is about ascending the vertical axis so that initiation and spiritual realisation become possible.
[193] Or at least, intentional 'blinds' were used by those that had integrity—for there were certain others that only used such methods of concealment to cover their own foul machinations.

The two spirals were in fact a double helix, so that the central *shushumna* between Ida and Pingala was always implied but never evoked directly. To put this another way, the two 'stairways' in fact occupy the same space in reality, or to be more precise, space that is immediately contiguous or otherwise separated by an indefinitely small degree.[194] This same flexibility of symbolism, which defies any attempt to be mastered by ordinary reason or converted to concrete knowledge, applied throughout Butler's course.

It is expressly part of the Hindu doctrines that the Tantras form a 'fifth Veda'. This is an adaptation particularly necessary in the Age of Kali Yuga, where the faculties once common to all in previous ages no longer exist. The Tantras are associated with the Kshatriyas in tradition, the warrior caste that has its reflection in Western chivalry, and the Bhaktas ('devotees'). With the romance of the Grail, or the poetry of love, there is inevitably a sentimental influence that has to be offset in other ways, but that is inevitable in the Kali Yuga.

The transmutation and finally the transformation of such a Great Symbol—passing beyond form altogether—is one aspect that remains to be considered. This cannot, by its nature, be written into a course and is only conveyed by the practice itself and initiatic transmission, should that be possible.[195] Once the level of Da'ath (*ajna*) is reached through the upward ascent of the 'tower' or other symbol and only if this is effectively realised—which can take some years at least—there is a threshold reached comparable to rising up to the surface of waters. The light of spirit shines upon the surface and is reflected into the depths. There it is subject to multitudinous modifications and contingencies. It is veiled by countless refractions of light—and it must be clearly understood that 'light' here has nothing to do with visible light or even what is termed the Astral Light.

Such a crossing point also takes place at the level of Tiphereth. The heart symbolism of the centre is upwardly transposed so that it exists on at least two levels, superior and inferior, as represented on the Tree of Life model. If the being is able to rise above the surface of these waters, whether celestial or inferior, a way is opened to the higher states. At the pinnacle or the crown of the microcosm, the *brahmarandra* chakra is such a 'door' or opening.

---

[194] A similar extension of the Cube of Space or three-dimensional cross is described in very great detail by Guénon in *The Symbolism of the Cross* [Sophia Perennis].
[195] As a general rule, neo-spiritualist organisations, especially those that place a heavy emphasis on 'psychic development', are unable to transmit anything of a spiritual nature. There are, however, rare exceptions.

This is sometimes represented symbolically by the doors to the roof, or ceiling, or otherwise the centre of the dome that is placed on the top of a square tower. The complexity of the exterior symbolism is necessarily simplified at higher levels. There is comparison to be made between the dual serpents of Kundalini entwined about the central canal or *shushumna* and the Hermetic Caduceus. The dual currents of sun and moon, and the central fire, are also contained within the central column itself.[196] This has a certain correspondence with the Hebrew letter Shin, of three flames.

The pyramid is also a very flexible figure, whether it has four sides raised above the base, is truncated so that it has five, or is tetrahedronal. The latter is particularly efficacious as it is the perfect unity of the 'three' and the 'four'. It therefore symbolises the 'crossing point' at any level, and so is a means of going forth in a certain way. Sometimes all this can be dispensed with and there is only the luminous body of the Shakti. This body mirrors the other symbolism, the Tree of Life and the chakra systems. In the final measure one must not be overly encumbered with the armour, shields and other equipment of the Knights of the Holy Grail.

---

[196] Cf. Guénon, *Studies in Hinduism* [Sophia Perennis].

Gradations of Samadhi

Although these following considerations on the states that are accessible through the practice of yoga have a basis in the works of Patanjali, there is general agreement among most schools of traditional yoga on the essential points. The *Yoga-Sutras* and Tantras have their basis in the Vedas. There is nothing 'mystical' about yoga or the states associated with it. It is an exact science. We hope this will become clear from what is said here, even though it is greatly simplified and the use of Sanskrit terms is kept to the very minimum of that which is necessary.

Samadhi is attained by the practice of *dharana* (concentration) and *dhyana* (true meditation). By it the True Self is known (*atma*), which is beyond the human individual state, without distortions of the mind. It is essentially the goal of yoga. Compared to normal thought, Samadhi is as a bright light to deep darkness. Its first realisation is 'unity', comparable to union with God or Ishvara, the first envelope of being. At further levels of the realisation of Atma, undetermined, it is pure knowledge. Through Samadhi, the yogin is able to touch upon the universal absolute that is even beyond this. Although there are various practices by which yoga Samadhi may be attained, practice or method alone cannot convey either Samadhi or ultimate liberation (*moksha*). Liberation is attained only by the grace (or bestowal) of the Guru or Shakti—and one must remember that the Shakti is the Guru or that which is termed the 'Holy Guardian Angel' in the Western tradition. There are three levels of Samadhi, of which the first has four degrees, gradations or refinements.

Savikalpa Samadhi

The first level is called Savikalpa Samadhi, which generally implies the yoga of discrimination, for the distractions of thought have been overcome. In Savikalpa Samadhi it is possible to access the lesser yogic or magical powers (*siddhis*). However, the only legitimate use of such powers is as a way of measuring progress. There may be exceptions when their use is valid on the path but all traditions warn against them being used for personal greed and ambition. Not least, the desire for such powers, and their use, can even permanently bar all spiritual development.

Savikalpa Samadhi includes four sub degrees. Firstly, in the silence of meditation one must transcend all mental activity. There is a temporary loss of all human consciousness but this has nothing to do with the psychological 'unconscious' and obviously it is not an unconscious state. The perceptions of time and space belong to the human state and are therefore altered. A minute might seem like an hour or an hour might seem like a minute. The practitioner does not perform any action, mental or otherwise, and is so unaffected by any thoughts or ideas; yet this must be understood as a dynamic not a static state. After meditation one naturally returns to the ordinary consciousness. With the Savikalpa Samadhi, the latent tendencies or conditioning factors (*samskaras*) are dissolved but they still remain in seed or latency. There is effort involved in holding to Savikalpa Samadhi so the practitioner should not be surprised if yoga seems like hard work at the beginning.

The first degree or the beginning of Savikalpa Samadhi is called *savitarka samadhi*. The name implies that an object is meditated upon. It is where prolonged *dharana* concentration has produced *dhyana* meditation and there is the first intimation of union between subject and object. The mind is focused on the gross aspect or form of a physical object, for example a *yantra* but it can be anything. This can include a name or symbol or sound. By *savitarka*, the nature of that thing is revealed or known fully.

The second degree of the Savikalpa Samadhi is called *savichara samadhi*. The name implies 'following' or 'furthering', and has a common root with the word for 'devotion'. Qualities such as colour, sound, beauty, love and so forth are understood. The meditation has passed from the gross contemplation to the subtle. The mind then passes to meditation upon the subtle roots of the elements, called *tanmatras*. For example *akasha*, equated with hearing, is known through the 'unstruck sound'—the principle, not audible in itself.

The third degree of the Savikalpa Samadhi is called *sa'ananda samadhi*, which implies 'bliss' or 'beatitude'. Here, the mind passes beyond the objective world and of reason. There is no reflection or reflected knowledge, only bliss and tranquility. The pure (*sattvic*) mind is aware only of its own bliss. Here the mind's inner powers of perception are known.

The fourth degree of the Savikalpa Samadhi is called *sa'asmita samadhi*. The name implies the non-existence of the ego (*ahankara*). Even the bliss of the previous stage is surpassed and there is only pure awareness. The pure (*sattvic*) sense of being is that which remains.

This fourth degree is comparable—though only through upward transposition—to the word that Moses heard on the mountain, 'I Am That I Am', or 'Being is Being'. It implies the state of Pure Being, which is essentially Ishvara as one step removed from pure Atma. The *sa'asmita samadhi* surpasses all desire and therefore all fear, and is sometimes called, rather imprecisely, cosmic consciousness. What is important is that divinity is known within the celestial realm.

Nirvikalpa Samadhi

We can now move on to the second level, called Nirvikalpa Samadhi, which transcends all degrees of Savikalpa Samadhi. In the Nirvikalpa Samadhi, the individual ego state (*ahankara*) and the conditioning determinations associated with it (*samskaras*) have been dissolved. The pure consciousness is all that remains. According to Patanjali, the material world becomes like a shadow that has no further hold upon us. The knower and the known become one Knower. It is essentially what is called 'divine ecstasy', though such terms are always misleading because of their emotional interpretation, which relegates it solely to the human individual state or a vague mysticism, which it is not. The Nirvikalpa Samadhi corresponds to the fuller awakening of *anahatha* (the heart) chakra. This may be experienced in various ways; for example, the whole universe may seem like a minute grain or seed within the vast heart of the Guru. It is not to experience bliss or beatitude (*ananda*) but to *be* bliss.

This Samadhi nonetheless has its dangers, for it approximates the celestial world and there, a deep love for the world and everything in it may be encountered; divinity is in everything. In what is called *ritambhara pragya*, thoughts spontaneously manifest and become real. The past and future are merged into the eternal present; time and space are transcended. This state may last for a few hours or a few days. There is an obvious correspondence between this state and what is called the 'Knowledge and Conversation of the Holy Guardian Angel' in the Western tradition, although that term has itself been subjected to degradation to a mere psychic or mystical phenomenon. Naturally one is reluctant to return to ordinary consciousness and the world. Therein is the great danger, for a person may become deluded in their efforts to remain in the state even when they are not any longer really in it, only a semblance of it. It is said though that through continued practice one may enter Nirvikalpa Samadhi and then leave it to function 'normally' in the world. Both Savikalpa and Nirvikalpa Samadhi are then considered to be temporary states as entering them necessitates withdrawal from ordinary life.

However, the life of the yogin—by which is meant 'adept' in Western language—includes the real awareness of all possibilities so that pure awareness is always within reach.

Dharmamegha Samadhi

Dharmamegha Samadhi is very rare indeed and is the most advanced level. The name translates as 'Cloud of Virtue'. There may be some comparison with the 'cloud' associated with the Shekinah in the Hebrew and other traditions, and certainly, the Shakti alone confers such a state on the practitioner; the Samadhi is a divine gift. Here there is no longer any desire even to know God or to be enlightened or liberated. This Samadhi cannot be gained by effort; it reveals itself when all effort has dissolved. The temptations of the magical or yogic powers cease to cause any distraction. It is said that pure knowledge (*jnana*) showers down (like a 'cloud of virtue'), bringing liberation (*moksha*) and beatitude. This is known as Jivanmukta—liberation attained while still in a physical body and life. The yogin is free of the burden of afflictions (or *karmas*) and shines in his own inner light. It is said that the yogin 'sees without eyes, tastes without tongue, hears without ears, smells without nose, and touches without skin'. He simply wills something and it comes into being; hence 'miracles' correspond to this level. It must also be said that all those who have legitimately produced such miracles have never attached any real significance or importance to them at all.

Of all the levels and degrees of Samadhi there is the development through yoga and there is the development through long practice, over time. These are not really separate, of course. The desire for magical powers or *siddhis* wears off naturally as they are seen for what they truly are. If that does not happen then the person is unable to pass beyond the level of the microcosm and enter the universal and higher states for so long as they remain attached to such desires. At the last one may lose even the desire to know God or to attain Deliverance (*moksha*) but this must not be confused with sheer slack or inertia, which is the vice at the mere entry level of yoga. The states of yoga Samadhi are all dynamic, not static.

In regard to Kundalini Yoga practice, there must also be clearly discerned a difference between 'the worship' and the yoga itself. For example, there is a whole world of difference between imagining (or visualising) that *kundalini* enters the crown chakra and this actually taking place.

The meditation on yantras, sounds or other things is a support to yoga; likewise, all imagined scenarios or visions, whether constructed at will or received spontaneously, are called 'worship', which is not yoga as such. The worship and devotion is essential nonetheless as a support to realisation. One may begin with worship as here defined, and by degrees this may become yoga in fact. One must though be able to clearly recognise the difference and this also comes about with continued practice, unless the person is deluding their self.

Likewise, when worshipping the Shakti there is a great difference between this worship, however exalted the feelings, and the *boddhi* perception of her real presence. It is the Shakti alone that confers the higher states; the entry into Samadhi 'proper' is marked by the joy or beatitude (*ananda*) that is her attribute and divine gift.

Darmamegha Samadhi	Ipsissimus	10 = 1
	Magus	9 = 2
	Magister Templi	8 = 3
Nirvikalpa Samadhi	Adeptus Exemptus	7 = 4
	Adeptus Major	6 = 5
Savikalpa Samadhi 4th Degree	Adeptus Minor	5 = 6
	Philosophus	4 = 7
Savikalpa Samadhi 3rd Degree	Practicus	3 = 8
Savikalpa Samadhi 2nd Degree	Zelator	2 = 9
Savikalpa Samadhi 1st Degree (entry level)	Neophyte	1 = 10

The table above is not exact, and neither would it be possible to make any exact tabulated or systematised representation of Samadhi. It may be helpful though as a rough guide as to how the degrees of initiation may generally correspond to the yogic states as a way of marking progress. However, it must clearly be understood first and foremost that the grades in neo-spiritualist (or occult) organisations in no way confer such states, and that those who claim high grades in such organisations frequently have no idea what initiation really is. It would be so unlikely as to be almost impossible for an actual Adeptus Minor, that has risen through ceremonies of initiation, psychism and 'pathworking', as is commonly used in such organisations, to know *savikalpa samadhi* to the fourth degree as shown on our own chart. And so it goes for all the grades, even more so the higher ones. What is said here below is in no way descriptive of the degrees in existing, or historical occult Orders. The purpose is to provide comparison that will be helpful to those well versed in the Qabalistic Tree of Life.

The inclusive brackets are used to show certain subtle relations that exist between some of the Order grades, as are the Egyptian hieroglyphs. For example, there is a special relation between the Adeptus Major and the Neophyte that owes to the correspondence with Malkuth the Kingdom, or Gate of Death, and so forth. There is a special relation between the Magister Templi and the Adeptus Minor through Nirvikalpa Samadhi, the 'Knowledge and Conversation of the Guardian Angel', and the lesser degrees of Samadhi.

The hieroglyph of the Votive Flame is placed here to show the devotion and sacrifice that the aspirant must be capable of so as to progress from Neophyte through to Adeptus Minor. The Ab or 'heart' vessel, including the seed principle and ark of heaven, is placed to mark the development from the completion of the first level of Samadhi to the initiation of the second level and Nirvikalpa Samadhi. The inverted Ankh is placed between the Adeptus Exemptus and all that is beyond that grade as signifying the Night. One must note that 'night' has a dual aspect, for there is the inferior chaos and darkness of the world and the general condition of the uninitiated soul, and there is the superior darkness of the unmanifest, which is beyond all manifestation and the worlds of being. The Star as the 'Hand of Orion' with the principial circle and point in the centre is placed between the Magister Templi and the Magus, although as Jivatma or the 'star' that is worshipped it could equally be placed at the level of Tiphereth and the Adeptus Minor.

Considerations on Yoga Practice

Only the Guru or the Shakti herself can assist the advancement of the yogin through Nirvikalpa, the second level of Samadhi. Although all forms of Samadhi are a divine gift, it is quite easily possible to give some practical advice on how to accomplish the four gradations of Savikalpa, the first level. For one that has already practiced various forms of *dharana* for some time, even some years, then it is easily possible to pass through the first and second level quickly, as we shall describe here. However, the veriest beginner will take much longer and will require expert guidance.[197]

1. *Savitarka*. In seated asana, after the relaxed control of breath, as learned, formulate any symbol; for example, the Red Cross and White Triangle of the Golden Dawn. Contemplate only the form of the symbol and restrain the mind from having thoughts about it. After several minutes of sustained concentration, note down any observations about the form of the symbol or the practice itself.

It should be noted, though, that if using the Cross and Triangle, for example, one that has incorporated it many times and in various ways in practice could easily write half a page or much more on what it means without any prompting. That is not the purpose of this yoga. One should contemplate the form alone and not have thoughts about it, otherwise true meditation (*dhyana*) will not be achieved.

2. *Savichara*. Using the same symbol, do not this time contemplate the form of it but hold only the idea of the symbol in mind—this may begin with a visualisation of the symbol, as with the first degree, but that should quickly be let go of completely until only a sense or impression remains. Continue with the *pranayama* and *dharana* as learned, restraining all thoughts whatsoever on the symbol but allow contemplation of subtle qualities of the symbol only. This can easily turn into having thoughts about the object but that must be reserved for when the Record is written up later. This facility of memory or recollection comes with practice. With experience, about five minutes of sustained concentration will be quite sufficient. Note down any observations about the subtle qualities of the symbol or the practice itself.

---

[197] Contrary to popular belief, 'self-initiation' is an impossibility.

3. *Sa'ananda*. It is much more difficult to get to this level than it is to get to the first and second and this requires persistence. It is the beginning of the real Samadhi. A symbol may be used to begin with, as an aid to getting started off, but as with the second level, it is soon let go of, and furthermore there must now be no thoughts at all. As this degree can lead to the first real Samadhi, it may be better to begin with meditation on the Shakti or one of her attributes. At this level, the Self is its own object. Simply breathe and prolong the concentration of mind as though there were an invisible 'point', or a seed or a star, some way vertically above the crown. Let the breath (*prana*) travel upward to the crown and beyond it. (Kundalini Yoga greatly assists this, but it is not the place here to try and teach how to do that.) Maintain stillness of body and mind and refuse to allow any intrusive thoughts whatsoever.

When the silence of meditation is prolonged enough—and how long may vary from person to person and from day to day—then there comes a sense like 'making the sun shine' from within. This is true *dhyana*, opening the gateway of possibility to a more perfect Samadhi. This phenomenon is what was meant, or what should have been meant in any case, by the generic name 'Order of the Golden Dawn', the 'Sun Rising above the Waters of Space'. It is also what is referred to as the 'Lamp that shines without wick or oil' of the Dominus Liminis intermediary grade after the 4 = 7. At this stage any excited feelings about having success or any disappointed feelings must be rigorously restrained for these have no significance at all. If ordinary thought recommences it is then necessary to start again from the beginning. Assuming that this can be held without any catastrophic break in the meditation, and by grace of Mahadevi Shakti, Isis, Hathoor or any form or attribute of her, there will be nothing but tranquility, joy and bliss or beatitude. At this level, the flower or lotus of the *boddhi* or higher intellect begins to emerge from latency.

4. *Sa'asmita*. It is more difficult yet again to pass from the third degree of Savikalpa Samadhi to the fourth, for at this level there is the ecstasy of the (temporary) dissolution of the ego. Begin as with the third degree, with the Shakti or one of her attributes (even Horus or Ra, for example, is an attribute of the Shakti as all forms belong to her). By now it should easily be possible to pass quickly beyond the visual stage and the subtle stage, so that the interior lamp is made luminous. With prolonged meditation, and by the generous grace of the Shakti or Guru, the luminosity and the bliss that accompanies it are now transcended.

This fourth degree is the exact equivalent of the 'Knowledge and Conversation of the Holy Guardian Angel'.[198] At this level, divinity is known with real certainty. Sometimes, when the practitioner has not knowingly renounced the bliss that accompanied the third degree of *sa'ananda*, or perhaps because they wanted to hold on to it, they mistakenly assume that they have 'lost the knack', that success is eluding them or that it is not possible for some reason. In fact, it may well be that the Shakti power has already withdrawn the bliss of the *sa'ananda* to help further the progress of the aspiring yogin, but the aspirant is retaining egoistic thoughts about the practice, the magical powers and so forth, and is being held back. When that is the case, then as soon as the egoistic tendencies are overcome the practitioner will realise they have already received the gift of the Sa'asmita Samadhi but their attention was previously going in the wrong direction! Once the full attention is redirected to its true and proper place, the aspirant becomes a yogin, one of the few persons in the world today that knows real Samadhi.

---

[198] Cf. 'Name and Form: Nama-Rupa'.

Kundalini Yoga

Yoga means 'union' (with God). Ritual magick is 'yoga in action' (*karma* yoga), when it is correctly practiced and understood. Various forms of yoga are used throughout the grades of initiation. Kundalini Yoga is a type of individual alchemy. It works by virtue of the analogous relation between the macrocosm and the microcosm, 'as above and so below'. It is first necessary to examine some of the obstructions that arise as soon as yoga is even attempted, and some of the false notions that also act as formidable barriers to the path of knowledge (Sanskrit *ynana*).

If a man is being dragged by two horses running in opposite directions, the only way he can save himself from destruction is to jump into one saddle or the other. The Neophyte imperative can be reduced to this: which horse is it going to be? The Neophyte either 'Quits the Material to seek the Spiritual' or they reverse this and quit the spiritual to seek the woven fabric of mundane existence, the tapestry of dream—in which contingencies form the very nature of the dream, and are without end. In practicing Kundalini Yoga there is all the more reason to be aware that the pressures and lures of the outer world must be avoided. These can become so great they are a real threat to even maintaining the discipline at all. The practitioner rarely suspects that the partially risen Serpent Power, combined with incomplete knowledge, has led them deeper into delusion, for all power has been sent out into the world and there is none available for yoga. Objects of desire become glamorised, enchanted, and their seductive lure is overwhelming.

With Kundalini Yoga a special kind of force or energy is released. But it is easy for all this to be poured away through placing attention on external and peripheral things—called 'contingent' because they are in reality random or chance elements, without substance. The rising of the Serpent Power will focus and magnify all glamours as it passes upward and if our attention follows these objects passively, without resistance, one obstruction after another will materialise. Such knowledge is 'built in' to our symbol of the Tree of Life. A man may ride the Serpent to the junction of the twenty-fifth and twenty-seventh paths, Samekh and Pé, the Angel and the Blasted Tower. Then the lightning hits him and if he should turn his attention downwards (or outwards) then in that flash, devastation is seen, and there is an urgent call to action after action, one thing after another.

If he fails to understand the need to practice indifference to phenomena and follows the call, thinking he is riding into battle like a brave knight, he is already lost in that instant; he has fallen into the world of Shells. The path of the Angel is the straight way upward. The path of the Tower is the horizontal—the 'fall' is to follow the tapestry or fabric of the dream instead of rising up on the warp that the weave is hung on.[199]

The seductions of the outer world come in many disguises. Sometimes we have to remove ourselves from profane influences, especially where these are predatory persons actively hostile to what they do not understand. Compassion is the vice of kings when we think we can help people by some action or pouring 'love' in their direction—but that is certainly a misdirection and only enflames the ego in a subversive way, creating even more loops and coils in the binding force of the Great Dragon of Restriction.[200] As well as being flattering to the self, it can even be flattering to other people and then we have real trouble on our hands.

All attempts to 'fix things' in ourselves, a sort of desire for self-improvement, is misdirected energy; it is directed towards the self instead of the goal of yoga. There is no end to that work of 'balancing' or 'working through things' as it is frequently referred to in pop psychological and therapeutic culture. Self-improvement is a force of anti-initiation because it limits everything to the individual state. If we contact the solar ray then we must let the solar ray work on us instead of trying to 'work on ourselves'—or even worse, working on other people.

Sometimes the mundane world is pitched against the practice of yoga, as though these are two things that are mutually antagonist. In fact, the division exists only in the self (Sanskrit *ahankara*). We have to maintain our existence in the world but if we attach ultimate importance to it, making it our sole concern, we then place ourselves under the power of Restriction that rules the material world.

Metaphysical reality can only be known metaphysically. There is no resolution or understanding of metaphysical realities at all in human rational thought because reason is by definition (as defined as 'rational') a realm that does not reach to the intellectual intuition (*boddhi*).

---

[199] Cf. 'The House of the Net', *Nu Hermetica*.
[200] Cf. 'Dragons and Serpents' [*ibid*].

The goal of yoga is outside of and beyond the human state, and it is only from the point of view of the human state that such things as success or failure can have any meaning at all. Even then, such meaning is strictly relative and as such is not in any way constant—it is subject to change or impermanence.

A further consideration is that it is an error to suppose that we do a Great Work only for ourselves. If we do that, we are limiting the Great Work to the domain of the *ahankara*, the human ego—and that is not even a small fraction of what the individuality truly is, let alone the integral individuality and that which is beyond the human state altogether.

Effective rites of an initiatic organisation are infallible. We are not infallible but the rites are infallible. Even if an Initiate has not attained the knowledge of the Supreme State in their physical life, by performing effective rites they undergo symbolic initiation. It is then possible that even in the posthumous state the symbolic initiation can be rendered fully effective and Deliverance attained. If a person does not have innate 'qualifications' (as may be shown in their natal horoscope) then it is unlikely they will go far on the knowledge path. It may nonetheless be beneficial for them to be attached either to orthodoxy or to an initiatic organisation.[201] When a person does have these qualifications then nothing is guaranteed by that fact alone, but the possibilities certainly exist within that person. It remains as to whether those possibilities will be developed.

Psychic phenomena has no use in initiation, which is always our goal; if such things occur it is purely contingent and it is best not to regard it as in any way significant or meaningful in itself. That which people usually call 'psychic phenomena' would be completely normal in a normal world. But our world is completely abnormal and most persons by now have lost the apprehension of the subtle domain let alone the spiritual reality that is far beyond that.

The realm of the psyche is not as far removed from that of the body as is often supposed. Psychic apparitions or visions may seem extraordinary but in fact they are very ordinary and are certainly not worth seeking after.

---

[201] At the advanced stage of the Kali Yuga we have arrived at, it is often better to have affiliation with one of the few remaining initiatic Orders than it is to have exoteric affiliation, for most religions of the world have by now separated themselves from the esotericism that validated them and kept them alive. Unfortunately, the same goes for the countless pseudo-initiatic organisations in the world today.

There is a notion of 'intuition' that we have previously alluded to, that has arisen from the New Age counter-initiatic culture and that sometimes afflicts beginners to such an extent they never persist with a discipline as they imagine that what they call their intuition 'guides them' this way and that.[202] Such intuition is instinctive, emotional or psychic. It has nothing to do with the intellectual intuition (Sanskrit *boddhi*) that must be developed before apprehension of metaphysical reality can take place. The conventional idea of intuition, whether that is taken to the psychic level or not, is totally unreliable and untrustworthy. Those who put trust in such things have no idea what it is they are really trusting in. The psychic intuition, which is a kind of parody of real intuition, is particularly devious when it becomes the habitual mode, and magnifies the level of delusion considerably.

The emotional or even romantic sense of association with an initiatic organisation is not something to be dismissed or disregarded altogether. Emotional states are in the domain of mysticism and so long as mystical experience has a basis in theoretical knowledge to guide it then it can still act as a support to initiation. Emotionalism or sentimentality, as such, is not encouraged in the praxis however. If the person dwells upon sentiment, recollections or thoughts of a sentimental nature, they are not meditating at all in the sense we mean it in relation to yoga. 'Meditation' here means more than ordinary thought and must involve concentration of the mind on a symbol or idea without deviation.

The bond existing between members of a fraternity after long years of association is more than can be put in words. There will be few persons of whom we could say we have a 'spiritual' relation, one that extends beyond the human domain, yet which is inclusive of all that is possible to the human. Such bonds exceed even those of normal family attachments. The last rite for an Initiate is performed by their friends and colleagues three days after physical death. The Rite of Ascension frees us from all earthly bonds and attachments. One should not think, though, that those who remain on earth do not grieve bitterly over the loss of their loved ones in this world. A 'rite' means 'ordinance', 'to set in order', and that is a large part of our work, ongoing through all of our lives and even after physical death.

---

[202] Cf. 'Postmodern Shamanism'.

Egyptian Yoga

In modern times yoga has become separated from its spiritual purpose. All focus is then placed upon the physicality of the yoga postures (*mudras*), breathing techniques and so forth. These were only added to Hatha Yoga when the sages wished to make a complete science of yoga, and were never intended to be separated from meditation or the goal, which is 'union with God'.

In the subtle human body tradition has it there are two forces at work, often symbolised by two serpents called *ida* and *pingala* in Sanskrit, or personified as Isis and Nephthys in Egypt.[203] These are likened to the solar and lunar force, the Sun and the Moon. Through their interactions we are able to perform all functions. We can live, breathe, eat and think, for example, by virtue of them. At various times one or the other force is dominant. When they are equilibrated, through yoga for example, it becomes possible to raise consciousness up through the chakras or 'wheels', centres of power, to the higher or supra-human states. This is brought about through the means of a 'central canal' called *shushumna* in Sanskrit, which has its equivalent in the central column of the Tree of Life or the trunk of the world tree in various cultures. This is described as the passage for a certain kind of fire and is otherwise called the Serpent Power. The vital force or Kundalini, that which keeps us alive, is said to be coiled sleeping at the base of the spine in the occult anatomy; the dream of existence arises therefrom. The Shakti or living power, which is personified as a goddess of the same name, is able to rise upward along the path of the *shushumna*. This is facilitated by *pranayama* or control of breath in the yoga practice, combined with fervent aspiration and sometimes the use of images (*yantras*) and sounds (*mantras*).

The primary aim of yoga is withdrawal of the senses from the physical body (and mind) to the subtle realm. The gross and subtle senses are then withdrawn so that true meditation and yoga union is possible. This alone makes possible the *moksha* ('liberation') of Laya Yoga when carried to its ultimate.[204] Shushumna ends at the top of the skull (*brahmarandra*) but continues through a 'solar ray', which must be followed to its source, which we posit as a 'star'.

---

[203] The chakras in yoga do not in any way exist in the physical anatomy as such. When they are 'located' in various parts of the body the placement is only to serve as an analogy, not literal fact.
[204] It should be noted that *moksha* liberation in the real sense, and while alive in a body of flesh, is usually only possible through total renunciation.

Comparison may readily be made between the chakras of Laya Yoga, as revealed to the West in Sir John Woodroffe's *The Serpent Power*, and the sephiroth of the Tree of Life schema. The speculative arrangement of chakras now widely known as the Middle Pillar Exercise bears only a passing relation to Kundalini Yoga. It does not rest on any traditional knowledge and has no doctrinal basis.[205] To make matters worse, this was taken out of the legacy of the Order of the Golden Dawn—which was already a very syncretic collection of knowledge—and placed in the context of the New Age movement, replete with psychological and 'healing' applications. Thus it was completely separated from any higher spiritual principle. This has unfortunate consequences for the practitioners, though they rarely if ever realise the fact. As with 'yoga for health', the denaturing of the practice means that while it may appear to be effective, the ego (Sanskrit *ahankara*) of the person remains in an unregenerate state and impervious to any real spiritual knowledge. Furthermore, such an attitude may easily become even more deeply entrenched. It is even harmful to the being in so far as the unleashed force, separated from the principle, can only manifest in the abode of the practitioner in an inferior or degraded form.

The arrangement of the Tree of Life and chakras described above confuses the positions of Da'ath and Malkuth. Da'ath, 'Knowledge', was associated with *vishuddha*, whereas Da'ath is not a sephira. The arrangement includes the peculiar notion of placing Malkuth as the base chakra, which is the equivalent to *muladhara*, but removed to our feet. All this introduces distortion and confusion.

In the preliminary form of Egyptian Yoga that we are about to present here, the chakras are arranged as though the Tree of Life is superimposed upon the subtle anatomy. There are other ways we can do this but at the beginning it is best to start with the model as described below in more detail.

---

[205] Israel Regardie is thought to have produced the particular arrangement known as the Middle Pillar Exercise. It was based on a diagram that appeared among the Golden Dawn papers, though it is more than possible the diagram was an invention of Regardie. Contrary to what is often supposed, this was not practiced in the Order of the Golden Dawn until counterfeit versions of the Order were created more than half a century after the original organisation was disbanded.

With this method, Hod and Netzach are on a horizontal plane, so Netzach is not 'above' Hod. Likewise with Chesed and Geburah and Chokmah and Binah, they are pairs on the same plane. Kether is posited as vertically above the top of the head. It is most interesting to discover that René Guénon posited a method of placing the chakras of Laya Yoga ('union towards the goal of dissolution') upon the Tree of Life that is more or less identical to ours. Da'ath is not a separate chakra from *ajna*, and has nothing to do with *vishuddha*. Yesod is also the base chakra corresponding to *svadhisthana*. It is best to quote directly from Guénon, as he is very clear on this:[206]

> We shall conclude here with an observation that we believe has never before been made anywhere ... By beginning at the top, there is at first no difficulty as concerns the assimilation of *sahasrara*, 'located' at the crown of the head, to the supreme Sephira—Kether—whose name means precisely 'crown'.
>
> Then comes the pair Chokmah and Binah, which must correspond to *ajna* and whose duality could even be represented by the two petals of that lotus; moreover, they have as their 'resultant' Da'ath, that is, 'knowledge', and we have seen that the localisation of *ajna* also refers to the 'eye of knowledge'.
>
> As regards man, the following pair, that is, Chesed and Geburah, can be linked to the two arms, according to a very general symbolism concerning the attributes of 'Mercy' and 'Justice'; these two sephiroth will thus be placed at the two shoulders, and consequently on a level with the region of the throat, and so correspond to *vishuddha*.
>
> As for Tiphereth, its central position obviously refers to the heart, which immediately shows its correspondence with *anahatha*.
>
> The pair Netzach and Hod will be placed at the hips, the points at which the lower limbs are attached, as are Chesed and Geburah, at the shoulders, the points where the upper limbs are attached; now the hips are on a level with the umbilical region, thus of *manipura*.
>
> Finally as regards the last two Sephiroth, it seems there is cause to envisage an inversion, for Yesod, according to the very significance of its name, is the 'foundation', which exactly corresponds to *muladhara*. It would then be necessary to assimilate Malkuth to *svadhisthana*, which moreover the meaning of the names seems to justify, for Malkuth is the 'kingdom' and *svadhisthana* literally means 'proper abode of the Shakti'.

---

[206] *Studies in Hinduism* [Sophia Perennis]. This is towards the end of a whole chapter that Guénon devoted to Woodroffe's *The Serpent Power*.

In the Egyptian Yoga we have eleven chakras altogether. Firstly, we posit Malkuth as the whole temple and body of the practitioner. The chakra of the Moon or Yesod, the 'proper abode of the Shakti', is where activation of the Serpent Power begins. The next six chakras take us to the level of Da'ath as the 'resultant' of *ajna*. Nuit and Wadjet complete the union in *ajna* so that the illuminated sun disc enables the solar ray received from 'outside' the human individuality. The solar ray begins where the central canal (Sanskrit *shushumna*) ends, so to speak. ISA, as primordial Throne, is then the centre of the triangle residing in *sahasrara*. This is how communication is made possible between the human and non-human states that are beyond. The triangle may also be summarised by the Sanskrit term *sat-chit-ananda*, and AUM.[207]

---

[207] Cf. 'Sat-Chit-Ananda'.

Dual Symbolism and Symbolic Inversion

The European folk tale Little Red Riding Hood is well known, but not so well known are its origins, which are of great antiquity. The story is certainly much older, at least in its antecedents, than biblical references to a wolf in sheep's clothing, but the singular etymological link between *leukos*, the Greek word for 'bright, shining' and the word for 'a wolf' may be explained.

The Greek word *lukos* (λυκος) means 'a wolf'. By the addition of the letter *epsilon*, the name becomes *leukos* (λευκος), which means 'bright, brilliant or white'. The word *leukos* is etymologically linked with other words for light including the Latin *lux* and the Hebrew *luz*. Over time, descriptive words became proper nouns.[208] Words for 'shining' or 'white' became names such as Luke, Logres, Loki, Lucia and Lucifer. The word *leukos* is used quite frequently in the New Testament in Greek. A most striking example is in Matthew 17: 1–3, where the word is used to describe the bright, shining whiteness of the transfiguration of Jesus on Mount Hermon.[209] The Hebrew name of the holy mountain means 'white' or 'dazzling brightness', which conveys a literal fact as well as a metaphorical one as the peaks of the mountain are snow-covered.[210]

> And after six days Jesus taketh Peter, James, and John his brother, and bringeth them up into an high mountain apart, And was transfigured before them: and his face did shine as the sun, and his raiment was white as the light. And, behold, there appeared unto them Moses and Elias talking with him.

This is an important biblical text that has profound esoteric import. When Jesus took three disciples up Mount Hermon to witness his transfiguration, it was said that his face shone like the sun—he is the solar principle.

---

[208] Cf. 'Brahmacharya'.
[209] Cf. *Nu Hermetica*, pp. 107, 108 and 181.
[210] The name is similar in Arabic (Jabal Haramun) and is Har Hermon (מון הר) in Hebrew. There is a possible link with the ancient Egyptian Theban God, Amoun or Amen, who was often depicted in shining white and was sometimes ithyphallic when associated with Min. One cannot ignore either the fact that HR or Hor is the Egyptian name of Horus, also associated with the sky and with high mountains. This might account for an alternative Arabic name, 'Mountain of the Sheikh', which is the mount of the Holy King. Hor or Har, the name of Horus, also has an etymological link with 'heart', *cor* in Latin or *kore* in Greek.

Even though the disciples saw this, they were terrified when the Shekinah or divine presence then descended upon them. Notably, these events transpired 'after six days', which is the fulfilment of the creation or manifestation that is followed by the seventh day of 'rest', symbolising the holy Shekinah. The narrative continues to weave a complex thread in which the prophets and John the Baptist are recalled.[211] There are three prophets mentioned including Jesus, and three disciples as witness, two of which were brothers, a symbolism that is by no means incidental. Together these make six, the triad and its lower inversion, which forms the holy hexagram. Furthermore, only three of the disciples were chosen as witnesses, signifying an *elect*. A man can only see what he is able to see and he will see it according to the degree of reality he knows, his level of initiation. When the disciples were afraid of the holy presence, which instructed them to hear the words of Jesus as the Son of God, they threw themselves to the ground and could only open their eyes again after Jesus had touched them. Touch is associated with the heart, the *anahatha* chakra, and only the Master could open their eyes. That is to say, the light of direct revelation is blinding to the profane, and an avatar or divine intermediary is required. It is to be 'touched' by the Heart of the Master, a theme that is repeated after the crucifixion when Magdalene wants to touch Jesus when he appears to her.[212] The heart is also the 'cave' or centre of the holy mountain, which must be reached before the celestial or higher intelligence can be touched upon or attained.

Peter is the 'rock', upon which the Church is built, as his name suggests, for the name means exactly that in several languages.[213] Further, the Egyptian God Ptah (PTH) is the equivalent of the Grand Architect of Freemasonry. Peter is also said to be the keeper of the keys of heaven, which means that he symbolically partakes of the attributes of Christ.[214] Ptah also has the meaning of 'sky', for the rock, stone or mountain unites heaven with earth.

---

[211] The disciples see Jesus talking with Moses and Elias, two other prophets. It is later revealed that Elias is John the Baptist, who had already laid the foundation or prepared the way, and so it was useless to await the coming of Elias, who would 'restore all things', because he had already come (17: 12).
[212] Cf. *Babalon Unveiled*, Lapis Philosophorum, 'Parable and Parabola'.
[213] Matthew, 16: 18: 'That thou art Peter, and upon this rock I will build my church; and the gates of hell shall not prevail against it.'
[214] The title was conferred on Peter by Jesus in Matthew 16: 19, prior to the ascent of the holy mountain: 'I will give you the keys of the kingdom of heaven, and whatever you bind on Earth shall be bound in heaven, and whatever you loose on Earth shall be loosed in heaven.'

The keys are frequently depicted as of silver and gold, especially as sacerdotal authority, and these are the two ways of the primordial tradition: the lesser way of Salvation (Egyptian Amentet) and the greater way of Deliverance (Sahu). James and John, the two brothers that witnessed the transfiguration, symbolise the dual current or twin serpents that must be witnesses to the truth. The mountain is the 'rock' or foundation and at the same time it is the seed principle itself, and the primordial summit (Atma). This is resumed later, after Jesus has cast out a devil from a man's child that was deranged and that would fall into fire and into water—a further symbolism of esoteric import.[215] Suffice to say that in alchemy the Lion and Eagle are figured and that these are the dual manifestation of the unitive principle in different modes of operation. Essentially, the child was subject to disequilibrium. In Matthew, 17: 20, the disciples ask of Jesus why it is that they could not themselves cast out the same devil, and the reply is very telling:

> Because of your unbelief: for verily I say unto you, If ye have faith as a grain of mustard seed, ye shall say unto this mountain, Remove hence to yonder place; and it shall remove; and nothing shall be impossible unto you.

It transpires then, that although unbelief is the ground, this is a matter of the greater mysteries, not the lesser. The word 'belief' is in any case derived from the Old English *lēof*, related to 'love', and therefore the true or original sense is 'heart' or higher intellect. It is the original meaning of the word that we should read in scriptures, not the conventional one, which is degraded. The grain of mustard seed is a symbol of the Atma or supreme principle in which all things are accomplished. Atma is the mover that is not moved by anything. Furthermore, in 17: 21, it is revealed that this way is only attained by meditation practice and self-sacrifice:

> Howbeit this kind goeth not out but by prayer and fasting.

As mentioned previously, there is a curious etymological link with *leukos*, the Greek word for 'light', and *lukos*, 'wolf'. The wolf is a symbol of the Hyperborean or primordial tradition, the source of all knowledge and learning. As with all symbolism, it has an inverse or negative meaning. In scriptural context, the wolf is ravenous, greedy, or voracious. According to Matthew, 7: 15,

> Beware of false prophets, which come to you in sheep's clothing, but inwardly they are ravening wolves.

---

[215] Matthew 17: 14–23; Mark 9: 30–32; Luke 9: 43–45.

The whiteness in this context is the outer appearance of things. We should beware then of those whose appearance is 'white' or 'shining', even if it should be of a dazzling brightness, but who are seething with corruption within. The Pharisees were similarly described in Luke, 11: 39. In Ezekiel, 22: 25, further detail is gone into concerning such anti-initiatic agencies as are symbolised by the ravenous wolf, whose white appearance is a trick. It is said of these that they destroy souls by taking all precious things from them, that 'they have made her many widows in the midst thereof'. In Ezekiel, 22: 27, this is again affirmed. While these words of wisdom are placed in a context of social prohibitions, it becomes evident that the nature of such a ravening beast compares to the force of Antichrist that has assumed control of our world at the end of the Age of Kali Yuga. It is therefore applicable to the present as much as it is to the past, so long as we understand the symbolism.

The meaning of the wolf dressed in sheep's clothing, sometimes applied to false prophets, is that a person can appear to be whiter than white but that is only the outward appearance. They may even be very concerned with 'purity'. The Pharisees were a merchant cult that, along with the scribes of the time, paid strict attention to the letter of the law but not the spirit, of which they had no knowledge whatsoever. The theme figures frequently in the Gospel narrative. A man who only sees the appearance of things does not know the Real. He may think that the wolf is a shining exemplar or rôle model. He may be the wolf himself, a ravenous, hungry devourer. He hungers and thirsts for more but only sees the appearance of things; and that is why he hungers, because of the nothingness inside him. He might serve the Antichrist, knowingly or not, and destroy other souls, in which case he is of the damned, leading others to the same fate.

In old Tarot decks such as the Marseille, the trump numbered 18 depicts two wolves on a desolate landscape and howling at the Moon. Lycanthrope, 'a werewolf', is derived from Greek *lukos*, 'wolf', and *anthropos*, 'man'. Dictionaries define lycanthropy as a 'delusional state', which sees no further than the psychological domain. In fact, the transformation of men into other creatures than man is a practice that became degenerate over time, due to ignorance, but it is no more delusional than man's ordinary state of mind. The two wolves in the Tarot picture could provide a clue to the inherent duality.[216]

---

[216] It cannot be a coincidence that in some countries all creatures once identified with the primordial such as the wolf, bear and wild boar, have been hunted to extinction.

The action of devouring has lunar as well as Jovian connotations. Cancer, the sign ruled by the Moon, is associated with vampirism in its inferior aspect, and Jupiter, also known for greed or gluttony, is exalted in the sign (by astrological dignity). Even the Moon herself, over time, came to have almost wholly negative meanings, although in the Egyptian, Hindu and other ancient traditions she is seen in her most positive aspect as the Great Mother, Isis, or Mahamaya Shakti. The Mother as Devourer is the unmanifest or supreme principle, the pure Atma, not limited, determined or moved by any other thing and which can hardly be said to be a thing in itself for it is not objectified.

The Moon, as a symbol, is dual, for there is the lower elemental aspect and higher principial aspect—where she is descriptive of the moon-flower or the crown chakra, *sahasrara*, *brahmarandra*, or the Kether of the Qabalah. The Moon is bright and shining and illumines the night sky. She is thus in earliest times the guide of the soul, the curer of sickness and the way-shower. The white wolf is particularly associated with the northern tradition of which the polar north, or a polar star, is a further symbolism.

In the book of Genesis, 49: 27, the tribe of Benjamin, which corresponds to Sagittarius (there are twelve tribes), is described as a ravening wolf:

> Benjamin shall ravin as a wolf: in the morning he shall devour the prey, and at night he shall divide the spoil.

The twelve signs of the Zodiac are best understood in opposite or complementary pairs. This description indicates Jupiter, the ruling planet of Sagittarius, as 'devouring', and the daytime aspect. The opposite sign of Gemini, ruled by Mercury, is then the night aspect and is described as a thief that divides up the loot. Division is the general principle of Gemini while the thief is the inverse aspect of Mercury.

As well as the wolf, and sometimes the lion, the crocodile is used in various ancient traditions to depict all aspects of the Devourer; in ancient Egypt this was sometimes combined with the hippo. Whether a symbol is viewed as positive or negative depends entirely on the point of view, for the principle itself is unchanged by anything. The crocodile that lurks behind the scales in the Hall of Ma'at is the devourer of the soul in time but to one that is able to pass beyond the 'second birth' to final Deliverance, its hungry mouth is the gateway to the dissolution of ultimate freedom.

The traditional virtues are powers of the soul. The vices are the inversion of the soul's power, through ignorance of the principle, as we have previously explained, so we will only mention one pair of vices and virtues here, which are those corresponding to Jupiter.[217] This has a further correspondence with the ravening wolf, as we shall see. The virtue of Jupiter is Obedience (to the path). Without faith and obedience no path truly exists so far as the ignorant person is concerned. This will be true however much they may want to think it is otherwise.

We will hear it said from aspirants, perhaps countless times, that 'this is my path', as though it were something unique and personal to their selves. In that case it is no spiritual path but a path of self-delusion, if it can then be called 'path'. Those who speak of 'my path' will also determine what is 'not my path', and in so doing they imagine they are practicing the soul's power of Discrimination, which is the first step on the path.[218] But the personal preferences, acquired likes and dislikes, have nothing to do at all with the true nature or *dharma*, especially in this Age of Kali Yuga. Such a choosing does not indicate any real path at all and is merely the exercise of a sort of criticism that everyone now learns in their ordinary education, used to cultivate a wolfish appetite for 'self expression' and 'creativity'. All of that pertains to the domain of the ego (*ahankara*) and all it can do is close the ears and eyes to the knowledge of the unitive principle of the Real. Such a person will think they are choosing freedom but they are choosing slavery and are shouting down the still voice of the soul. The consequence is that Obedience will only be known through the exclusive vices of Bigotry, Hypocrisy, Gluttony and Tyranny. These all relate to an inverse form of surrender that only means following the very ordinary wishes and desires of the individual ego.

Gluttony is then symbolised by *lukos*, the ravening wolf. Such greed can take countless forms, for example there is hunger for information, data, statistics, research, evidence and the fake 'proving' required by profane sciences. It can even parody the hunger for knowledge, a kind of inverse substitution for the knowledge (*jnana*) of the Real. An appetite for profane knowledge can never develop the individual beyond facts and information for their own sake, which is, as it were, a nothingness seeking after more nothingness.

---

[217] See 'Powers of the Soul', *Nu Hermetica*.
[218] Discrimination corresponds to Malkuth, the Kingdom of Earth. See *Nu Hermetica* [ibid].

Devils and demons are the manifestations of the metaphysical Principle (Atma Itself) at the lowest, most degraded level. Or to put it another way, the demons of the path only have a degree of existence as relative to the person lacking knowledge of the higher principle involved.

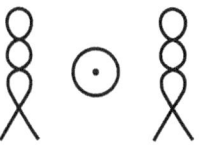

One example is that of the ancient Egyptian hieroglyph for 'Eternity'. It is called Heh (or *hech*) and is formed from two spiralic lamp-wicks on either side of a metaphysical point within a circle.

As Eternity, it is the principle itself. The spiralic threads on either side encompass all possibilities of Being and the worlds. This could be viewed as a more ancient form of Jesus, Moses and Elias, reflected as 'below' by the disciples Peter, James and John on the holy mountain. When there is total ignorance of the eternal principle, it manifests as three Demons, two of which take the form of serpents. The first serpent ties us up, binding us through our thoughts and actions. The second devours us through our desire for the appearance of things, a desire that leads to the delusion that the appearance of things is real or even in any way significant. The third, which is the inversion of the pure, undetermined Principle Itself, is a type of the Demon Whose Face Cannot be Seen. This has taken on very particular significance in the present time, as we near the end of the Kali Yuga. It is of course the principle, the Real, that cannot be seen, that is not known. The consequence, when this is completely obscure to humans, who will even deny and attack the possibility of it, is a Nameless Fear, a phobic rejection of all else outside the most restricted elements of the ego self. It is spiritual blindness and even a kind of wilful ignorance or incomprehension.

Brahmacharya

The Hindu doctrines, comprising various *darshanas* or 'points of view', have the most complete and exact metaphysics of all wisdom traditions. This is not because the Egyptians, for example, lacked such a complete metaphysics, but their language was no longer spoken or understood two thousand years ago or more. Those who translate the hieroglyphs are not in any way qualified to construe anything but the most basic, literal meaning. When a literal translation of symbols results in nonsense the Egyptologists say it is because the Egyptians were confused or the texts were badly written. They will not see that it is their own lack of comprehension of ancient metaphysics that stands in the way.

> The glory of the Vedas is their universal and timeless quality. The subtle and symbolic invocations of the Śruti, and the mystic and melodic music of the celestial hymns, have hallowed human consciousness through trackless centuries with a sublime glow.[219]

The Vedas and Vedanta, the ancient commentaries on them by sages, hold the keys to the universal primordial tradition. But how can we even begin to become a *brahmacharya*, a student of the Vedas, without spending years learning Sanskrit? Modern commentaries, even those supplied by Hindu scholars, use the prejudiced language of conventional or profane sciences. Fortunately, René Guénon can act as a guide to our understanding the true meaning of the Vedic literature.[220] Once equipped, we can proceed to the source texts and will then immediately see the errors or inaccurate English terms and translations of modern commentaries. What follows here serves as a general introduction to the *trayi-vidya*, the 'threefold knowledge', of which the first, Rigveda, is the oldest of the four Vedas: Rigveda (Knowledge of the Verses), Yajurveda, Samaveda and Atharvaveda.

The Vedas comprise complete knowledge. The study takes us back to the origin of language itself. The divine origin of language is either accepted without question but without comprehension, or it is rejected and then a false 'scientific' explanation given, also without comprehension.

---

[219] Foreword to *The Four Vedas: Mantras in Sanskrit with Transliteration and English Translation* (Set of 22 Volumes), DAV Publication Division, New Delhi (2008 Edition).
[220] We may refer the student to the three books dealing specifically with Hindu Studies, and in particular, *Man and His Becoming according to the Vedānta*.

The non-human origin of all true symbols is scarcely understood, if it is known about at all. Yet it is perfectly clear from the Vedas exactly where the limits of the human individual and formal order are set, and that the corporeal or physical world, which is all that conventional science admits to having existence, amounts to a tiny fraction of even the limited human domain.

We may say that 'in the beginning' there was the mode of speech called *para-vak* in Sanskrit. The feminine noun *vāk* can mean both the voice and the word it utters, and is also the 'sound' of any thing whatsoever. At the supreme level this is Cosmic Ideation, an attribute of Ishvara as the divine Word or Logos. Those with an evolutionary bias will unfortunately then call this 'primitive speech', rendering real understanding completely impossible. In fact the word 'para' means 'beyond' or 'above'. As *para-vak* came first in the order of things, it is superior, not inferior, as modern science will have us believe. Neither is *para-vak* 'psychological', as the apologists will have it. Rather, it pertains to the subtle non-corporeal state and is made possible in the human by what is called the *manas* or 'inward sense'. Thus this inward sense is the root of thought as we know it. The mode of speech we are discussing, which is not in any way articulated as physical sound, is called *manomaya-kosha*. It is the 'thought-forming' (or producing) envelope of the self, of which there are five in total, this one being the third. As we are concerned here for the time being only with speech, the matter of the five envelopes of the self and all their modifications will be dealt with in another place. Let it suffice to say here that it is no accident that what we call the Khabs 'star' in Esoteric Thelema has five radials from the centre, and for that reason is sometimes likened to the 'Hand of Orion'.[221]

There is a mode of *para-vak* called *pasyanti-vak*, which is an agent of manifestation or production that goes forth (*iksana*) by 'seeing'. One may recall to mind the same mode that is attributed to the Eye of Ra in the Egyptian tradition that 'goes forth' as Hadit, or is sometimes personified as his daughter Hathoor. By this means, a word, intention or thought may be transmitted without sound, by the envelope of *manomaya-kosha*. Distance is no object here; in fact such thought may travel to the limits of the universe and back, for this is taking place at the subtle level, we should remember, and not in the physical world at all. Such a transmission is activated by the power of will (*samkalpa*).

---

[221] See 'The Star of Man', that follows this chapter.

Here it will be readily seen that we have the origin of initiatic tradition, where *transmission* is often the very word used to describe it, for example, 'Qabalah'. Perhaps needless to say, such a power, although in vastly ancient times common to all humans, is not in any way within the scope of anyone that has not developed it through long practice of yoga of the breath, concentration and contemplation. From here arises the well-known but little understood phenomenon of *guru-darshana,* where the guru 'point of view' may be transmitted whether by touch, a sound (*mantra*) or by soundless vibration where physical distance is no object at all.

After *para-vak* comes *apara-vak*, the 'non-primordial' speech. Here, speech is translated and articulated by means of physical utterance. This requires two stages, of which the first is *pasyanti*, the image-forming or visual aspect already mentioned above. While this may be particular to an individual—since we have by now entered the level of the human individuality and formal state—the true symbols, as for example are recorded in the Pyramid Texts of Egypt, derive from a non-human source as is the case with *para-vak*, for nothing can exist in separation from its higher principle. The second stage is *madhyama-vak*, where the physical action or the object itself, be it animal, mineral or vegetable, becomes an impression (*samskara*) in the mind. This is the beginning of conceptual awareness (*pratyaya*).

In the many diverse applications of traditional sciences, collected together and called 'magick', which our students are well familiar with, the image-making faculty is made much use of—sometimes, it must be said, to a rather excessive degree. As pure or real meditation involves non-conceptual awareness it should be easy to see that though it is necessary at the beginning, the use of images, if seen as an end in itself, tends to arrest all development at the formal level of manifestation. Such conceptual thought requires sound vibration. It might be objected that postmodern 'conceptual art' can surely be done without sound being involved at all? It must be understood then that such art, so-called, takes ordinary thought as existing in separation from any higher principle, then produces an image or a structure to represent it—it is thus a facile inversion of the natural order. True or real conceptualisation on the other hand requires sound or vocal utterance and this faculty is common to men and all other creatures. When the action, creature or thing itself is determined by its vocalisation then we may say that what takes place on the mental level is translated into physicality (viz., articulate speech). The determined action or object is *bhava*, and this word also refers to that principle which is behind the formation of the word or name.

When the action or the source of the vocalisation becomes a determined thing, the adjective or attributive is formed into a verb, the verb is translated into a noun, and the 'name' is born. Thus, for example, the drawing up of water into vapours and clouds by the heat of the sun means that words for clouds, dew, rain, water and even fire or lightning, through the solar action, have come to be interchangeable in meaning, or identified with the sun as the visible agent for the action. The sun is not only the brightest orb in the sky but is also the agency for distillation. So it is that verbs such as 'to live', 'to reside', 'to dwell', 'to pray', 'to appear', 'to speak' and so on, were embodied in the names of various objects, things or creatures. The Vedic idea of sacrifice is commonly misunderstood, for it did not originally imply any killing, physical offering or oblation; any ritual that is done before a consecrated fire is called a 'sacrifice'. When a state of being is transposed to a higher one it necessarily involves destruction of the previous state.

It is said, and wisely, that the Vedas came to be written down after humanity descended or fell from the primordial state and there was a need for utterances to be symbolised in written language. This is comparable with the 'two Adams' in the biblical book of Genesis. It is the second Adam, not the primordial Adam Kadmon, that gave names to the creatures. It is only when Adam became separate from Eve that there was a need for it to be so, otherwise he would have plunged headlong into the abyss.[222]

As the 'name' or noun is derived from an action, with the passage of time the embodied action fades into the background and becomes lost. We then have the proper noun, which is rarely if ever used as an attributive in later Vedic texts or those that came after them. Thus 'lightning' assumed the proper noun Indra in later texts, whereas originally it was the attributive, *indratame*, 'lighting the darkness' or 'descending to earth'. In the Rigveda, the Shakti Devi Sarasvati is called Paviravi or 'Daughter of the Lightning', a name that refers to the supreme Vajra that sustains all of the worlds. The universe is in fact not a collection of objects and things so much as speech or language.

---

[222] Cf. 'The Two Adams'.

It may thus be seen that over the course of time there was a 'solidification' of language; its flexibility was sacrificed in favour of the need to find definitive names for all things. There is a movement from the primary or direct knowledge to the reflected or secondary knowledge.

We should note that *para-vak*, the primordial or direct language, was common to all creatures, human and animal. The earliest and most direct or transmissive mode of communication, by analogy, is comparable to the 'language of birds' or the 'language of the angels'. It is the language that was taught to Adam in the Garden of Eden. The Veda couplets called *chandas*, or mantras, emerged from direct perception of the 'luminous ether' and are the origin of the Vedas, sometimes also called Dharmas. The word *dharma* has no equivalent in modern languages but approximates divine and natural law or ordinance, as appropriate to each creature and individual, each type of being or species or any group or any collective whatsoever. The *chandas* were from earliest times regarded as divine revelation. Those who could receive these or expound on them were called Rasis, a word that has associations with 'beauty' and 'mystery'. The truth revealed therein is called *devata*, which refers directly to the divine or celestial (angelic) world (*paraloka*).

Once any oral tradition of great antiquity is written down and so made subject to the many refinements of grammar and philology, it becomes removed from the root meaning once understood by all. Vedic seers described the standardisation of Sanskrit, the work of millennia, as a grand operation akin to a ritual sacrifice. No material oblation was made, as previously explained. The sacrifice was made in the form of the vocalisation of the mantras. According to Rigveda 10.71.2, the work of suffix and prefix was like 'putting grains through a sieve'.

The mantras, Brahma or Veda couplets, were classified according to the three worlds: Agni, 'fire', governing the terrestrial realm; Vayu 'wind', 'air', governing the middle world between earth and heaven; Surya, 'sun' or 'solar light', as governing the celestial sphere. Agni and various associated deities therefore govern the latent or subtle aspect of earth and to this belongs the mantras of the Rigveda. Vayu, Indra and others govern the intermediary world as a sudden, mobile force like lightning, and to this belongs the mantras of the Samaveda. To complete the *trayi-vidya* or 'threefold knowledge', the Yajaveda is classified according to Surya, the celestial world or heavens and the luminosity of the solar force. This is not, of course, to be confused with the visible light of the sun itself.

From all this is should at once be seen that the earliest roots of language, far from being 'primitive', are in fact very sophisticated and that, unfortunately, much of the subtle meaning of ancient texts is completely obscure not only to linguists of today but also to those who study them in the hope of availing themselves of wisdom. It remains to be said then, that the Upanishads, which are the second or last part of each Veda, comprise the inner knowledge and science of the complete doctrine. To truly avail oneself of wisdom, the study of the Upanishads, as with any sacred texts, must be supported by yoga. By 'yoga' here we do not refer to the diverse physical postures and breathing exercises that were a later development of Hatha Yoga. Yoga, in the real and original sense, is concentration of the mind and meditation that is aimed solely towards the goal of union with God or the Real (Atma).[223]

---

[223] *The Upanishads*, translated by Eknath Easwaran (Arkana 1988), is an excellent, clearly written introduction to this sacred science that the modern reader will have no difficulty assimilating, and will even find pleasing.

The Star of Man

In a previous work we gave an explanation of the Egyptian Khabs or 'star' from a metaphysical point of view.[224] The declaration by Aiwass in the (Egyptian) Book of the Law, I: 8, regarding the Khabs as being 'in the Khu' and not vice versa indicates a complete doctrine, but of course that book in itself falls far short of being in any way a complete doctrine in itself. As we have showed, no simple explanation suffices even to cover adequately this one line of text. What we can do now, by way of a further and more detailed study, is to look at this from the particular point of view of man. To do this we must make use of the Vedantic knowledge concerning the 'envelopes of the self' that cover or clothe Atma, the Real.[225]

Firstly, it must be said that the Egyptian Khabs is not usually spelled with a 'star' determinative.[226] Most often it is spelled with a type of bird, presumably a wader, which, as if to demonstrate the complexity of what is being hinted at in the Book of the Law, is frequently associated with the Khu. The Khu is sometimes given as 'a spirit', but the word in fact has many levels of meaning. Khabs is also spelled with a flower (possibly a lotus), seen from one side. The hieroglyphs shown above and to the left here indicate a particular form of the Khabs, where it is a 'living star or intelligence'. We should note also that this flower hieroglyph is used to indicate the female generally, and sometimes even specifically the yoni or other things that share a common symbolism. Now, we have taken the Khabs as 'star' generally in context of the opening of the Book of the Law, I: 2–3.

The unveiling of the company of heaven.
Every man and every woman is a star.

Other meanings of the Khabs include 'to worship', 'to give light or radiance'. We can then see the play on words, typical of the ancient Egyptian tradition, conveyed by verses 7, 8 and 9:

---

[224] 'The Star of the Order', *Nu Hermetica*.
[225] A more detailed study of the 'envelopes of the self', strictly in the context of the Vedanta, may be found in *Man and His Becoming according to the Vedānta*, René Guénon [Sophia Perennis].
[226] For various spellings of 'khabs' see the Appendices, *Nu Hermetica*.

Behold! it is revealed by Aiwass the minister of Hoor-paar-kraat.
The Khabs is in the Khu, not the Khu in the Khabs.
Worship then the Khabs, and behold my light shed over you!

The latter verse, 'worship then the Khabs, and behold my light shed over you!' includes all three of the main meanings of 'Khabs'. The giving off of light is usually thought to be the light of a star, but as it has been stated that 'Every man and every woman is a star', clearly the instruction is not to worship our selves! In fact, it must be said that the many profane commentators and practitioners of the anti-metaphysical interpretations of Thelema effectively do that. We need not waste time with such infantilism, so can instead consider what was previously said, that the hieroglyphs of the Khabs often denote the feminine principle. Furthermore, Khabset is the proper name of the Goddess of the Star. Some find it puzzling that the Gods of the Egyptians are so 'interchangeable', so that for example Hathoor can be invoked 'in her name of Isis', or 'in her name of Mut'. There is nothing strange in this at all; it is only bewildering to those who want to think of the Egyptian tradition, which they even insist on calling a 'religion', as pantheistic or polytheistic. It is no more pantheistic than is the Hindu tradition, with its many Gods, all aspects of Ishvara or, more precisely, different attributes or powers of Ishvara. To the Egyptians, Ishvara was known as Sekher Neter, the 'God of all Gods'.

Therefore Nuit herself, the subject of the first chapter of the Book of the Law, can be known as Khabset in the particular sense of that chapter. It is her light that is clearly referred to, not the light of any person and not the light of any star in the ordinary sense of that word. The stars, plural, are the beings of her manifestation, for Nuit herself is at the formless level, Pure Being, and even beyond that, as the principle itself equal to Brahma.

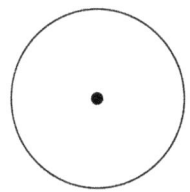

When the Khabs is regarded as a 'star', though it is never in the literal sense, that star is always shown as five-rayed. It was likened to the 'Hand of Orion', in which case the metaphysical point in the circle was shown in the palm. According to the Hindu doctrines, the Self or pure Atma is not determined by anything, and is the principle Itself. It is not within manifestation but nothing can exist without it. It is the Real.[227] The circumference of the circle may be regarded as the first envelope of the Self and in a certain sense might be referred to the 'hiding of Hadit' of the Book of the Law, II: 79.

---

[227] Cf. 'Sat-Chit-Ananda'.

The first envelope of the Self, at the primary and formless level of manifestation, is called *anandamaya-kosha*, 'the envelope (*kosha*) made (*maya*) of beatitude (*ananda*) or bliss'. It is the realm of Pure Being, and also corresponds to Ishvara.

The second envelope of being is only possible through the *boddhi* or higher intellectual state, formless in nature. Looking at this the other way, in terms of ascension of being, the *boddhi* is the only way that an individual can attain knowledge of formless reality, and even verily God (Ishvara) and the principle or True Self (Atma). Below the *boddhi*, the second envelope of being, called *vijnanamaya-kosha* or 'reflected knowledge', is the first in the individual order, which is known generally as *ahankara*.[228] Now this 'reflected knowledge' is in essence the reflection of Atma, which we have here symbolised as the metaphysical point in the circle. This reflection takes place at the level of non-corporeal subtle form.

The reflection of Atma is *jivatma*, which forms the very centre of the individuality, for example, in man.[229] This has a certain relation with Tiphereth in the Qabalistic schema, in which case we can posit the *boddhi* as being somewhat beyond the threshold of Da'ath and the link to the supernal trinity, the Godhead and that which lies beyond it. The second envelope includes five *tanmatras* or 'determinations', the subtle principles of the sense perceptions. The word *tanmatra* literally means 'an assignment', from *matra*, 'measure', 'determination', and has very close similarity in meaning and sound with other languages such as Egyptian, Greek and Hebrew. It delimits the assignment of any particular modality, making that thing what it is.

We can now see, by means of the symbol of the Khabs star or Hand of Orion (above), how Atma (or Hadit) is reflected downward into subtle form. While this is merely a reflection of the True Self, by upward transposition it can be realised as identical to Atma Itself, unextended. Thus, as it is said in the oracle of Nuit in the Book of the Law, I: 15,

They shall gather my children into their fold: they shall bring the glory of the stars into the hearts of men.

---

[228] Ibid.
[229] There are countless forms of individuality; the human being is merely one particular type of individuality.

And it is said in the Upanishads,

> Hear, O children of immortal bliss,
> You are born to be united with the Lord.
> Follow the path of the illumined ones
> And be united with the Lord of Life.[230]

And again, according to the oracle of Hadit, II: 6,

> *I am the flame that burns in every heart of man, and in the core of every star.*

We can thus understand the importance of the Khabs star as the very embodiment of the principle, and the practice itself, by which man can reach upward to the higher intellectual intuition (*boddhi*) and so touch upon the knowledge of the Real. Can man do this alone? No! So long as he thinks he is alone, he is separated from all else, including the knowledge of the Real. Nuit, the Goddess of the Star, can lead us to herself, through the great power of her love, and she can lead us even to the final deliverance (*moksha*), the knowledge of the supreme Reality.

The third envelope of the self is called *manomaya-kosha*, the envelope of the mental modality. Through *manas*, 'inward sense', we have the modification of the mentality, the principal of thought. The subtle sense perceptions or *tanmatras*, which we have shown as the radiations of the Khabs or the Hand of Orion, are here translated downwardly into the subtle principles of hearing, touch, sight, taste and smell—we are not yet at the level of physical senses.

The fourth envelope is called *pranamaya-kosha*, the envelope that is (literally) 'made of prana', the vital breath at the subtle level. The *prana* forms five *vayus*, principles of perception, plus two more, action and sensation. While the word *vayu* can be taken as meaning 'air', or 'wind', it has a correspondence with the Hebrew *ruach*, which is 'mind' in the particular sense of a mobile force ('that which flows', which is common to both Sanskrit and Hebrew words). These have a further correspondence with the five lowest chakras in the occult or subtle anatomy.

---

[230] Shvetashvatara Upanishad, 2: 5, translated by Eknath Easwaran.

The fifth envelope is called *annamaya-kosha*, the gross body or the corporeal form itself. At the substantial level, the five *vayus* here translate as the *bhutas* or elemental *tattvas*, *akasha* (ether), *vayu* (air), *tejas* (fire), *apas* (water) and *prithivi* (earth). It can be seen by this that the Hindu doctrines do not include an equivalent word for the modern conception of 'matter', as though it were something separate and self-causal, even though that word is often used quite incorrectly in the English translations and commentaries. The fifth envelope is thus best understood as the 'clothing of the body' that gives rise to the appearance itself, which is all that is known by modern sciences.

It becomes evident that the five envelopes of being have their source with the Khabs star at the level of subtle form, within reach of the higher intellectual intuition, by which the Real can alone be apprehended in the way of direct knowledge. Through reflection, the radiations of the fivefold star of the individuality become the five senses at the subtle and elemental levels, which are the means of ordinary perception. There is thus correspondence with the number 15, which is a product of five: $\sum (1-5) = 15$. When the number 15 is itself multiplied by 5, the result is 75, the number of Nuit's name.[231]

This now opens the question as to what happens to the envelopes of the Self after physical mortality? While we treated of the envelopes here as beginning from around the principial 'point', in death there is naturally a dissolution of each vehicle in reverse order. Speech, of the verbal utterance, is the first of the faculties to withdraw into the *manas* or inward sense, as previously defined. The five faculties of sensation and five faculties of action then follow this. The *manas* is then withdrawn into the *prana* or vital breath along with all of its vital functions. This includes the five *vayus*, which are modifications or modalities of the *prana*. These all return to the undifferentiated state, which is no different from that of life itself. This is also what occurs in the state of deep sleep, or dreamless sleep. There is a cessation of all external modes of consciousness. Similarly, this can take place in certain trance states.[232]

Now that all the faculties and functions have been withdrawn into the vital breath, so that they subsist as possibilities or latency, the vital breath along with all its functions is in turn subsumed into the *jivatma*, the 'living soul'. Jivatma is the most central principle of the individuality and is itself a reflection of the Atma or True Self.

---

[231] NVIT = 75 by standard Qabalistic values.
[232] Chandogya Upanishad V.1:8:6.

Jivatma is properly regarded as the governor of all the functions in the integral state, not merely in their relationship with the physical mentality and perceptions.[233] This is likened to a king's servants that are gathered about him that is embarking on a journey, for the functions and faculties, both internal and external, all gather about, or within, the living soul—for it is from the *jivatma* that they are manifested and then withdrawn. These are all then withdrawn into a luminous individual essence, which is of the nature of a subtle state. Now all, including the vital breath, is subsumed into the light, which is not to be regarded exclusively in its fiery or igneous aspect, since we are dealing here with a reflection of the Intelligible Light. The reflection we speak of is no different in essence from the mental faculty during the physical life, which requires all five elements as a support or vehicle of manifestation.[234]

We can now see why it is the Khabs star is also called the Hand of Orion. Orion, the constellation that rises in the east and dominates the heavens, symbolises the Egyptian Sahu, sometimes called the 'body of the risen king'. This is more accurately understood not as a body as such but the divine 'breath' when that is understood as the luminous individual essence.

It is now necessary to deal with some popular confusions that have arisen from all this. Some commentators, including even Hindu scholars, will say there is 'a divine spark in every creature'. This is not a total contradiction of the Hindu doctrines but it is a simplification that brings about real confusions, and this has been put about and used by those who wilfully subvert all spiritual knowledge. Similarly, since men and women are essentially 'stars', which we explained in detail already, subversion arises to turn many away from the path. Atma cannot be contained by anything otherwise Atma would be limited by the containment. Atma is therefore not 'in' anything, and to think so also gives rise to 'divine immanence'. The question we would then put to those who insist on the 'divine spark' theory is this: If there is a divine spark in every creature then please tell us exactly where it is? The question cannot be answered of course, because the 'divine' or 'the spirit' does not occupy space, as does the corporeal human or other being. Neither does it occupy time, and neither does it occupy the subtle realms of form.

---

[233] Brihadaranyaka Upanishad IV.3.58.
[234] Cf. *Man and His Becoming according to the Vedānta*, p. 61.

Furthermore, it is most certainly not hidden in the psychological structures of man, as defined by profane science, which deal only with infra or 'unconscious' levels even below that of reason. Neither is it 'in' the elemental or subtle faculties as all these are reflections or appearances, as is all else but Atma Itself. As we have explained, the first envelope of the self is the first veil upon Atma and corresponds to Ishvara, whose function is that of Logos, the Word that orders all of creation. Ishvara is Pure Being.

It is verily through Nuit's 'star' that it becomes possible to enter the 'company of heaven' and to realise the supreme identity or True Self. Every man and every woman is truly a star, otherwise they could not exist at all—the *jivatma* is the core of the individuality at the level of the second envelope of being. However, while each individual is a kind of 'centre' in itself, there can be no plurality of infinites as that would be a contradiction in terms and a metaphysical impossibility. The true state of affairs exists as latency only, or virtuality, until the knowledge and full realisation of Atma, or the supreme centre, takes place. There is then a corresponding and permanent change of state in the being.[235]

---

[235] It might be worth noting here that Crowley's notion of each individual star as a centre in itself was flawed for this very reason, and this owes to the fact that he took the notion from Leibnitz and pretended it was his own. It is only mathematical points, as spatial determinations, that can be said to in any way constitute the 'different points of view'. The declaration of Nuit in the Book of the Law, I: 22, 'Since I am Infinite Space, and the Infinite Stars thereof', must be taken as analogy and not as ordinary physics, for space as such can never be infinite, only indeterminate. See Guénon, *Symbolism of the Cross*, p. 88 foonote 4 in particular.

Selected Works of Oliver St. John

Hermetic Astrology (2015)
Magical Theurgy (2015)
The Enterer of the Threshold (2016)
Liber 373 Astrum Draconis (2017)
Hermetic Qabalah Foundation—Complete Course (2018)
Babalon Unveiled! Thelemic Monographs (2019)
Ritual Magick—Initiation of the Star and Snake (2019)
Nu Hermetica—Initiation and Metaphysical Reality (2021)
Thirty-two paths of Wisdom (2023)
Thunder Perfect Gnosis—Intellectual Flower of Mind (2023)
Law of Thelema—Hidden Alchemy (2024)
Metamorphosis—Hermetic Science and Yoga Power (2024)
Advaita Vedanta—Question of the Real (2025)
Egyptian Tarot and Guidebook (2025)

Contact the O∴A∴

Universal Gnostic Collegium: Contact details and information is posted on our website at www.ordoastri.org

www.ingramcontent.com/pod-product-compliance
Lightning Source LLC
Chambersburg PA
CBHW072129160426
43197CB00012B/2046